The Effects of the Eurozone Sovereign Debt Crisis

T0316047

The book analyses the emerging centre–periphery divisions within the European Union which result from the unprecedented conditions created by the 2008–09 global financial crisis and the subsequent Eurozone sovereign debt crisis. The multiple layers of policy coordination which emerged in response to the crisis have initiated a process by which the EU is increasingly divided in terms of the level of vertical integration between the Eurozone core group and differentiated peripheries amongst the outsiders. At the same time the sovereign debt crisis has created a periphery of predominantly Southern European countries within the Eurozone that became dependent on external financial support from the other member states. The contributions in this book critically examine various aspects of the emerging internal post-crisis constellation of the EU. The main focus lies on national and supranational governance issues, national dynamics and dynamics in the Eurozone core as well as in the periphery.

This book was originally published as a special issue of *Perspectives on European Politics and Society*.

Christian Schweiger is Senior Lecturer in the School of Government and International Affairs at Durham University, UK. His main research interests are the political economy of the EU, national varieties of economic and social development in the member states and transatlantic relations.

José M. Magone is Professor of Regional and Global Governance at the Berlin School of Economics and Law, Germany. He has published widely on European politics, particularly on Southern Europe and European integration.

The Effects of the Eurozone Sovereign Debt Crisis

Differentiated Integration between the Centre and the New Peripheries of the EU

Edited by
Christian Schweiger and José M. Magone

LONDON AND NEW YORK

First published 2015
by Routledge
2 Park Square, Milton Park, Abingdon, Oxfordshire OX14 4RN

and by Routledge
711 Third Avenue, New York, NY 10017, USA

First issued in paperback 2017

Routledge is an imprint of the Taylor & Francis Group, an informa business

© 2015 Taylor & Francis

British Library Cataloguing in Publication Data
A catalogue record for this book is available from the British Library

ISBN 13: 978-1-138-05749-4 (pbk)
ISBN 13: 978-1-138-85109-2 (hbk)

Typeset in Times New Roman
by RefineCatch Limited, Bungay, Suffolk

Publisher's Note
The publisher accepts responsibility for any inconsistencies that may have
arisen during the conversion of this book from journal articles to book chapters,
namely the possible inclusion of journal terminology.

Disclaimer
Every effort has been made to contact copyright holders for their permission to
reprint material in this book. The publishers would be grateful to hear from any
copyright holder who is not here acknowledged and will undertake to rectify
any errors or omissions in future editions of this book.

Contents

CONTENTS

Citation Information

The chapters in this book were originally published in *Perspectives on European Politics and Society*, volume 15, issue 3 (September 2014). When citing this material, please use the original page numbering for each article, as follows:

Chapter 6
The Limits of Transnational Solidarity and the Eurozone Crisis in Germany, Ireland and Slovakia
Stefan Auer
Perspectives on European Politics and Society, volume 15, issue 3 (September 2014)
pp. 322–334

Chapter 7
From Grexit *to* Grecovery: *The Paradox of the Troika's Engagement with Greece*
Anna Visvizi
Perspectives on European Politics and Society, volume 15, issue 3 (September 2014)
pp. 335–345

Chapter 8
Portugal Is Not Greece: Policy Responses to the Sovereign Debt Crisis and the Consequences for the Portuguese Political Economy
José M. Magone
Perspectives on European Politics and Society, volume 15, issue 3 (September 2014)
pp. 346–360

Chapter 9
The Tale of Two Peripheries in a Divided Europe
Bela Galgoczi
Perspectives on European Politics and Society, volume 15, issue 3 (September 2014)
pp. 361–369

Chapter 10
Poland under Economic Crisis Conditions
Maciej Duszczyk
Perspectives on European Politics and Society, volume 15, issue 3 (September 2014)
pp. 370–384

Chapter 11
Hungary and the Eurozone – the Need for a More Systemic Approach
Olivér Kovács
Perspectives on European Politics and Society, volume 15, issue 3 (September 2014)
pp. 385–399

Please direct any queries you may have about the citations to
clsuk.permissions@cengage.com

Notes on Contributors

Stefan Auer is an Associate Professor and Director of European Studies in the School of Modern Languages and Culture at the University of Hong Kong.

Maciej Duszczyk is Deputy Director of the Institute of Social Policy and Member of the Board of the Centre of Migration Research at the University of Warsaw, Poland.

Lothar Funk is a Professor in International Economic Relations at the University of Applied Sciences, Düsseldorf, Germany.

Bela Galgoczi is a Senior Researcher in the field of Economic and Labour Market Policy at the European Trade Union Institute, Brussels, Belgium.

Olivér Kovács is a Research Fellow at the ICEG European Center, Budapest, Hungary.

Brigid Laffan is Director and Professor at the Robert Schuman Centre for Advanced Studies and Director of the Global Governance Programme, European University Institute, Florence, Italy.

José M. Magone is Professor of Regional and Global Governance at the Berlin School of Economics and Law, Germany.

Philippe Pochet is General Director of the European Trade Union Institute, Brussels, Belgium.

Caroline de la Porte is an Associate Professor in the Department of Society and Globalisation at Roskilde University, Denmark.

Christian Schweiger is Senior Lecturer in the School of Government and International Affairs at Durham University, UK.

Anna Visvizi is an Associate Professor in the International Business & European Affairs Department at The American College of Greece, Athens, Greece.

Introduction

Differentiated Integration and Cleavage in the EU under Crisis Conditions

CHRISTIAN SCHWEIGER* & JOSÉ M. MAGONE**

*School of Government and International Affairs, Durham University, UK;
**Department of Business and Economics, Berlin School of Economics and Law, Germany

ABSTRACT   This special issue, which is published on behalf of the UACES Collaborative Research Network The EU Single Market in the Global Economy and supported by the Fritz Thyssen Foundation, addresses the various aspects of the emerging centre–periphery cleavages in the European Union (EU) which result from unprecedented conditions of the 2008–09 global financial crisis and the subsequent eurozone sovereign debt crisis. The multiple layers of policy coordination which emerged in response to the crisis have initiated a process where the EU is increasingly internally divided in terms of the level of vertical integration between the eurozone core group and differentiated peripheries amongst the outsiders. At the same time the sovereign debt crisis has created a periphery group of predominantly Southern European countries within the eurozone that became dependent on external financial support from the other member states. The contributions in the special issue critically examine various aspects of the emerging internal post-crisis constellation of the EU. The main focus lies on national and supranational governance issues, as well as national perspectives and dynamics in the eurozone-18 core and the outside periphery.

The European Union (EU) approaches the sixth decade of its existence since the signing of the Treaty of Rome in 1957 in a state of profound political disorientation and widespread economic instability. Rattled by ongoing effects of the sovereign debt problems in the eurozone, EU governments struggle to come to terms with the most profound crisis in the history of the organisation. The eurozone crisis has accentuated an ongoing debate about the nature and the scope of European integration which had originated in the early 1990s. After the end of the Cold War and the fall of the iron curtain that had artificially divided Europe for over 40 years, the EU was facing the prospect of its biggest ever enlargement towards the former communist countries in Central and Eastern Europe. This raised substantial questions about the internal set-up of the EU, both in terms of its institutions and policies. The resulting internal debate on the need for institutional reform was accompanied by an emerging split between those who advocated the continuation of the traditional Community method of integration towards an eventual federal union and others who adopted a more realist perspective on how an enlarged EU could maintain institutional and procedural efficiency (Andréani, 2002, p. 4). The paper published by Wolfgang Schäuble and Karl Lamers, two leading German Christian Democrat politicians, in 1994 had a crucial impact on this debate. Schäuble and Lamers argued that differentiated integration in the enlarging EU would become inevitable as not all countries were willing and able to move at the same speed towards deeper integration. Both envisaged the development of a core group of countries around France and Germany that would move towards a federal political union with others potentially joining at a later stage (Schäuble & Lamers, 1994).

The notion of differentiated integration was unpopular at the time of the publication of the paper but has since become increasingly prominent as it reflects the reality of the integration process in the EU. Since Maastricht and the creation of the EU in 1993, the evolvement of cleavages between groups of member states have become a fact. This was shown by the establishment of the Schengen area in 1995, the opt out mechanisms introduced under the Treaty of Amsterdam in 1998 and ultimately the creation of monetary union with 12 out of the total of 25 member states in 2002. It is certainly true that the EU generally managed to combine horizontal integration (widening its membership base) with vertical integration (deepening individual policy areas). Horizontal integration even occurred when the process of vertical integration began to stagnate (Leuffen et al., 2013, p. 21). This was the case during the first enlargement in 1973 and again in the period after the creation of the euro. The eastward enlargement in 2004 and 2007 took place against the background of a profound institutional crisis of the EU, which culminated in the rejection of the EU constitutional treaty in public referenda in France and the Netherlands in 2005 and a further public dismissal of the revised Lisbon Treaty in the Irish Republic in 2007. In the eyes of many observers this was a clear sign of a growing mismatch between the technocratic vision of the EU put forward by the political elite and the perception amongst citizens on the national level (Hayward, 2012, p. 10). It also explains why the EU-15 member states were less generous towards the new cohort of Central and Eastern European (CEE) members than it had been during the past waves of enlargement. The CEE countries had to accept lower levels of pre-accession support than those countries that had joined during previous waves of enlargement (Jovanović, 2004, p. 841)

The lack of public support and the increasing disunion between member state governments on the future institutional shape of the EU seemed to lead to a situation where further treaty changes beyond the rather limited consensus on institutional reform and policy development manifested in the Lisbon Treaty (Christiansen & Dobbels, 2013) seemed almost impossible. In addition to the deepening Euroscepticism in the UK, the obvious rift between French and German perspectives on the future of the EU, which had emerged under Chirac and Schröder and seem to prevail under Merkel and Sarkozy (Paterson, 2012, pp. 239–242), made it unlikely that Lisbon would be followed up by any substantial deepening of the EU's *acquis*. On the occasion of the official signing of the Lisbon Treaty member states consequently collectively emphasised that the treaty potentially represented the final stage in the process of European institutional integration. The December 2007 EU Council conclusions stated that 'the Lisbon Treaty provides the Union with a stable and lasting institutional framework' and that member state governments expected 'no change in the foreseeable future' (Council of the European Union, 2007, article 6, p. 2).

The onset of the financial crisis in the USA and the subsequent sovereign debt crisis in the eurozone dramatically changed the perspective of EU leaders. Driven by the urgent need to reinstall market confidence in the crisis economies of the eurozone and to avoid the collapse of the single currency, France and Germany formed a renewed alliance of necessity to establish new mechanisms which would ensure the supervision and implementation of budgetary and macroeconomic stability in the eurozone. The resulting *European Semester* annual cycle of policy coordination under the post-Lisbon Europe 2020 Strategy, the *Euro Plus Pact* and the *Fiscal Compact* are practical manifestations of the new level of policy coordination in the eurozone itself and beyond which emerged from the crisis. It is accompanied by the institutionalisation of financial support between the eurozone countries through the temporary *European Financial Stability Facility* (2010–13) and the subsequent permanent *European Stability Mechanism*, which has been in operation since 2012. The next step is likely to be the eurozone banking union, which member states are currently in the process of finalising. The banking union is likely to transfer the supervision of major national banks towards the European Central Bank with a *single supervisory mechanism* (Council of the European Union, 2013, p. 1). These policy developments have created a situation where the eurozone core is gradually moving towards a quasi-federation. The renewed focus on fiscal and macroeconomic stability in response to the eurozone sovereign debt crisis makes it likely that eurozone countries will give the Commission greater independent supervisory powers and that they expand the coordination of domestic policy-making towards further areas such as taxation. The latter prospect is supported by a group of aspiring eurozone members who have agreed to link their national policy coordination in core areas such as education, training, wages, taxes and banking legislation to the eurozone under the *Euro Plus Pact* (European Commission, 2011). The Euro Plus Pact (EPP) group of countries (Bulgaria, Lithuania, Poland, Romania and Denmark) consequently currently represents a semi-periphery in the EU which is closely associated with the eurozone core. Denmark is the odd one out in this group as it is the only country that does not have a clear aspiration to join the eurozone but nevertheless joined the EPP in an attempt to avoid being sidelined if it did not participate in the new policy mechanisms (Parello-Plesner & Friis, 2012). On the outer periphery of the EU one can find Czech Republic, the UK, Hungary and Sweden. The latter two countries are not part of the EPP but have signed the intergovernmental *Fiscal Compact*. This requires both countries to abide by the Compact's 'golden rule' of limiting national structural deficits, even though they are not part of the eurozone. The UK and the Czech Republic on the other hand have refused to sign up to any form of binding policy coordination beyond the annual *European Semester*, which remains loose for non-eurozone countries.

The contributions in this special issue examine the emerging divide of the EU into a eurozone core with increasingly differentiated peripheries, depending on the level of integration. The selected papers were first presented and discussed at the conference *Centre-periphery relations as an emerging cleavage in European politics and policy-making? Empirical studies on differentiated integration*, which took place at the Berlin School of Economics and Law in October 2013. The conference represented an Anglo-German project funded largely by the Fritz Thyssen Foundation with additional support by the University Association of Contemporary European Studies and the Berlin School of Economics and Law. It was also organised on behalf of the interdisciplinary UACES collaborative research network *The EU Single Market in the Global Economy*. The network was founded in 2009 with the purpose of instilling a continuous dialogue between academic scholars from various disciplines, national and EU level policy-makers and other stakeholders. The dialogue became the basis for the overall goal to develop effective practical proposals on how the EU should deal the challenge of economic globalisation and in particular the effects of the financial crisis. Participants at the Berlin conference attempted an early analysis of the emerging effects of the eurozone sovereign debt crisis on the EU's internal coherence and external scope. The papers in this special issue concentrate on examining the supranational policy response and the resulting national dynamics and perspectives inside the eurozone-18 core and the semi-periphery groups.

The contributions in the special issue are divided into three thematic parts which all refer to the new differentiated centre–periphery division in the EU. Part 1 concentrates on the mechanisms and the effects of the emerging policy agenda in response to the crisis in the context of diverging national interests. Laffan concentrates on what she considers to be an emerging cleavage within the eurozone core between the stronger economies, spearheaded by Germany, that have essentially become creditor states and the periphery of debtor countries with a sovereign debt crisis. Schweiger analyses the origins and the scope of the Fiscal Compact which was developed in 2012 under substantial political controversy due to the veto of the British government against its inclusion in the EU's treaty structure. He argues that the intergovernmental Fiscal Compact illustrates the new dominance of differentiated intergovernmental policy coordination in the EU which in effect has led to the emergence of an outer periphery of countries that chose to detach themselves from this process.

Part 2 offers an analysis of differences in the national perspectives and policy responses to the crisis inside the eurozone-17 core. Funk's contribution concentrates on Germany which, at least temporarily, has moved into the position of a 'reluctant hegemon' in the EU under the crisis conditions and has therefore taken the leading role in determining the shape of the policy mechanisms in response to the eurozone crisis (Paterson, 2011; Bulmer & Paterson, 2013). Against this background Funk provides a detailed analysis of the factors which contributed to Germany's ability to recover its economic role model status, which it seemed to have lost in the wake of reunification. Funk particularly concentrates on the recovery in the German labour market, which contrary to the expectations of many, could be maintained under the external crisis conditions. Auer provides a comparative case study of reactions to the eurozone crisis in Germany, Ireland and the Slovak Republic. He argues that the stark differences in their perceptions of the root causes of the crisis and the political responses are a reflection of a wider malaise in the European project which puts a profound question mark over the future of the eurozone and the EU as a whole. Visvizi offers an insight into the domestic circumstances of the severe sovereign debt crisis in Greece, which has moved the country centre stage in the group of eurozone crisis countries. In this respect Visvizi highlights the curious position Greece finds itself in under these conditions, where it is formally positioned in the eurozone core but nevertheless widely perceived as a periphery country. This is the result of Greece's deepening economic malaise and the widespread concerns in the EU about the ability of the Greek political elite to put the country on a long-term course towards economic and social consolidation. Magone sheds light on the case of Portugal which he considers to be positioned in the EU's semi-periphery due to its weakening economic performance, which had become obvious way before the financial crisis took effect. Magone shows how Portuguese political elites tried to differentiate their country from Greece by making efforts to meet the reform targets which were prescribed by the EU troika. In spite of these efforts, Magone raises doubts about the viability of Portugal's economic and budgetary performance and considers it to remain firmly in the group of eurozone crisis countries.

The contributions in Part 3 concentrate on the performance of the Central and Eastern European member states during the eurozone crisis and offer detailed case studies on the perspective of two eurozone outsiders on the crisis. The two country case studies present Poland as a key representative of the semi-periphery group and Hungary as a member state that is positioned on the margins between the semi-periphery and the outer periphery of countries that are detached from the mechanisms of binding policy coordination. Galgoczi initiates this part with a crucial analysis of the differences between the Southern and Eastern periphery in the EU. He argues that a large part of the CEE periphery is closely associated with the eurozone core led by Germany. This explains why the CEE countries, in stark contrast to the Southern European states, are able to maintain balanced trade figures, albeit on the basis of a strong dependence on foreign direct investment which poses fundamental questions about the long-term viability of the CEE economies. Duszc- zyk presents the case study on Poland with a focus on the background of Poland's unique status as the only EU member state that did not fall into recession when the financial crisis hit Europe. Duszczyk shows that the combination of Poland's close economic ties with Germany, whilst at the same time being outside the constraints of eurozone membership, helped to maintain a strong Polish trade performance. At the same time the Polish govern- ment made prudent use of EU structural funds to stimulate growth in the economy and Poland's labour market in the overall context of having managed to achieve a consensual approach between the social partners on how to respond to the external crisis conditions. Kovács presents the more problematic case of Hungary, which has consistently lagged behind the economic performance of other CEE member states since its accession to the EU in 2004.

Kovács explains the background to what is perceived as Hungary's overall macroeco- nomic instability. He shows that successive Hungarian governments have for some time struggled to rectify a growing structural deficit problem under conditions of declining real investments and low levels of domestic demand. Kovács points out that Hungary needs a more systematic political approach towards regaining macroeconomic stability, especially through a consistent and targeted approach towards eurozone entry.

The essential question for the future of the European project is to what extent the new phase of differentiated integration which emerges in response to the eurozone sovereign debt crisis will undermine the EU's long-term cohesion and ultimately also its viability as a major regional organisation (Piris, 2011). The danger for the EU in its current situation is that the crisis may lead to the consolidation of its current internal configuration. The instability in the eurozone core could lead to a situation where the at present 18 member states may decide to continue down the path of deeper horizontal integration at the expense of pursuing the vertical widening of the core towards new members. A consolida- tion of the insider–outsider cleavage between eurozone members and outsiders on the basis of an exclusive rather than an inclusive approach towards the future design of the eurozone would pose a grave risk for the future viability of the Single European Market. The contri- butions in this special issue illustrate the stark differences in the national challenges and perspectives in the EU which result from the crisis. They also raise profound doubts about the ability of the new policy mechanisms which were adopted since 2010 to maintain the EU's internal political and economic cohesion. The special issue is published at a time where it is only possible to offer a glimpse of the potential future impact of the decisions that EU leaders took under unprecedented crisis conditions. In spite of the current uncertainty on how the EU will evolve in the foreseeable future, recent developments point towards the phasing out of the traditional Community method which aspired to gradually deepen collective policy harmonisation. In its place the EU has started to put a more flexible approach of differentiated integration. This approach is likely to be firmly orientated towards strengthening the intergovernmental coordination of national policies with the support of enhanced supervisory capabilities on the part of the EU institutional level. The level of policy coordination is unlikely to be the same for all EU member states and will undoubtedly be strongest within the eurozone core. At the same time the emergence of other core integrative groups of selected member states remains a possibility in areas such as defence and security, where we have already witnessed enhanced cooperation between individual member states (such as France, Germany and the UK and most recently the Visegrád four countries). This does not necessarily have to pose a risk for the EU's cohesion. On the contrary, greater differentiation of policy cooperation amongst different groups of member states offers an opportunity for the EU to overcome the stagnation in the integration process which has beset most policy areas other than economic and monetary affairs. Differentiation consequently has the potential to offer a viable future perspective for the EU in the aftermath of the global financial crisis, provided that it emerges on the basis of a 'horizontal federalism' (Buonanno & Nugent, 2013, p. 326), where the differentiated core groups remain principally open towards the inclusion of new members and refrain from moving into a direction which undermines the existing collective principles of the EU's *acquis*.

References

Andréani, G. (2002) *What Future for Federalism?* (London: Centre for European Reform).

Bulmer, S. & Paterson, W. E. (2013) Germany as the EU's reluctant hegemon? Of economic strength and political constraints, *Journal of European Public Policy*, 20(10), pp. 1387–1405.

Buonanno, L. & Nugent, N. (2013) *Policies and Policy Processes of the European Union* (Basingstoke: Palgrave MacMillan).

Christiansen, T. & Dobbels, M. (2013) Delegated powers and inter-institutional relations in the EU after Lisbon: A normative assessment, *West European Politics*, 36(6), pp. 1159–1177.

Council of the European Union (2007, December 14) Brussels European Council Presidency Conclusions. Available at http://www.consilium.europa.eu/ueDocs/cms_Data/docs/pressData/en/ec/97669.pdf (accessed 20 February 2014).

Council of the European Union (2013) Single Resolution Mechanism Texts Agreed at ECOFIN on 18 December 2013. Available at http://register.consilium.europa.eu/doc/srv?l=EN&t=PDF&gc=true&sc=false&f=ST% 2018137%202013%20INIT (accessed 22 February 2014).

European Commission (2011, December 9) Background on the Euro Plus Pact. Available at http://ec.europa.eu/ europe2020/pdf/euro_plus_pact_background_december_2011_en.pdf (accessed 22 February 2014).

Hayward, J. (2012) Union without consensus, in: J. Hayward & R. Wurzel (Eds) *European Disunion: Between Sovereignty and Solidarity*, pp. 5–16 (Basingstoke: Palgrave MacMillan).

Jovanović, M. N. (2004) Eastern enlargement of the EU: A Topsy-Turvy endgame or permanent disillusionment, *Journal of Economic Integration*, 19(4), pp. 830–868.

Leuffen, D., Rittberger, B. & Schimmelfennig, F. (2013) *Differentiated Integration: Explaining Variation in the European Union* (Basingstoke: Palgrave MacMillan).

Parello-Plesner, J. & Friis, L. (2012) *Reinventing Europe: Denmark Caught Between 'Ins' and 'Outs'* (European Council on Foreign Relations). Available at http://ecfr.eu/content/entry/reinventing_europe_denmark_caught_ between_ins_and_outs (accessed 24 February 2014).

Paterson, W. E. (2011) The reluctant hegemon? Germany moves centre stage in the European Union, *Journal of Common Market Studies*, 49(Annual Review), pp. 55–75.

Paterson, W. E. (2012) A contested Franco-German duumvirate, in: J. Hayward & R. Wurzel (Eds) *European Disunion: Between Sovereignty and Solidarity*, pp. 234–251 (Basingstoke: Palgrave MacMillan).

Piris, J. C. (2011) *The Future of Europe. Towards a Two-Speed EU?* (Cambridge: Cambridge University Press).

Schäuble, W. & Lamers, K. (1994) *Considerations on European Politics* (Bonn: CDU/CSU).

Framing the Crisis, Defining the Problems: Decoding the Euro Area Crisis

BRIGID LAFFAN

Robert Schuman Centre for Advanced Studies, European University Institute, Florence, Italy

ABSTRACT   *From autumn 2009 onwards, the euro area has experienced a sustained economic crisis that has mutated into a social and political crisis. In 'hard times', existing paradigms come under strain and a high level of contestation concerning policy prescriptions is to be expected. Crises tend to act as focal points for institutional, policy and political change that leave significant legacies. European Union and euro area actors had to engage in a process of collectively decoding the crisis and the problems it engendered given the strong and sustained signals emanating from the financial markets, rating agencies and Europe's international partners. The crisis opened up a deep cleavage within the euro area between creditor and debtor states or Europe's core and periphery. The objective of this paper is to analyse how the crisis was decoded as this had a major impact on the choice of policy instruments and policy responses.*

Introduction

The global financial crisis took on a distinctive euro area character in autumn 2009, when the Greek government identified a serious 'fiscal gap' following the October election that saw George Papandreau return to power. As the crisis unfolded, debtors and creditors, core and periphery, were pitted against each other. The European Union (EU) and the euro area have had to engage in a process of collectively decoding the crisis and the problems that they faced given the strong and sustained signals emanating from the financial markets, rating agencies and Europe's international partners. The objective of this paper is to map how the euro crisis and its attendant problems were interpreted. The focus is on the meta-narrative of the crisis and the problem frame that evolved not on the process of framing itself. There is a substantial agreement in the literatures on agenda setting and crises, that the manner in which a crisis is framed and the problems that are identified as needing attention, impacts on the choice of policy instruments and on the selection of issues to be addressed. Schmidt (2008, p. 306) identified ideas in the policy process as operating at three levels, policies, programmes and philosophies. This paper focuses on a fourth level, namely, the frames that are developed in tandem with policy and programme solutions. The paper has three sections. Section I explores crisis and problem framing in theoretical context. Section II analyses how the crisis and its problems were framed. Section III links this analysis to the meta-narrative causal stories and issues that were masked.

Section I: Crisis and Problem Framing in Theoretical Context

The ideational turn in international political economy drew attention to the political and policy significance of the understandings actors develop about the challenges they face. From a constructivist perspective, 'a crisis is not a natural event, but a social event and, therefore, is always socially constructed and highly political' (Gamble, 2009, p. 38). A crisis is a decisive moment that pressurises political actors to develop understandings of the events they encounter and the nature and extent of the challenges they face (Blyth, 2007; Khong, 1992; Widmaier, Blyth, & Seabrooke, 2007). Political actors do not just respond to a crisis but crucially identify and define it through framing a crisis narrative and discourse (Hay, 1996, p. 255; Schmidt, 2002, 2008). Framing through language is a crucial part of crisis management because 'those who are able to define what the crisis is all about also hold the key to defining the appropriate strategies for resolution' ('t Hart, 1993, p. 41). Masking may also play an important role in crisis management as political actors seek to downplay the extent of the problems or keep crucial aspects of the crisis off the public agenda ('t Hart, 1993).

Financial crises are particularly challenging for political actors as financial markets operate to a very different temporal cycle to politics, and if there is an implosion of the financial system, the costs to the economy and society are high and prolonged. The smooth operation of the financial system is a part taken for granted character of a functioning market economy and modern society. Severe stress in the financial system generates panics, manias and heightened uncertainty (Cassis, 2011; Kindleberger, 1989). Hence in addressing financial crises, political actors operate in the shadow of panic and fear and in the context of financial markets that are nervous and uncertain. Investors look to political actors to provide them with a convincing narrative that they know what they are doing and can handle the problems; market players want to be convinced that there is no need to press the panic button.

Beyond the meta-narrative of a crisis, the attendant policy problems that are generated during a crisis do not appear neatly packaged on the political agenda with a clear definition of what is at stake and what issues need to be addressed. Policy problems, according to Cobb and Elder, 'are not simply givens, nor are they matters of the facts of the situation, they are matters of interpretation and social definition' (Cobb & Elder, 1983, p. 172). Issues must be detected and interpreted as problems before they receive political attention (Jones & Baumgartner, 2005). When and on what terms an issue is elevated to the political agenda has consequences for how a problem is portrayed and responded to. Some dimensions of a problem may be highlighted, whereas others receive less attention (Cobb & Ross, 1997).

The significance of what is called issue definition or problem framing is highlighted in the literature on agenda setting and is part of a wider focus on policy frames (Baumgartner & Jones, 2009, 2nd ed.; Cobb & Ross, 1997; Kindgon, 2011, 3rd ed). There is substantial agreement in the public policy literature that problem definition and framing is an inherently political process (Stone, 1989) and that there are 'great political stakes in problem definition' (Kindgon, 2011, p. 110). Stone (1989, p. 282) argues that the process of defining problems is a 'process of image making, where the images have to do fundamentally with attributing cause, blame and responsibility'. Crucial to image making for Stone is the use of language whereby political actors make use of 'several different methods, or languages, of problem definition' (Stone, 2002, p. 134). The problem frame, for the purposes of this paper, is defined as the package of issues that were construed by political actors as problematic and thus requiring attention and action. The language by which these issues were depicted is explored as are the narrative story lines that were deployed to explain what this was about.

This paper begins from the premise that the framing of a crisis and the policy problems it throws up is a crucial part of the politics of policy making and that crisis and problem framing has consequences for how problems are understood and addressed. The paper distinguishes between the meta-narrative of the crisis defined as the overarching narrative, and the problem frame, the definition of the issues that were identified by the core institutions as requiring a response. The meta-narrative and the problem frame intersected around the issue of sovereign debt that emerged both as the central issue in the crisis narrative and the problem frame. Adopting an inductive discovery-led approach, this paper seeks to decode how European institutions detected the problems in the euro area, developed a narrative of the crisis and defined the issues to be addressed in the period from autumn 2009 onwards. The evolution of the frame is linked to different periods. The focus is on two questions.

(1) How was the crisis construed by the key European institutions and what issues constituted the problem frame as the crisis unfolded?
(2) What was masked in the process of framing? See Figure 1.

Two institutional arenas at EU level were to the fore in decoding the crisis and its attendant problems. The design of the single currency established which institutions would have primacy in decoding the crisis. The first was the European Council of the 27 member states or its subset, Euro Heads of State and Government (HoSG) and second, the European Central Bank (ECB). Within the European Council, Angela Merkel, German Chancellor was the dominant political force. During phases of the crisis, the chancellor worked intensively with the French President, Nicolas Sarkozy through bilateral channels. Germany was, however, the dominant force because of the size and performance of its economy, on the one hand, and its very strong perferences concerning economic governance, on

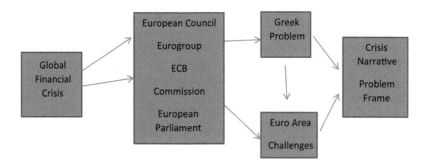

Figure 1. Institutional arenas

the other. The Council of Ministers in its Eco-Fin (Economic and Finance Minsiters) format and a subset, the Eurogroup, engaged in detailed technical work but acted under the direction of the HoSG. The Council of Ministers did not act as agenda setters on the euro crisis. Nor did the European Commission or the European Parliament. The Commission, just like the Finance Ministers, largely acted under the direction of the HoSG. Only the European Council (full or euro area configuration) and the ECB could frame, act or induce action. Europe's central bankers operated through the ECB and the HoSG were the central actors in the European Council and Euro Summits. The ECB was responsible for the 'M' in EMU and the HoSG, representing the national governments, were responsible for the 'E', economic policy. Both institutions were composite institutions involving national and EU level actors. The President of the ECB was its major spokesperson and primary interlocutor with the HoSG. The European Council and the Euro summits were the central arena for a collective response from the national governments. The HoSG deliberated on the euro crisis in many different institutional arenas, at domestic level and in bilaterals with partners but their collective response was contained in the formal statements and conclusions of their joint meetings. The response to the crisis and crisis management within the euro area was concentrated and hierarchical unlike the EU's legislative system which is characterised by multiple access points and in which the Commission has a central role (Princen, 2009; Rhinard, 2010). The two peak organisations were fundamental to developing both the meta-narrative of the crisis and its attendant problem frame. This was the 'co-ordinative' sphere within which the political actors generated ideas about the crisis and its attendant problems (Schmidt, 2002). The meta-narrative and the problem frame evolved in tandem during in the early phase of the crisis as the euro states and the ECB grappled with the mutation of the global financial crisis into a euro area crisis.

Question 1 is addressed by analysing the key texts that were agreed by both the HoSG and the ECB as the crisis unfolded.[1] A thematic reading of the texts allowed us to identify the bundle of issues that were identified by the HoSG as requiring atttention. European Council conclusions and statements from the Eurogroup HoSG, although they invariably involve rhetorical and political positioning, represented agreement among the member states on the issues they were committed to addressing and the actions that they were undertaking. The conclusions took stock of how deliberations in other fora were evolving and they provided the impetus for further work. They were the subject of considerable negotiation, drafting and redrafting both before and during the meetings. A reading of the texts enabled us to map the crisis narrative and the problem frame, the package of issues that the HoSG construed as requiring attention. The ECB President was the spokesperson for the Central Bank and his speeches, statements at the European Parliament (EP) and interviews provided an insight into how the problem was construed by the Central Bank, notwithstanding the reticence of central bankers. The second question was addressed by identifying issues that struggled for attention on the agenda. Masking not just framing was part of crisis management.

Section II: Framing the Crisis and its Attendant Problems

The EU appeared to manage the early phase of the global financial crisis beginning in 2007 in a reasonably effective manner but struggled to manage the crisis from autumn 2009 onwards (Schelke, 2011). Acknowledging that there were serious problems to be addressed proved very challenging to Europe's political actors in autumn 2009? Just two years earlier, the EU had celebrated the 10th anniversary of the introduction of the euro in glowing terms. The Commission in a 2008 communication to the EP concluded that the euro had been 'a resounding success' and had improved Europe's resilience against adverse external developments.[2] In addition, when the global financial crisis began in 2007 and intensified following the collapse of Lehman Brothers, the crisis was interpreted as a problem of the Anglo-Saxon model of capitalism rather than one that might call into question the design and survival of the Euro. It was not until May 2010 that the HoSG fully acknowledged that there was a 'crisis' when they issued a statement following the first Greek bailout on the 7th of May.[3] One month later, in a European Council Conclusion, they referred again to the 'worldwide financial crisis' rather than acknowledging that the global crisis had assumed a distinctive euro area character. Elite perceptions of the success of the euro and the absence of financial crises in Western Europe in the postwar period inured Europe's political and administrative elites to the possibility of a euro area crisis. When it emerged, there was an initial period of denial as the euro states and the ECB grappled with a rapidly evolving situation. Throughout the crisis, the president of the ECB, M. Trichet was adamant that this was not a crisis of the euro rather 'what we have is a crisis related to the public finances of a number of euro area countries' (Interview with Das Bild, 15 January 2011). In a similar vein, M. Trichet in another interview argued that 'There are important problems at present which are related to bad public finances, by way of consequence, to financial stability. But these problems are the responsibility of the governments in question. Each government must keep its own house in order (FTD, 18 July 2011). When asked about dissatisfaction with the euro, M. Trichet suggested that he did not think that 'the criticism concerns the single currency, which is a clear success' (Interview with El Pias, 15 May 2011).

What was initially interpreted as a Greek problem to be solved by Greece was transformed into a euro area problem in the first half of 2010. Because Greece had an excess of sovereign debt and was fiscally profligate, this quickly became the dominant frame within the euro area. Greece dominated the discussions in the euro area up to the first bailout in May 2010 and was back on the agenda in spring 2011 as it became clear that the first rescue package had failed. Within weeks of establishing the new Greek Government, the prime minister announced an upwards revision of the 2009 Greek budget deficit from 6 per cent to 12.7 per cent of GDP. The scale of the upwards revision led to a strong signal, in the form of downgrades, from all three rating agencies.[4] In its accompanying statement to the December 2009 downgrade, S&P stated that, 'the fiscal consolidation plans outlined by the new government are unlikely to secure a sustained reduction in fiscal deficits and the public debt burden' (S&P, 16 December 2009). From mid-November 2009 to April 2010, the spread of Greek bonds over German ones increased from 135 to 586 bp by April 22 (Arghyrou & Stoukalas, 2011, p. 174). As spreads began to widen further, the cost of insuring against a Greek default (price of Credit Default Swaps [CDS]) increased and stocks, particularly banking stocks, on the Athens exchange fell. Investors were rapidly losing faith in Greece (Lynn, 2011, p. 128). Graphs of bond spreads, CDS swaps and debt burdens became the leitmotiv of the crisis from then on.

Although the Greek problem was beginning to surface on the EU agenda, there was as yet no evidence that EU institutions and the euro member states, neither grasped the danger nor were they prepared to act at this stage. The Commission issued statements to the effect that it was willing to work with Greece to develop its reform programme. At the December 2009 European Council, the Swedish Prime Minister, who chaired the Summit, said to reporters on the way into the meeting, that the situation was 'basically a domestic problem that has to be addressed by domestic decisions' (quoted in Lynn, 2011, p. 130). The focus of the Summit was on the implementation of the Lisbon Treaty. Although there is reference in the Conclusions to bringing deficits under control, the situation in Greece was not mentioned. By mid-January, the Greek Government announced another budget designed to stem the crisis and convince markets that the deficit was being brought under control and that its debt was sustainable. This and a number of further austerity measures in Spring 2010 set the pattern for the management of the situation in Greece.

By 21 January, Martin Wolf in the Financial Times referred to the developing situation as a Greek Tragedy, emphasising that Greece's problems were extreme (FT, 21 January 2010).[5] The euro area was ill-equipped to deal with looming insolvency in Greece because of the no-bail rules and the deep unpopularity of any such bailouts in the creditor states. The situation in Greece deteriorated to such an extent that a European Council meeting called for 11 February intended by the new President of the European Council, Herman Van Rompuy, as an occasion to discuss Europe's long-term economic and social agenda became the first of many statements from the HoSG on the problems in the euro area. This marked the Europeanisation of the Greek problem and the beginning of a problem frame within the euro area. For the next two years, four issues, namely, sovereign debt, contagion, systemic threat and economic governance represented the package of issues that the euro area identified as the problem frame. A fifth issue, growth, began to emerge on the agenda two years after the crisis began but by then sovereign debt was embedded as the meta-narrative about the crisis and also a key component of the problem frame. See Figure 2.

Issue I: Sovereign Debt

The meeting on 11th of February was the first of many devoted to the crisis. The statement issued was entirely devoted to Greece. The President of the Council announced at his press conference after the meeting, that a support package for Greece was being put together but no details of what that might consist of were given. The short statement issued by the Euro

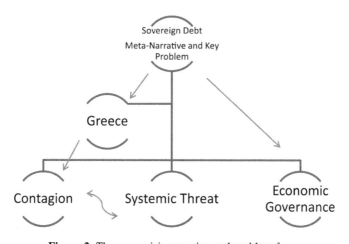

Figure 2. The euro crisis narrative and problem frame

Summit underlined the extent to which the situation was still being couched as a Greek problem. It stated:

> All euro area members must conduct sound national policies in line with the agreed rules. They have a shared responsibility for the economic and financial stability in the area.
>
> we fully support the efforts of the Greek government and their commitment to do whatever is necessary, including adopting additional measures to ensure that the ambitious targets set in the stability programme for 2010 and the following years are met. We call on the Greek government to implement all these measures in a rigorous and determined manner to effectively reduce the budgetary deficit by 4% in 2010.[6]

The statement ended by saying that the Greek government had not requested any financial support. In press conferences and statements after the meeting, an outline of the actions that might be deployed to assist Greece was not forthcoming. Asking the markets to assess a strategy that had not been made public was unlikely to ease their nervousness about Greece or the capacity of the euro area to manage the crisis. In her press conference, Chancellor Merkel said Greece 'will not be left on its own, but there are rules and these rules must be adhered to'.[7] The statement contained the pledge that 'Euro area Member states will take determined and coordinated action, *if needed*, to safeguard financial stability in the euro area as a whole'.[8] This represented a commitment to the euro but action only if *needed*. The euro states, particularly Germany, had not yet conceded that action would be necessary. Following the summit, the Finance Ministers asked Greece to submit a report by 15 March on the further measures it planned to take to make progress on bringing its deficit under control. By March, there was a growing realisation that with mounting pressure on Greece, collective action was necessary but on what terms and by whom.[9] There was considerable debate and disagreement about the potential involvement of the International Monetary Fund (IMF) in any rescue package. Less than seven weeks after the February statement from the Euro HOS, there was a second on 25 March which opened with the following:

> We reaffirm that all euro area members must conduct sound national policies in line with the agreed rules and should be aware of their shared responsibility for the economic and financial stability in the area.

The statement continued as follows:

> We fully support the efforts of the Greek government and welcome the additional measures announced on 3 March which are sufficient to safeguard the 2010 budgetary targets. We recognise that the Greek authorities have taken ambitious and decisive action which should allow Greece to regain the full confidence of the markets.[10]

On 23 April, the Greek Prime Minister finally requested the activation of bilateral loans. In April, Eco-Fin and the Eurogroup concentrated on agreeing a package which was enlarged by IMF participation. There was a considerable contestation about the involvement of the IMF notwithstanding its expertise. By 2 May, an EU/IMF rescue package amounting to 110 billion Euros in emergency loans was agreed and Greece became the first Euro state to become a programme country.[11] The three-year rescue package came with strong conditionality and a commitment to a further 30 billion in budget cuts. The age of rescue and retrenchment had arrived (Scharpf, 2011). The language used in HoSG statements during this phase was replete with references to fiscal sustainability, acceleration of plans for fiscal consolidation, frontloaded budgetary consolidation measures, fiscal responsibility, correcting excessive deficits, fiscal, financial and structural reforms, restoring sound budgets, adhering strictly to fiscal targets and debt reduction and fiscal imbalances (European Council, 2010). The language of the rescue package was strong on conditionality and non-concessional loans.

Issue 2: Contagion to the Vulnerable

Although the epicentre of the crisis was in Greece, the focus began to mutate from a problem in one country to concern about contagion to other euro member states. The prospect of contagion which could undermine the 'macro-financial stability of the EU as a whole' was a crucial issue from May 2010 onwards and was one of the core challenges identified by EU institutions. Investors, analysts and rating agencies highlighted the euro states that were vulnerable to contagion as the so-called PIIGS (Portugal, Ireland/Italy, Greece and Spain), all on the periphery of the EU. In providing a rationale for the Greek package in May, the EU Commissioner for Economic and Monetary Affairs, Olli Rhen, argued that 'It is absolutely essential to contain the bush fire in Greece so that it will not become a forest fire and a threat to financial stability for the European Union and its economy as a whole'.[12] In an interview with Der Spiegel President, Trichet expressed his concern about contagion when saying: 'In the market, there is always a danger of contagion – like the contagion we saw among the private institutions in 2008. And it can occur quickly. Sometimes it is a question of half days'.[13] By May, evidence of the potential for contagion was apparent. The process of downgrades which had contributed to the closing of market access to Greece began to affect others. Ireland and Portugal were entering the vicious cycle of nervous markets, widening spreads, a rise in the cost of borrowing, further downgrades, all of which contributed to a downward spiral into a funding crisis.[14] Ireland lost market access in November 2010 and Portugal by April 2011.

Issue 3: Systemic Stability

Fear of the disintegration of the currency union was acute in the first week of May 2010 as the euro area finally agreed a Greek bailout. Sentiment in the financial markets worsened creating alarm in Frankfurt and in the Euro member capitals. All indicators, spreads on sovereign bonds, CDS spreads and the interbank market pointed to acute financial instability and concern about the future of the Euro itself. Agreement on the Greek bailout on the 2nd of May did not calm the markets. On the contrary according to M. Trichet on the 7th of May:

> we were facing a situation that we regarded as fundamentally abnormal. That situation deteriorated abruptly, sharply and extensively. The very moment where the agreement was reached in Europe to provide Greece with financial support and the imminent decision of the International Monetary Fund (IMF) to approve the Greek

standby should have contributed on the contrary to ease tensions in the markets. (Interview with Handlesblatt, 12 May 2010)[15]

From the perspective of the ECB, 'A number of markets were no longer functioning correctly; it looked somewhat like the situation in mid-September 2008 after the Lehman Brothers' bankruptcy'.[16] M. Trichet brought his concerns to the HoSG at dinner on the Friday evening, 7 May, in Brussels. He demonstrated the interconnections across the European financial system with illustrative graphs that had a major impact on Europe's political leaders. The HoSG having committed themselves to the 'stability, unity and integrity' of the Euro area, now had to match that commitment with financial resources to protect the euro. [17]This came in the form of 750 million euro shield, called the European Financial Stability Facility (EFSF) that was finalised by the euro group Finance Ministers before the markets opened on Monday, 10th of May. The ECB also began its controversial Securities Market Programme (SMP) on the same day. These policy measures represented a new phase in the framing of the problem. The stability and even future of the euro was at stake and the euro states had moved from a position of taking action 'if needed' to affirming 'our commitment to ensure the stability, unity and integrity of the euro area. All the institutions of the euro area (Council, Commission, ECB) as well as all euro area member states agreed to use the full range of means available to ensure the stability of the euro area' (Emergency Euro Area Summit, 7 May 2010).[18] The member states and European institutions would be asked to greatly expand their 'toolkit' over the next 20 months.

From the time that the threat of contagion was first identified, the situation of Spain and Italy was to the fore. These countries represented a significant proportion of the euro economy and were both considered 'too big to bail' but also 'too big to fail'. If either of these countries could not access the markets, the problems facing the euro would deepen dramatically. In May 2011, the IMF in its Regional Economic Outlook warned that contagion from the periphery to the core eurozone remained a serious risk (IMF, 13 May 2011).[19] There was tangible evidence of that risk in July and August as Italian and Spanish spreads widened. By August 7, the ECB President announced steps to reassure the markets by saying that the ECB would 'actively implement its SMP'. In that week, the ECB bought Italian and Spanish bonds on the secondary market for the first time.[20] The President of the ECB, M. Trichet, at a hearing at the Economic and Monetary Affairs Committee of the EP said in his role as Chair of the European Systemic Risk Board: 'Over the past three weeks, the situation has continued to be very demanding. The crisis is systemic and must be tackled decisively: national governments and authorities, as well as European institutions, must rise to the challenge and act together swiftly.'[21] The ECB injected 1 trillion euros into the European financial system in two tranches (December 2011 and January 2012) to maintain liquidity and to lower the cost of borrowing in Spain and Italy. It achieved its goal for a short time, but by May, both Spain and Italy were again under severe market pressure with their costs of borrowing rising to levels that triggered bailouts in the smaller euro states. By June 2012, Spain acknowledged that it required assistance to recapitalise its banks and Cyprus requested assistance. Concern about the stability of the euro area was not just about the single currency. The link between the euro and European integration was a central theme. Failure of the euro could trigger disintegrative forces in the wider EU and internal market. The December 2010 European Council reiterated that 'The euro is and will remain a central part of European integration'.[22] For political leaders in Europe, the widening and deepening of integration and the governance structures that the EU has generated are part of their 'deep core' or worldview (Sabatier & Jenkins, 1993). Europe's elites, if not publics, had internalised the EU as central to how they govern.

Issue 4: Euro Area Governance

Greece, the weakest link in the euro, exposed the fault lines in the single currency as the gaps in its institutional and policy design were brought sharply into focus. A major focus, driven by Germany and the ECB, was not just on addressing the current crisis but preventing its reoccurrence. The economic governance of the euro was firmly placed on the agenda as an issue to be addressed. This in turn has led to institution building, the addition of new financial instruments and legislative packages known as the 'six pack' and 'two pack'.

   Running though the proposals on economic governance was a focus on macro-economic surveillance and competitiveness, greater fiscal discipline and debt monitoring, enhanced enforcement through sanctions, budgetary surveillance via the European Semester and stronger institutions within the eurozone. Notwithstanding the development of new rules and measures on economic governance, the measures were still not considered adequate by Germany. The question of a new European treaty dominated the December 2011 European Council and when the UK decided to veto treaty change within the EU framework, the Euro states and others agreed to go outside the formal framework and concluded what has been called the *Treaty on Stability, Coordination and Governance of Economic and Monetary Union*, usually referred to as a Stability Pact.[23] The language was a language of discipline, rigorous surveillance, scrutiny, monitoring and sanctions. It all points to greatly enhanced intrusion by the euro area into the budgetary and fiscal policies of the member states.

A Challenge Frame: Growth

The dominant focus on debt, budgetary consolidation and surveillance crowded out attention to growth in the European debate at the highest level. Because of the attention that was being paid to crisis management and crisis prevention, the effects of the policies of retrenchment on growth struggled for attention on the agenda. However, the deterioration of the economies on the periphery and the social consequences of the crisis forced change in the dominant frame. The Conclusions of the October 2011 European Council notably led with an acknowledgement that: '*it is essential to intensify efforts to secure sustainable and job-creating growth*'.[24] The signal that something had to be done about the economy in the short term was a significant shift in terms of the positioning of issues on the European Council agenda. This was followed by a statement of the European Council on 30 January 2012 entitled *Towards Growth-Friendly Consolidation and Job-Friendly Growth*.[25]

   Prior to the March 2012 European Council, the HoSG of 12 member states sent a letter entitled 'A Plan for Growth in Europe' to the President of the European Council. It was noteworthy for its content but also the fact that it was sent by a group of states that were members and non-members of the euro. The two large states represented on the list, Italy and the UK, were joined by Netherlands, Estonia, Latvia, Finland, Ireland, the Czech Republic, Slovakia, Spain, Sweden and Poland. This was a deliberate and coordinated attempt to shift the EU agenda from austerity to growth and from the euro area exclusively to EU 27. For Italy, it served the Monti strategy of reframing the EU agenda to focus on growth and for the UK, it represented an effort to regain some leverage at the table following the December European Council meeting. The letter was also a reminder to the Franco-German core that there were limits to its domination of the agenda and to the presence of a *de facto* if not *de jure* directoire in the Union. The combination of two large states and a number of medium and small states underlined the importance of alternative coalitions within the EU. The election of M. Hollande in France in May 2012 shifted the coalition dynamics within the Union. He did not lead a coalition against Germany but was more distant from the Berlin orthodoxy than his predecessor. Growth was added to the policy agenda but it did not replace the focus on fiscal consolidation and austerity as the dominant frame.

Section III: Causal Stories Accompanied by Masking

From the outbreak of the Greek crisis, sovereign debt constituted the core of both the meta-narrative and problem frame in the euro area until the end of 2011 and its dominance although eroded has not been replaced by another narrative. A narrative story line dominated the packaging of the issues associated with the crisis, characterised by strong normative underpinnings. The first story line identified fiscal profligacy as the underlying cause of the crisis, attributed blame to the peripheral states and assigned primary responsibility to the euro states themselves. In response to the systemic threat, responsibility was elevated to a shared one within the euro area. This story line was characterised by a strong emphasis on core/periphery and north/south divergence of economic and fiscal performance; Club Med profligacy in contrast to northern prudence. The morality tale was captured by Tilford and Whyte in the following: 'Ever since the eurozone crisis broke out, the North European interpretation of it has prevailed. It essentially sees the crisis as a morality tale, pitting those who sinned against those who stuck to the path of virtue' (Tilford & Whyte, 2011). The future lay with redemption and prevention. If the cause of the crisis was fiscal profligacy, then the cure was fiscal consolidation to be achieved through austerity policies. Responsibility for redemption was assigned to individual euro states but within a framework of economic governance that had the power to sanction the transgressors. The meta-narrative of the crisis and the problem frame, however, served to mask two significant dimensions of the crisis.

The first was the European banking system. States with excessive sovereign debt did not borrow all of the money from their own citizens or banks. In fact, the establishment of the euro had led to an explosion of credit across the eurozone which was part of the wider global increase of credit. For countries such as Spain and Ireland, the underlying problems were in the banking system not the sovereign signature. For every debtor, there was a lender and in the case of the PIIGS, the lenders included banks in the core. From the outset, the problem was an interlinked sovereign debt and banking crisis, a crisis of interdependence and financial integration. When responding to the May 2010 policy interventions in Greece, former Bundesbank chief, Pohl suggested that the rescue

> was about protecting German banks, but especially the French banks, from debt write offs. On the day that the rescue package was agreed on, shares of French banks rose

by up to 24 per cent. Looking at that, you can see what this was really about – namely, rescuing the banks and the rich Greeks. (Der Spiegel, 18.5.2011, http://www.spiegel.de/international/germany/0,1518,695245,00.html)

Banks owe primary responsibility to their shareholders not to taxpayers either of creditor or debtor states. Like all commercial organisations, banks did not want to face losses and if those losses could be offloaded, they could protect their balance sheets. Governments in Europe had just come through a phase, following Lehman Brothers, of injecting capital into troubled banks. This was deeply unpopular with their citizens and they did not want to face another period of recapitalising banks. Moreover, the core countries could shift some of the burden of maintaining the financial system and their banks to the taxpayers on the periphery. The strategy was to buy time in the hope that the banking problem could be contained and that their banks would get sufficient time to strengthen their capital reserves and balance sheets. The problems in the European banking system were disguised in two rounds of limited stress tests (Summer, 2010 and 2011). In February 2011, Barry Eichengreen, among others, was warning of the problems in the European Banking system. In an interview with Der Spiegel, he suggested that:

The present bailout attempts have never made sense. Essentially, all Germany and France want to achieve with these measures is to protect their own banks from collapsing. Now people are beginning to realize that there is no way around rescheduling Greece's debt – and that will also involve the banks. For this to happen, there is only one solution: Europe needs to strengthen its banks! Greece lived beyond its means, but in Ireland and Spain it is the banks that are the problem. The euro crisis is first and foremost a banking crisis. (Der Spiegel, 3.2.2011, http://www.spiegel.de/international/world/0,1518,748239,00.html)

It took until the rescue of Dexia in September 2011, which had passed a stress test in July 2011, for the banking dimension to be highlighted. It was not until June 2012 that the Euro area in a statement affirmed 'that it is imperative to break the vicious circle between banks and sovereigns' (Euro area statement, 29 June 2012).

The second issue that was masked was the role of current account imbalances that had developed, particularly since the creation of the euro, within the euro area. Current account imbalances had deep structural roots and the issue struggled for attention as the crisis unfolded. Current account imbalances were and are particularly problematic in the euro area because of the design of the single currency. The absence of fiscal federalism and the elimination of the policy tool of devaluation greatly narrowed the range of options available to countries in current account deficit. Regaining competitiveness must come through internal adjustment which is politically very difficult, potentially economically damaging and takes a considerable amount of time. In this crisis, the cost of adjustment was borne by the peripheral states. It is not shared between the surplus and deficit countries and there is no fiscal compensation available in the absence of a fiscal union.

Conclusions

Because the euro area crisis first manifested itself in Greece and it had a serious debt problem, the predominant frame that took hold was and remains that the euro area faced a sovereign debt crisis. The narrative of fiscal excess was characterised by a depiction of the profligate Club Med with Ireland as an honorary member and the prudent north. The use of the acronym, PIIGS, in the media although never in official documents underlined the depiction of these countries as dissolute. The language of fiscal imbalances and profligacy acted as a serious conceptual blockage to learning within the euro area and prevented deeper structural issues such as banking, current account imbalances and fiscal federalism receiving serious attention. The issue of growth struggled for space on the agenda. By October 2011, the HoSG highlighted growth but this frame remained subordinate to the debt and fiscal retrenchment frame that predominated throughout the crisis.

The cleavage between creditor and debtor states, which pitted the core against the periphery, was crucial to how the crisis and attendant problems were framed. The countries in the eye in the storm, first Greece, then Ireland and Portugal were small, vulnerable and dependent with little room for manoeuvre in negotiations. For Greece, there was the added problem of deliberately masking the level of debt for many years. The small peripheral states were in the position of *demandeurs*. States that cannot borrow on the financial markets face stark choices; either they receive assistance or they run out of money. Default which is the outcome of overwhelming debt brings with it serious economic and societal dislocation. The creditor states wanted to limit their exposure to indebted states and were reluctant to subsidise other states using taxpayers' money. When the crisis became systemic, through the prospect of contagion, Spain and Italy found themselves in the eye of the storm. Although significant member states, they could not shift the narrative or the policy prescriptions emanating from the European system. The asymmetric relationship between creditor and debtor states disguised an underlying interdependence when banks are brought into the equation. Europe's banks wanted to avoid taking losses or at least avoid losses until they thought that their balance sheets could absorb those losses. Masking the banking issue and the predominant focus on sovereign debt transformed this crisis into a crisis between euro area states and their peoples, creditors and debtors rather than a crisis of interdependence.

Notes

[1] The European Council and the HoSG issued 23 statements, conclusions on the crisis between February 2010 and March 2012. Given the number of texts and their size, it was decided not to do a formal content analysis but to engage in a thematic reading of the texts.

[2] Commission 2008, EMU@10: successes and challenges after 10 years of Economic and Monetary Union, http://ec.europa.eu/economy_finance/publications/publication12682_en.pdf

[3] Statement of the Heads of State and Government of the Euro area, May 7 Brussels http://ec.europa.eu /commission_2010-2014/president/news/speeches-statements/pdf/114295.pdf

[4] Fitch responded by downgrading Greece from A to A−. This was followed by further downgrades in quick succession: from A− to BBB + (Fitch, December 8), S&P to BBB + (December 16) and Moodys from A1 to A2 (December 22).

[5] http://www.ft.com/cms/s/0/eeef5996-0532-11df-a85e-00144feabdc0.html)

[6] http://www.consilium.europa.eu/uedocs/cms_data/docs/pressdata/en/ec/112856.pdf

[7] http://news.bbc.co.uk/2/hi/8508688.stm

[8] http://www.consilium.europa.eu/uedocs/cms_data/docs/pressdata/en/ec/112856.pdf

[9] In early March 2010, Prime Minister Papandreou embarked on a round of meetings with the key players, Chancellor Merkel on the 5th of March, followed by a meeting with Jean Claude Juncker, Chair of Euro-Group on the same day and with President Sarkozy (7th of March). Chancellor Merkel offered political support but said that financial aid was not on the table as it was not needed. Prime Minister Juncker said that Europe was ready

to assist Greece but he did not think assistance would be needed. President Sarkozy in his press conference said that Europe's Finance Ministers were working on a set of measures in case Greece needed them.

[10] Statement by the Euro Heads of State and Government, 25 March 2010 http://www.consilium.europa.eu/uedocs/cms_data/docs/pressdata/en/ec/113563.pdf

[11] http://www.consilium.europa.eu/media/6977/100502-%20eurogroup_statement%20greece.pdf. Providing a loan was justified to safeguard the financial stability of the euro area as a whole and to avoid a Greek default.

[12] http://www.bbc.co.uk/news/10098179.

[13] Trichet, J. C., Der Spiegel http://www.spiegel.de/international/europe/european-central-bank-president-jean-claude-trichet-a-quantum-leap-in-governance-of-the-euro-zone-is-needed-a-694960.html

[14] The dynamic of contagion intensified with downgrades of Spain (Fitch 29 May, Moody's 30 September), Portugal (Moody's 13 July) and Ireland (Moody's 19 July, S&P 24 August).

[15] http://www.ecb.int/press/key/date/2010/html/sp100514.en.html

[16] Interview with Der Spiegel, http://www.ecb.int/press/key/date/2010/html/sp100515.en.html

[17] http://www.consilium.europa.eu/uedocs/cms_data/docs/pressdata/en/ec/114296.pdf

[18] http://www.reuters.com/article/2010/05/07/eurozone-idUSLDE6462FG20100507

[19] http://www.imf.org/external/pubs/ft/reo/2011/eur/eng/ereo0511.pdf)

[20] www.ecb.int/press/pr/date/2011/html/pr110807.en.html

[21] http://www.esrb.europa.eu/news/pr/2011/html/sp111011.en.html

[22] Statement by the HoSG of the Euro Area, Annex 3 of European Council Conclusions, 16/17 December 2010.

[23] http://european-council.europa.eu/media/639235/st00tscg26_en12.pdf

[24] http://www.consilium.europa.eu/uedocs/cms_data/docs/pressdata/en/ec/125496.pdf

[25] Statement of Members of the European Council, 30 January 2012, http://www.consilium.europa.eu/uedocs/cms_Data/docs/pressdata/en/ec/127599.pdf

References

Arghyrou, M. D. & Stoukalas, J. D. (2011) The Greek debt crisis: likely causes mechanics and outcomes, *The World Economy*, 34(2), pp. 173–191.

Baumgartner F. R. & Jones, B. D. (2009) *Agendas and Instability in American Politics*, 2nd ed. (Chicago, IL: University of Chicago Press).

Blyth, M. (2007) Powering puzzling or persuading? The mechanisms of building institutional orders, *International Studies Quarterly*, 51(4), pp. 761–777.

Cassis, Y. (2011) *Crises and Opportunities: The Shaping of Modern Finance* (Oxford, UK: OUP).

Cobb, R. W. & Elder, C. D. (1983) *Participation in American Politics: The Dynamics of Agenda Building* (Baltimore, MD: John Hopkins University Press).

Cobb, R. W. & Ross, M. H. (1997) *Cultural Strategies of Agenda Denial: Avoidance, Attack and Redefinition* (Kansas, KS: University of Kansas Press).

European Council. (2010) *The European Council in 2010*. Available at http://www.european-council.europa.eu/the-president/the-ec-in-2010 (accessed 26 April 2014).

Gamble, A. (2009) *The Spectre at the Feast: Capitalist Crisis and the Politics of Recession* (London: Palgrave Macmillan).

't Hart, P. (1993) Symbols Rituals and Power: The Lost Dimensions of Crisis Management, *Journal of Contingencies and Crisis Management*, 1(1), pp. 36–50.

Hay, C. (1996) Narrating crisis: The discursive construction of the winter of discontent, *Sociology*, 30(2), pp. 253–277.

Jones, B. D. & Baumgartner, F. R. (2005) *The Politics of Attention: How Government Prioritizes Problems* (Chicago, IL: University of Chicago Press).

Khong, Y. F. (1992) *Analogies at War* (Princeton, NJ: Princeton University Press).

Kindgon, J. W. (2011) *Agendas Alternatives and Public Policies*, 3rd ed. (Boston: Longman).

Kindleberger, C. P. (1989) *Manias Panics and Crashes: A history of Financial Crises* (New York, NY: Basic Books).

Lynn, M. (2011) *Bust: Greece the Euro and the Sovereign Debt Crisis* (London, UK: Bloomberg).

Princen, S. (2009) *Agenda-Setting in the European Union* (London, UK: Palgrave).

Rhinard, M. (2010) *Framing Europe: The Policy Shaping Strategies of the European Commission* (Dordrecht, The Netherlands: Martinus Nijhoff).

Sabatier, P. A. & Jenkins, H. C. (1993) *Policy Change and Learning: An Advocacy Coalition Approach* (Boulder: Westview Press).

Scharpf, F. W. (2011) Monetary Union, Fiscal Crisis and the Preemption of Democracy. MPIfG Discussion Paper, (11/11).

Schelke, W. (2011) A tale of two crises: The Euro area in 2008/09 and in 2010, *European Political Science*, 10(3), pp. 375–383.

Schmidt, V. (2002) Does discourse matter in the politics of welfare state adjustment? *Comparative Political Studies*, 35(2), pp. 168–193.

Schmidt, V. (2008) Discursive Institutionalism: The Explanatory Power of Ideas and Discourse, *American Review of Political Science*, 11, pp. 303–326.

Stone, D. A. (1989) Causal Stories and the Formation of Policy Agendas, *Political Science Quarterly*, 104(2), pp. 281–300.

Stone, D. (2002) *Policy Paradox: The Art of Political Decision Making*, 3rd ed. (New York, NY: Norton and Co).

Tilford, P. & Whyte, P. (2011) *Why stricter rules threaten the Eurozone*, Center for European Reform. Available at http://www.cer.org.uk/sites/default/files/publications/attachments/pdf/2011/essay_eurozone_9nov11–4084.pdf (accessed 25 January 2012).

Widmaier, W. W., Blyth, M. & Seabrooke, L. (2007) Exogenous shocks or endogenous constructions? The meanings of wars and crises, *International Studies Quarterly*, 51(4), pp. 747–759.

Boundaries of Welfare between the EU and Member States during the 'Great Recession'

CAROLINE DE LA PORTE* & PHILIPPE POCHET**

*Department of Globalisation and Society, Roskilde University, Denmark; **EuropeanTrade Union Insiliuie, Belglum

ABSTRACT   This paper focuses on the changing boundaries of welfare between EU and national levels by developing a dynamic and actor-centred approach, where different groups of actors compete to influence the social and economic dimensions of EU social policy. The success of ideas and policies around welfare-state reform changes over time in line with socio-economic conditions as well as shifting political-party governmental coalitions in the Council. We argue that in particular the economically oriented actors, including the European Central Bank, have been successful in the context of the Great Recession. More recently, social priorities around notions such as social investment are becoming more central in the EU debate on economic and social policy.

1.   Introduction

Since 2010, not a month has gone by without an EU member state embarking on major reform of its welfare state, due to the crisis of public finances. Some of the structural reforms have arguably been necessary, particularly in the countries with high levels of public debt. The policy response at the national level, encouraged by the EU and international levels, has by and large been to implement austerity policies. While this may have reassured markets in the very short term, the depth of austerity has in some cases stifled growth (Krugman, 2012). But this context of increased economic vulnerability has created the possibility for carrying through reforms that were unthinkable prior to the crisis, such as pension reform. At the same time, social investment policies still prevail in most European countries, although the quality may be decreasing (Morel, Palier & Palme, 2012; Kvist, 2013).

At the EU level, there have been ongoing discussions over the last two decades about whether, and if so how to modernize the European social model. The economically oriented actors, that are mainly the Directorate-General for Economic and Financial Affairs (DG ECFIN), the European Central Bank (ECB), Business Europe and their networks at the national level, have insisted on the need to have sustainable public finances. The socially oriented actors, that are DG employment and social affairs (DG EMPL), the European Trade Union Confederation and social NGOs with weaker networks at the national level, have supported this agenda but have equally put forward the need to ensure the solidarity, fairness and equity in European welfare states. The instruments used at the European level for economic and social governance were initially, in the 1990s and 2000s, rather flexible and soft, but have since 2010 been made tougher and at least theoretically more coercive, around the European Semester and various new legislative initiatives aimed at strengthening it (de la Porte & Heins, forthcoming). Parallel to the strengthening of economic governance, the European social model was put on the sidelines due to the emphasis on preventing a sovereign debt crisis. However, there is now a renewed effort by socially oriented actors to re-launch thinking on the European social model. In particular, the ideas around social investment have led to various policy initiatives in the Commission, although they are much less constraining than the initiatives for containing public debt (Kvist, 2013). A further problem is that in a context of austerity, there is not much money to 'invest' socially, making it difficult to have high-quality social investment.

Much has been written about the crisis, welfare-state reform and the new European instruments. One, mainly consisting of economists or political economists, has focused on the creation (or absence) of new economic institutions at the EU level for accompanying, re-balancing or mitigating the previous institutional framework, which was considered to be incomplete. The other, composed mainly of sociologists, political scientists and lawyers, has centred on the consequences of the crisis on the national welfare state (Farnsworth & Irving, 2011).

The literature thus far assesses that the attempt by international actors to re-launch growth and regulate international finance is insufficient and has, thus far, failed. It also underscores the fact that governments have developed crisis responses behind closed doors to a large extent excluding traditional industrial actors, in particular trade unions, although business interests are taken into account. The literature has also shown that the patterns of response follow recent paths of institutional change. These new paths include the development of employment at the margins, which re-enforces patterns of labour market segmentation, toughening access to unemployment and other benefits, as well as curtailing public expenditure in the areas of health care, pensions and education. Finally, the literature underscores that it is necessary to move beyond the theories mainly focusing on the nation-state, i.e. the worlds of welfare capitalism or varieties of capitalism (Farnsworth, & Irving, 2011; Bermeo & Pontusson, 2012). Our ambition is to bring in the EU level by considering changing boundaries of welfare in complex processes of interaction between the EU and national levels (Ferrera, 2005). In this perspective, our contribution focuses in particular on actors, politics, and ideas, and the institutional context they are embedded in. We analyse changes at European and national levels longitudinally, throughout a 20-year period.

The remainder of the paper is organized as follows. The following (second) section lays down the theoretical framework used to analyse the EU – national level developments with regard to the welfare state over time. The third section presents the period from the 1990s and the fourth section centres on the developments since the crisis. The final section concludes.

2. Theoretical Approach

We adopt a broad theoretical approach about changes to welfare-state boundaries, combining insights from Rokkan (centre formation, system building, political structuring) as adapted by Ferrera (2005). With regard to boundary formation, what is central is the dismantling and restructuring of old boundaries and restructuring along new, wider boundaries (Ferrera, 2005). We focus mostly on the latter. As put by Ferrera (2005, p. 210)

> At the EU level restructuring would imply dynamics of institutional reforms or experimentation aimed at stabilizing the complex web of spatial interactions which is emerging in the wider and reconfigured EU space, with a view to gradually 'Europeanizing' the sphere of social sharing.

The dynamics are not only vertical but also horizontal between actors from different fields. As Martin and Ross (2004) underline:

> Social models are a complex of institutions and interconnected social contracts that morally engage actors. However much they may disagree on specific issues, a critical mass of these actors will normally act to preserve the broader engagements of the contract. The institutions are interconnected, or clustered, such that actors often perceive threats to particular arrangements as threats to others, even if the functional relationships are apparently different.

Another fundamental element is the political dimension of tensions between left and right at EU level, which we will take account of in our analysis. In this regard, Manow, Schäfer and Zorn (2004) have found that 1995 represented a turning point in EU social policy, since it was the first time that there was a majority of left-leaning governments. However, the manifestos of these left parties all indicated a shift towards more support of market policies. This political context opened up the development of multiple OMC processes reflecting the ideas of these more market-friendly left-leaning parties around issues such as social inclusion, quality in work and a balance between social and economic aims.

In summary, our approach is a dynamic and actor-centred one, where different groups of actors compete to influence the social dimension, parallel to the economic and political dimensions of EU social policy. In this process, the relationship between national and supranational levels is an ongoing political process that alters the boundaries between the EU and the nation-state in an area considered to be in the realm of national sovereignty – the welfare state and social policies.

3. 1990s to 2007: A Balance in Economic and Social Policies

The Maastricht Treaty (signed in 1992) creating the Economic and Monetary Union (EMU), marks a change in EU-nation states boundaries. Monetary policy was pooled at the EU level, with the independent ECB as the key player, setting interest rates based on the average performances of EMU economies. The Treaty of Lisbon highlights that the ECB's main role is to ensure a policy of price stability and also to support the general economic policy of the Union, including economic growth as well as a high level of employment and social progress. The belief was that the EMU would have an integrative effect with spillover effects from monetary to economic policy and eventually to other areas, such as social policy (Scharpf, 2002; Degryse, 2012). Since policy areas are increasingly inter-related in this context, both economically and socially oriented actors mobilized in order to influence the policy process.

This is in turn influenced strongly by the political orientation of member state governments (see Table 1). In order to analyse this, we have used the situation in March each year, when the yearly European Council Spring meeting that deals with socio-economic affairs is held. In case of coalitions, we have taken the political colour of the Prime Minister, which is relevant because the EU Council is composed of Prime ministers that have the key positions to decide about the broad directions.

From the late 1990s to mid-2000s, left-leaning governments prevailed. It is to be noted that the eastern enlargement of 2007 changed the political party leaning of the governments. At the beginning, the negative impact was not so strong, as the new members had a weak political clout, but this changed progressively after 2005.

In the political context that prevailed in the preparation of monetary union, a series of political, social and trade union actors, aware of the risk of social policies being turned into an adjustment variable in the case of economic shocks in the eurozone, sought to develop a social dimension of economic and monetary integration. At the national level, the 1990s also saw the conclusion of numerous national social pacts among political, economic and social actors (Fajertag & Pochet, 2000). In the majority of EMU accession countries, a great deal of thought was being given during this period to the new framework of constraints represented by monetary union, particularly in relation to inflation and wage policy (including the national-level structuring of collective bargaining) (Pochet, 1999).

At the EU level, the period between 1995 and 2004, that might be described as 'the social moment', results firstly from a concern that the Maastricht Treaty was underdeveloped with regard to employment and social policies, compared with tighter convergence criteria for economic and monetary policies in the development of the monetary union. Second, it was actively brought to the agenda by coming to power in the member states, as from 1995, of a majority of centre-left parties and an advocacy coalition in favour of rebalancing economic and social integration (Van riel & Van der Meer, 2002; Jenson & Pochet, 2006). This concern to have social policies more integrated at the EU level in the context of EMU culminated with the Amsterdam Treaty (1997) and the European Employment Strategy initiated by it. The process was taken further with the Lisbon Strategy (2000) and the development of the open methods of coordination for a range of social policy issues (employment, poverty, pensions, etc.) (de la Porte & Pochet, 2012; Barcevicius et al., 2014).

Table 1. Left-leaning governments among EU member states 1994–2005

	1994	1995	1996	1997	1998	1999	2000	2001	2002	2003	2004	2005
Number of left leaning government	4	7	7	6[a]	8	11	9	9	7	4[b]	9	9
Number of EU member states	12	15	15	15	15	15	15	15	15	15	15	25

[a]The UK and France will both change to left-leaning governments in the late spring of 1997. UK and after France will turn left in April/May.
[b]Germany, UK, Greece, Sweden.

The ECB's policy, grounded in supply-side economics supports 'structural reforms', such as tax cuts, privatization, labour market flexibilization and deregulation Formally, the ECB does not have the power to propose such policies (Scharpf, 2011). Nevertheless, social policy came under pressure via the fiscal consolidation aims necessary for the establishment and functioning of the EMU.[1] In 1999, European macroeconomic dialogue was developed by Oscar Lafontaine, then Finance Minister, to organize a dialogue among the social partners, the ECB and the Commission. The basic idea was to have a signalling process between the different parties around wage and monetary policy around the German model.

As the socially oriented actors were dynamic and their initiatives were backed by a supporting political environment, the economically oriented actors that formed an epistemic community around monetarist ideas (Verdun, 1996) were taken by surprise. As noted by Dyson (2002, p. 101)

> the ECB-centric Eurozone policy community had to absorb and accommodate the so-called Luxembourg 'process' – with its annual employment guidelines and national action plans – and the Cologne 'process' – the Employment Pact and the macroeconomic dialogue. These developments opened up the dialogue about EMU by transforming the definition of who was in the policy domain.

At the same time, national governments were increasingly trying to enhance labour market participation in order to address the burden of ageing populations. Over the last two decades, policy-makers have introduced flexibility at the margins in countries with increasingly flexible labour markets, particularly in some sectors to enable employers to adjust rapidly and at low cost to fluctuations in economic demands (Emmenegger et al., 2012). As a result, there is an increasing proportion of the population that is on atypical contracts, with less protection than workers on contracts of indeterminate duration, and these workers are more vulnerable in a crisis situation. Contrasting with the reforms in the crisis period, at the end of the 2000s the reforms from the mid-1990s until the crisis were negotiated in a context where social partners were key players (Fajertag & Pochet, 2000).

At the beginning of the 2000s, a series of initiatives were to be undertaken by the ECB, DG ECFIN, the Ecofin Council and its subordinate Economic Policy Committee (EPC). Their focus was to analyse labour markets and wage development, especially in the Eurozone. In many respects, they entered the territory of the more socially oriented actors (DG employment, the Social Affairs Council and its two supporting committees: the Employment committee and the Social Protection Committee.

After 2005, the 'social' dynamic was halted to a great extent because the left-leaning political parties had lost ground. This is reflected in the report on the mid-term evaluation of the Lisbon strategy, 'Jobs, jobs, jobs', which refocused the whole debate on growth, competitiveness and flexibility. In this context, the economically oriented actors developed multiple initiatives in order to create networks and knowledge, but always around the aim of labour market restructuring and wage developments. In 2005, the ECB set up a 'Wage dynamic network' to assess the risks of, in particular, wage divergence. The network was structured into three working groups, namely, 'macro', 'micro' and 'survey'. Since 2005, DG ECFIN has annually published a report entitled 'Labour market and wage development'. This draws on two in-depth databases developed by the economically oriented actors. Started in December 2005, the LABREF database is a joint project managed by the European Commission DG ECFIN and the EPC to systematically record factual information on policy measures affecting the labour market institutions and thus likely to have an impact on labour market performance as part of the general economic surveillance of Member States . The AMECO database, on wages and wage developments, is another area where economically oriented actors are active. Another EPC sub-group deals with structural reforms linked to the Lisbon Strategy (the so-called 'LIME group') and bases its work on the assessment of the impacts of structural reforms in a major database known as MACMIC.

One could argue that collecting data and accumulating knowledge in order to analyse the likely impact of labour market reforms and wages in the context of monetary union do not indicate what reforms were supported in normative terms. However, the concern with labour markets and wages among the economically oriented actors has always built up around the over-arching concern of optimizing the functioning of the single market. We see this, for example, in an annex to a recent report by DG ECFIN. In the area of collective bargaining, the policy advice includes the following: decrease the bargaining coverage or (automatic) extension of collective agreements, decentralise the bargaining system, for instance by introducing/extending the possibility to derogate from higher level agreements or negotiate firm-level agreements, and reduce the wage-setting power of trade unions (European Commission, 2012a, p. 113).

In this period, welfare states are still primarily nationally bounded, although the common monetarist policy strongly affects economic and social policy.

4.   Financial Crisis, Altered Governance and Welfare Models

When the crisis broke out in 2008, it brought to the fore the inbuilt asymmetry in the euro project – the inherent problem of a monetary union without a full fiscal union. The first response to this at the EU level was focused on reducing excessive public debt, and since 2010 on preventing a sovereign debt crisis. It was in this political context that the social developments and achievements of the 1990s and early 2000s came to be unravelled and that the economically oriented actors, well informed about wage policies, labour markets and social protection, became powerful ideational agenda-setters.

Indeed, the transformation of the crisis of bank debts into a sovereign debt crisis from 2010 enabled the economically oriented actors (ECB, economic and finance ministers, DG ECFIN) to put their ideas into practice around labour market and wage policies as well as social protection reform. It was in the context of the monetarist paradigm that the principle of internal devaluation was proposed and applied in practice in the countries that entered a recession and were in a sovereign debt crisis (i.e. Greece and Ireland). In the context of the crisis, the economically oriented actors were increasingly perceived as legit-imate, even in terms of policy advice. This was not the case before the crisis.

The policy perspectives of the economically oriented actors are favoured in a political context where there is a minority of left-leaning governments among EU member states. Table 2 shows their relative weakness, particularly in 2010–11 when the most important decisions on changes to economic governance were made.

As a response to the crisis, the economically oriented actors (especially the ECB, DG ECFIN and the Ecofin Council) have sought to increase coherence between economic, financial and fiscal policies in an attempt to restore financial stability in the eurozone. We focus here on the ECB, which has taken on an unprecedented role, able for the first time since its creation to enact its policy ideas. In terms of knowledge production in the

Table 2. Left-leaning governments 2005–2014

Year	2005	2006	2007	2008	2009	2010	2011	2012	2013	2014
Number of left leaning governments	9	9	10	10	9	9	6[a]	4[b]	8	10
Number of EU member states	25	25	25	27	27	27	27	27	27	28

[a]Portugal, Spain, Greece, Cyprus, Slovenia, Austria.
[b]Belgium, Austria, Denmark, Cyprus.

period between 2009 and 2011, not less than 51 Working Papers were published by the ECB covering an impressive number of issues relating to the links between labour markets, wages and the euro (see Degryse *et al.*, 2013). As mentioned previously, its knowledge production role is not new.

But what is new is that it indicated what structural reforms were required at the national level in return for its intervention on the sovereign debt market. In fact, the ECB, in the absence of any credible coordinated political response, became the only body capable of exerting a firm influence on the financial markets that had become decisive in the global financial crisis. The ECB's new position was therefore right at the centre of gravity of the normative apparatus, located mid-way between the markets and the political sphere. Torres (2013, pp. 293–294) poignantly argues that:

> For the ECB, this 'invasion of other policy domains' – by calling for sound economic policy management, in particular in the fiscal domain, for structural reforms and for reinforced economic governance in general – is motivated by the fact that the euro area is at the epicentre of sovereign debt crisis.

In the following, we analyse the features of the new economic governance structure developed after 2010. The most important change is that the instruments used to suggest 'structural reforms' have become more binding. We have been witnessing a series of radical and rather similar reforms in a number of countries, though not in all. These reforms are imposed by the European Union, or the 'troika' (Commission, ECB and IMF) for those countries that are in receipt of financial assistance from the EU, by way of a set of new procedures put in place between 2010 and 2012. Memoranda of understanding (MoU) involve financial assistance provide by the EU-IMF, in exchange for carrying through specified reforms. Furthermore, this is monitored very closely by the European authorities, with on-site visits and the scrutiny of reforms effectively carried out.

For other EU countries as well, the tools have become more stringent than previously, which are designed to keep member states more under control. These changes are organized around the European Semester and have become more intrusive (see table in annex). This has altered the interrelationship between the EU and the member state actors and restrains member states in welfare reforms, weakening the national boundaries of welfare further.

In 2010, the European Semester was developed in order to coordinate *ex ante* the budgetary and economic policies of member states and to increase coherence among different policies. The Six Pack and the Fiscal Compact aim to reinforce the policy aims of the European Semester and to enhance EU surveillance of member state policies and coercion in the case of non-compliance. Both initiatives provide the European institutions with more surveillance power vis-à-vis member states' national budgets compared to pre-crisis and are designed to reinforce the implementation of the Stability and Growth Pact (SGP) and the European Semester within which they are embedded. The Six Pack does not only cover fiscal, but also macroeconomic surveillance under the new 'Macroeconomic Imbalance Procedure' (MIP), which aims to be more broad-ranging than the former focus only on public finances. Under the Six Pack, member states budget balance shall converge towards country-specific medium-term objectives (MTOs) (relating to the SGP's preventative arm). Stricter application of fiscal rules should be ensured by defining quantitatively what a 'significant deviation' from the MTO or the adjustment path towards it means.

The Six Pack also reinforces the corrective arm of the SGP, that is, the EDP, which applies to member states that have breached either the deficit *or* debt criterion (the latter not being operational before the Six Pack). Another important novelty is that the Six Pack introduces reverse qualified majority vote (RQMV) for deciding on sanctions. This means that a qualified majority of member states (in ECOFIN) must be against a Commission (DG ECFIN) proposal for an EDP or for a sanction to be overturned. This constitutes a very clear increase in power for the European Commission, especially DG ECFIN.

The Fiscal Compact applies to all EU countries except the UK and the Czech Republic. It requires them to ensure convergence towards country-specific MTOs, as well as to the balanced budget rules of the SGP, with an additional limit of 0.5 per cent of GDP on structural deficits (that can be extended to 1 per cent in exceptional circumstances). The Fiscal Compact requires these budget rules to be integrated in national law. Corrective mechanisms at the national level will be triggered automatically in case of deviation from the MTO or the adjustment path towards it. Likewise, the automatism of the EDP has been strengthened. Two benchmarks were changed: the annual deficit which is now linked to the economic cycle and the move towards the global debt (60 per cent) as a key indicator. That should not be a problem as the latter indicator better encompasses the past events (global debt is the sum of deficits and surpluses in the past) that the annual deficit. Nevertheless, a mandatory reduction by 5 per cent put severe pressure on countries highly indebted (for example Italy) but also for those with growing global debt (Greece, Ireland, Portugal and Spain). For these countries with a debt higher or close to 100 per cent, it means a reduction of 2 per cent a year. So, they will be forced to have a high primary surplus to be able to reach this ambitious goal. Should a country fail to transpose the budget rules and the correction mechanism on time, the European Court of Justice has the jurisdiction to take a decision on the matter, including the imposition of a financial sanction (up to 0.1 per cent of GDP).

In summary, contrasting with the pre-crisis period, the European Semester now takes account of the whole economy via the MIP, with new targets for budget deficits and public debt. This is because it became clear to European actors that taking account of budgetary discipline alone would not suffice for economic growth or crisis prevention. Since the MIP is the central instrument on which European actors formulate national recommendations and, more crucially, launch an EDP in the case of non-compliance, intrusion in member state policies could be high, as policy prescriptions may include the privatization of public services, labour market flexibilization, tax reforms, liberalization of product and service markets as well as social spending cuts. Also, sanctions can be implemented quite early on if certain targets are missed (de la Porte & Heins, forthcoming).

The crisis has led to a situation whereby there is more EU *interference* in national policy, where EU competencies are marginal, but where particularly the ECB and other financial actors require policy change, particularly for the countries under Memorandum of Understanding. There is also more surveillance activity by the EU to control whether member states are implementing the agreed policies and respecting or moving towards EU benchmarks and/or national targets.

Concerning the social dimension, 'Europe 2020' replaced the Lisbon Strategy, within which the instruments for re-calibrating social policy are now embedded. The link with the SGP is much closer as well, since Europe 2020 is integrated into the European semester. The assessment of the cause of the crisis by European economic elites is that some countries have not paid sufficient attention to structural reforms. The main aim stipulated is therefore to undertake structural reforms 'of pensions, health care, social protection and education systems' (European Commission, 2012b, p. 26) in order to achieve 'fiscal consolidation and long-term financial sustainability' (European Commission, 2012b, p. 26). Thus, even within processes more interested in social equity and solidarity, the genuine policy attention to issues of inequality is addressed within a framework aiming at macro-economic and financial sustainability (de la Porte & Heins, forthcoming).

As we have seen, the ECB and DG ECFIN have increased their knowledge of labour markets (and the national reforms on this score) and are in a position to exert much stronger and more precisely targeted pressure than was previously the case, partly because of their greater expertise but above all because the crisis has placed the ECB at the centre of the stage. It is mid-way between the markets which it has managed to reassure and the political actors whom it tells what they must do so as to ensure that the markets remain calm and that the ECB will take action to stabilize the system in the event of crisis.

5. Conclusions

The asymmetry in the institutional structure of EMU as adopted under the Maastricht Treaty was met at the national level in the 1990s and early 2000s by the conclusion of social pacts in the member states. Parallel to this, social strategies were put in place at the European level and included the development of the European social dialogue, the European employment strategy, the Lisbon strategy as well as multiple open methods of coordination in social policy. The EMU thus had, to a certain extent, its social dimension, even if this was weak, contradictory and fragile. In a sense, it was the recognition of the fact that the borders between EU and national levels were *de facto* more permeable, but that there was a concern of maintaining intergenerational solidarity and increasing equality. At the same time, it was clear that European welfare states had to be reformed, to decrease passive benefits, while at the same time including more people into the labour market in order to maintain welfare societies.

From the mid-2000s, this aim to maintain and to reform social policy was altered with a change in national governments from the centre-right and right, as well as the arrival of Mr Barroso as President of the European Commission. The open methods of coordination were gradually voided of their substance, the European social dialogue was no longer fed, the social goals of the Lisbon Strategy were neglected, while there were few new European legislative initiatives in the social policy field. In the wake of the 2008 financial crisis, the European Union as a whole underwent the second phase of weakening and little remained of the social dimension of the EMU. After first tackling the onset of crisis in

2008–09 with measures to boost economic activity and employment, the member states subsequently embarked upon major programmes to reduce public expenditure and to introduce structural reforms.

The reforms in question related principally to labour law and social protection. At the level of content, they followed mainstream economists, who generally regard the European social model as the main reason for the deterioration in the member states' public finances. If the content of these reforms was not new, the political and socio-economic context opened up, by contrast, an unexpected window of opportunity for the proponents of draconian reforms.

These reforms have been undertaken in the framework of strengthened economic governance. While it is not possible to draw conclusions on the impact of these, what is perfectly clear is that the social policy recommendations are developing a new message containing specific ideas about how a national social model should operate. The tenets of this message are as follows: the costs of health care and pension systems should be pegged or even reduced; the wage formation systems should be brought within the realm of competition; the social benefit systems create disincentives to labour market participation and labour costs must be reduced. This message contains nothing or very little about how social models are intended to reduce inequality, to supply assistance and protection, nor about the ways in which they could contribute to the operation of a regulated market economy.

Because of a failure to commit to a real economic union, that is to say, a voluntary process of convergence of the economic performance and social cohesion of the eurozone member states, social policies – in the broad sense – have today been designated as the main adjustment variables of monetary union. What the dominant discourse states is that internal devaluations – which will affect wages, labour law and social protection – must from now on replace the practice of currency devaluation, as it was practised in the past.

More recently, there have been efforts to re-launch a social agenda, notably via the European Commission's social investment package. This embodies an effort not only to maintain European social models, but also to adjust them so as to maintain competitiveness. In essence, it aims to invest in human capabilities and is designed to do so across the life-course. It aims to be intergenerational and takes account of gender. However, one of the main limitations is that the quality of social investment is not likely to increase in the context of the Great Recession.

The boundaries of welfare between EU and national levels have changed from semi-permeable to permeable in a crisis context, where the economically oriented actors have had the upper hand. This has been possible due to the political context, where left-leaning governments had virtually no voice.

Note

[1] This is reflected by the views of Jean-Claude Trichet, who was to become the ECB President in 2001. He underscores that in the context of the single market, increased capital mobility and EMU, it is necessary to decrease labour cost differentials and to de-regulate labour markets (see Barbier, 2012)

References

Barcevicius, E., Weishaupt, T. & Zeitlin, J. (eds.) (2014) *Assessing the Open Method of Coordination: Institutional Design and National Influence of EU Social Policy Coordination* (Basingstoke: Palgrave).

Bermeo, N. & Pontusson, J. (Eds.) (2012) *Coping with Crisis: Government Reactions to the Great Recession* (New York: Russell Sage Foundation).

Degryse, C. (2012) La nouvelle gouvernance économique européenne. Courrier Hebdomadaire du Crisp No 2148–49, Brussels.

de la Porte, C. & et Heins, E. (forthcoming) Game change in EU social policy: From optional re-calibration to Coercive retrenchment, in: E. Xiarchogiannopoulou & M. J. et Rodrigues (Eds.) *The Eurozone Crisis and the Transformation of Democracy* (Ashgate).

de la Porte, C. & Pochet, P. (2012) 'Why and how (still) study the OMC?', *Journal of European Social Policy*, 22 (2): 336–349.

Degryse, C., Jepsen, M. & Pochet, P. (2013) The Euro crisis and its impact on national and European social policies, Working Papers 05. European Trade Union Institute (ETUI).

Dyson, K. (2002) EMU as Europeanisation: Convergence diversity and contengency, in: A. Verdun (Ed.) *The Euro European Integration Theory and Economic and Monetary Union*, pp. 91–108 (Lanham: Rowman & Litlefield Publishers).

Emmenegger, P., Häusermann, S., Palier, B. & Seeleib-Kaiser, M. (2012) *The Age of Dualization: The Changing Face of inequality in De-industrializing Societies* (Oxford: Oxford University Press).

European Commission (2012a) Labour Market Developments in Europe, European Economy paper series no. 5, 2012, Brussels.

European Commission (2012b), Annual Growth Survey 2013, COM(2012) 750 final, 28.11.2012.

Fajertag, G. & Pochet, P. (Eds.) (2000) *Social Pacts in Europe – New Dynamics* (Brussels: European Trade Union Institute – Observatoire Social Européen).

Farnsworth, K. & Irving, Z. (Eds.) (2011) *Social Policy in Challenging Times: Economic Crisis and Welfare Systems* (Bristol: Policy Press).

Ferrera, M. (2005) The Boundaries of Welfare. European Integration and the New Spatial Politics of Social Protection (Oxford: Oxford University Press).

Jenson, J. & Pochet, P. (2006) Employment and social policy since maastricht: Standing up to the European Monetary Union, in: R. Fishman & A. Messina (Eds) (2006) The Year of the Euro. The cultural, social, and political import of Europe's Common currency, pp. 161–185 (Notre Dame: University of Notre Dame Press).

Krugman, P. (2012) *End This Depression Now!* Norton.

Kvist, J. (2013) The post-crisis European social model: Developing or dismantling social investments? *Journal of International and Comparative Social Policy*, 29(1), pp. 91–107.

Manow, P., Schäfer, A. & Zorn, H. (2004) European social policy and Europe's party-political center of gravity. MPIfG Discussion Paper 04/6, Cologne.

Martin, A. & Ross, G. (Eds.) (2004) *Euros and Europeans: Monetary Integration and the European Model of Society* (Cambridge: Cambridge University Press).

Morel, N., Palier, B. & Palme, J. (Eds.) (2012) *Towards a Social Investment State? Ideas Policies and Challenges* (Bristol: The Policy Press).

Pochet, P. (Dir.) (1999) *Monetary Union and Collective Bargaining in Europe* (Brussels: P- I-E Peter Lang).

van Riel, B. & van der Meer, M. (2002) The advocacy coalition for European employment policy – The European integration process after EMU, Marburg.

Scharpf, F. (2002) The European social model, *Journal of Common Market Studies*, 40(4), pp. 645–670.

Scharpf, F. (2011) Monetary union fiscal crisis and the preemption of democracy. Discussion Paper 11/11, Max Planck Institute for the Study of Societies, Cologne.

Torres, F. (2013) The EMU's legitimacy and the ECB as a strategic political player in the crisis context, *Journal of European Integration*, 35(3), pp. 287–300.

Verdun, A. (1996) An asymmetrical economic and monetary union in the EU: Perceptions of monetary authorities and social partners, *Journal of European Integration*, 20(1), pp. 59–81.

Annex. Typology of 'intrusiveness' of EU instruments

Dimension of intrusiveness	*Degree of intrusiveness*			
	Low	Medium	High	Very high
Interference NB. *This may differ according to the type of welfare state (and policy area)*	Uncontroversial objectives, not challenging existent member state policies or institutional arrangements, merely suggesting some minor adjustments in a particular policy area	Objectives challenging some existing policies, but not the underlying institutional structure of a policy area	Objectives requiring comprehensive policy reform, with the potential for undermining the existing institutional structure and fundamental principles of a policy area	Objectives requiring far-reaching structural policy reform, with a high potential for undermining the existing institutional structure and for changing the fundamental principles of a policy area
Surveillance	Infrequent *ex-post* EU surveillance of national policy reports	Frequent *ex-post* surveillance of national reports that specify policy which should meet common benchmarks and/or own national targets	Regular ex-ante and *ex-post* EU surveillance of national policy reports. member states are held accountable to EU benchmarks and are required to specify national targets and action plan to meet these	Frequent ex-ante and *ex-post* EU surveillance of national policy reports. member states are held accountable to their own policies (which must aim to meet European targets and/or policy)
Coercion	'Naming and shaming' and/or soft recommendations (with a weak treaty base)	Strong Treaty-based recommendations, but no sanctions	Treaty-based recommendations and ultimately financial sanctions in the case of non-compliance	Treaty-based corrective action and/or conditionality in order to receive financial assistance

Source: Reproduced and adapted from de la Porte and Heins (forthcoming).

The EU-25 *Fiscal Compact*: Differentiated *Spillover* Effects under Crisis Conditions

CHRISTIAN SCHWEIGER

School of Government and International Affairs, Durham University, Durham, UK

ABSTRACT   *This article analyses the intergovernmental Fiscal Compact, which represents the latest layer in the emerging new governance framework European Union (EU) governments have adopted in response to the sovereign debt crisis in the eurozone. The crisis has initiated a new wave of selective functionalist spillover towards noticeably different levels of policy coordination between the eurozone-18 core and the remaining EU member states, who are divided into a semi-periphery and an outer periphery group. As an intergovernmental contract with currently 25 EU member states the Fiscal Compact signifies the decline of the traditional community method of universal supranational integration in favour of a more differentiated form of intergovernmental policy coordination between groups of member states.*

The 2008–9 global financial crisis severely affected the economies of the eurozone, particularly those of Southern Europe. The collapse of major US financial institutions such as Freddie Mac, Fannie Mae and Lehman Brothers had profound ripple effects on the economies of Ireland and Greece who suffered drastic liquidity problems in the course of 2009. In the same year markets became increasingly shaky about the stability of other eurozone economies, which raised questions about the long-term stability of the single currency. In March 2010 the European Union (EU) lead by an initially reluctant Germany responded with the initiation of the new annual cycle of policy coordination under the post-Lisbon *Europe 2020 Strategy*. This was followed by a *Euro Plus Pact* in spring 2011, which established enhanced policy coordination between the eurozone and six outsiders. At the EU summit in Brussels in December 2011 German Chancellor Angela Merkel and French president Nicholas Sarkozy went one step further and suggested a new treaty which would require member states to determine a fiscal spending brake in their national constitutions. This plan was rejected by the British Prime Minister David Cameron who argued that 'what is on offer isn't in Britain's interests' on the basis that he could not accept a 'treaty within a treaty' which would ultimately affect Britain's sovereign economic policy-making (Traynor et al., 2012). Cameron had made his agreement on the inclusion of the treaty in the EU's *acquis* dependent on the inclusion of a protocol which would guarantee Britain safeguards against an expansion of EU regulatory powers over Britain's financial services sector (Grant, 2011).

The British veto against the Franco-German desire to instil budgetary stability in the EU treaty structure represents a significant development for the future of the EU. In effect it decouples Britain and currently also the Czech Republic from the emerging deepening policy coordination between the eurozone core and the outside periphery of non-euro members. The countries who signed up to the *Euro Plus Pact* (Bulgaria, Denmark, Latvia Lithuania, Poland and Romania) therefore emerged as the new *semi-periphery* which is closely associated to the deepening policy coordination in the eurozone-18 core. Latvia has in the meantime left the EPP and become a full member of the eurozone. The *semi-periphery* includes Hungary and Sweden, who are both not part of the EPP but nevertheless signatories of the March 2012 intergovernmental *Treaty on Stability, Coordination and Governance (Fiscal Compact)* which came into effect on 1 January 2013. Britain and the Czech Republic, who both opted out from the EPP and the *Fiscal Compact* currently represent the outer fringe of the EU's periphery.

The Institutional Failures of Econimic and Monetary Union

The divisions which emerged amongst EU member states with regard to the participation in the different layers of policy coordination illustrate the limitations of the classic Community method of integration. This has been evident for some time, most noticeably in the fact that Economic and Monetary Union (EMU) in 2002 had created a group of countries who voluntarily agreed to transfer the control over their monetary policy to the newly established supranational European Central Bank. The group of eurozone countries hence had moved further than those on the outside whose pooling of national sovereignty remained limited to the areas of binding Single Market legislation and limited areas of judicial and police cooperation.

The emerging eurozone had clearly become the core project of the EU. It was widely expected that policy coordination would be extended to further areas such as employment policy, education, welfare and taxation and could even result in at least partial harmonisation in these areas (Hantrais, 2007, p. 26). In reality the member states of the eurozone remained reluctant to accompany monetary union with deeper economic policy integration beyond the liberalisation agenda of the internal market. What was branded as a project which would combine monetary integration with the gradual binding coordination of core economic policy areas essentially ended up as a currency union with a set of budgetary rules which were after all interpreted in an extremely flexible manner. The original design of EMU consequently suffered from the fundamental flaw of taking away control over monetary policy from member states whilst practically failing to exercise an effective supervision of budgetary spending and a binding coordination of crucial policy areas such as wages, taxes and welfare (McCann, 2010, p. 36). The adoption of the *open method of coordination* (OMC) under the Lisbon Strategy in 2000 and its revised version in 2005 determined a set of targets which member states were expected to meet by engaging in a system of mutual policy learning under the OMC. The strategy essentially relied on the willingness of national governments to engage in best-practice benchmarking on the basis of peer pressure through a system which limited sanctions to being named and shamed in progress reports. In practice this resulted in insufficient progress towards national policy coordination and most significantly in the persistence of stark differences in the overall performance of member states in the policy areas which were operated under the OMC (Hodson, 2010, p. 173).

Philippe C. Schmitter has repeatedly argued that over time the *spillover* towards deeper integration did not emerge on the basis of internal pressures (such as demands by existing supranational actors to expand their powers) but in fact were caused by external factors: 'Much of what has happened since the mid-1970s can be better attributed to external trends and shocks than to purely internal processes and functional engrenages' (Schmitter, 1996a, p. 13). Schmitter's interpretation of neofunctionalism also rejected the initial assumption made by Haas that *spillover* would ultimately take a linear progression of the transfer of powers from the national towards the supranational institutional level. Instead Schmitter spoke of the likelihood that the European integration process would progress erratically. In practice this would boil down to the direction of the integration process remaining multidirectional. Haas later followed Schmitter by adopting a more fine-tuned neofunctionalist approach in which he acknowledged that political actors in most cases fail to pursue a strategic long-term vision. Instead they would 'stumble from one set of decisions into the next as a result of not having been able to foresee many of the implications and consequences of the earlier decisions' (Haas, 1970, p. 627). As a result, Community institutions and policies emerge incrementally and involve many twists and turns. From the perspective of Schmitter this included the possibility of the return of powers from the Community towards the national level ('spillback'). Most importantly for the analysis of the EU's current situation, Schmitter anticipated the likelihood that political elites would decide to adapt existing Community policies and institutions to new challenges ('encapsulate') rather than to follow a quasi-automatic progression towards deeper integration (Schmitter, 1970, p. 846). Schmitter also considered the post-Maastricht era to be much more likely to be characterised by a more flexible form of integration:

> For the MAT [Maastricht Treaty] opens the way for a multitude of relatively independent European arrangements with distinct statutes, functions, resources and memberships, not coordinated by a single central organization and operating under different decision rules'. (Schmitter, 1996b, pp. 121–150)

The creation of EMU seemed to prove Haas's original neofunctionalist approach right. Under the budgetary limits set in the EMU *Stability and Growth Pact (SGP)* member states had initiated a process were the transfer of their national sovereignty in the area of monetary policy to the European Central Bank would be accompanied by an increasing intrusion of the EU into national fiscal policies (Börzel, 2006, p. 224). The reality turned out to be starkly different. In practice the SGP turned out to be a soft gentleman's agreement which was de facto operated under the same open method of cooperation as other policy areas such as employment, education and environmental policy under the Lisbon Strategy (Borrás & Jacobsson, 2004, p. 193). Member state governments were consequently given substantial leeway in arguing against the execution of financial penalties under the excessive deficit procedure. This occurred most prominently when the European Commission dealt with the fact that France and Germany were unable to abide by the three per cent spending limit to annual borrowing and the 60 per cent limit to the structural deficit (both in relation to a country's annual gross domestic product, GDP). In 2002 both countries started to breach the first criteria and continuously did so until 2005. By 2003 they also had started to exceed the 60 per cent limit of structural debt but nevertheless in both cases no proper excessive deficit procedure was initiated (Hay & Wincott, 2012, p. 158). The background to this was that the European Commission under the leadership of former Italian prime minister and economics professor Romano Prodi adopted a very relaxed attitude towards the practical implementation of the SGP budgetary rules. Prodi himself had famously denounced the pact as 'stupid' and a straightjacket in an article in the *Le Monde* newspaper published on 17 October 2002 (Osborn, 2002).

The widespread perception was therefore that the SGP failed to instil the fiscal rigidity it was supposed to deliver (Wyplosz, Nickell, & Wolf, 2006, p. 231). Instead budgetary laxity prevailed and those countries in the Southern periphery of the eurozone who entered the eurozone with existing structural deficit problems (such as Italy and Greece) made little efforts to rectify them. Rather than to be pushed towards fiscal consolidation by the supposed institutional constraints of the SGP, membership of the eurozone created a free rider syndrome. This manifested itself in additional layer of security for countries with budgetary imbalances who assumed that the eurozone countries would collectively come to their rescue if their fiscal position worsened rather than to risk the overall stability or even the collapse of the eurozone. Figure 1 illustrates this free rider problem as it shows that amongst the founding members of the eurozone Belgium, Greece, Italy and even Austria consistently maintained a level of gross debt which exceeded 60 per cent of the national GDP between 1999 and 2006. From 2003 they were joined by France, Germany and Portugal. In the case of Belgium, Greece and Italy the levels of gross

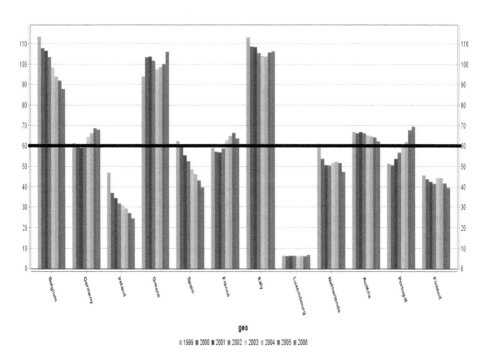

Figure 1. General government gross debt (per cent of GDP) in the Eurozone 12, 1999–2006
Source: EUROSTAT. Available at http://epp.eurostat.ec.europa.eu/tgm/graph.do?tab=graph&plugin=1&pcode=tsdde410&language=en&toolbox=data (accessed 27 February 2014).

structural debt consistently ranged between 90 and 110 per cent of the national GDP. Italy never managed to lower the debt level below 100 per cent without facing any consequences under the excessive deficit procedure.

The Fiscal Compact and the New Phase of Political *Spillover*

On 2 March 2012 the 17 countries of the eurozone plus eight new member states signed the *Treaty on Stability, Coordination and Governance in the EMU* which has since been more informally referred to as the 'Fiscal Compact'. The German chancellor Angela Merkel had intended to incorporate the compact into the EU's existing treaty structure. The purpose of this was to establish it as a foundation for the stronger coordination of fiscal and macroeconomic policies in the eurozone but also to link the latter with those EU member states who have not adopted the euro. It was Merkel's and Sarkozy's joint aspiration that the constitutional embedment of a debt brake on the national level would be more acceptable to member states than moves to expand the powers of the Commission to influence domestic budgetary decision-making:

> In the face of the non-existing budgetary competence of the European Commission the inherent link of the debt rule with national law is best suited to make it compulsory for all of us ... I therefore believe that it is the biggest sanction to be condemned in your own country. (Merkel and Sarkozy, 2011)

British Prime Minister David Cameron was not convinced of this argument and moved to veto the incorporation of the treaty into the EU's *acquis* because of his refusal to agree to the deepening of political integration beyond the eurozone core. The Fiscal Compact therefore ended up as an intergovernmental treaty between 25 of the member states, with the UK and the Czech Republic remaining on the outside. David Cameron tried to justify his veto against the Fiscal Compact to become a binding treaty for all EU member states by arguing that from his perspective the content of the treaty represents a decisive step towards the long-term goal of a European political federation, which he believes should be limited to the eurozone:

> Those of us outside the euro recognise that those in it are likely to need to make some big institutional changes. By the same token, the members of the eurozone should accept that we, and indeed all member states, will have changes that we need to safeguard our interests and strengthen democratic legitimacy. (Cameron, 2013, https://www.gov.uk/government/speeches/eu-speech-at-bloomberg)

Cameron's veto has to be considered in the context of the origins of the policy mechanisms which emerged in response to the eurozone sovereign debt crisis. It is obvious that these mechanisms are not part of a long-term visionary strategy for the future institutional shape of the EU. Instead they emerged on the basis of relatively ad hoc reactions to worsening economic circumstances in the eurozone and resulting adverse market reaction. This is illustrated by the German approach during the eurozone crisis, which was characterised by a hesitant and slow acceptance of the need to take a leading role in shaping a collective EU response to the crisis. In the initial stages of the emerging sovereign debt crisis in the eurozone Merkel did not share the view of British Prime Minister Gordon Brown and French president Sarkozy who both called for the EU to address the crisis collectively.

Brown, who was struggling to bring a deepening banking crisis under control in the course of 2008, spearheaded calls for a collective EU strategy. Brown voiced his frustrations with the attitude of other EU leaders, whom he considered to be in denial about the true scale of the emerging crisis:

> I sensed that most of Europe still considered the problem an essentially American one, even in spite of everything that was happening across Europe (...) I argued that European banks were more highly leveraged than banks in the US, and I argued that concerted European Union action was vital. (Brown, 2010, pp. 52–53)

Sarkozy quickly moved to support Brown in this endeavour and started to publicly distance himself from Merkel's reluctance to consider EU for the ailing economies of Ireland and Greece in the form of recapitalisation or stimulus programmes. During the joint press conference with Merkel in November 2008, Sarkozy stunned the assembled journalists when he stated that France under his leadership was working on the crisis while Germany would remain in a deliberative position (Sarkozy & Merkel, 2008). In the course of 2009 Merkel was forced to change her stance as the worsening economic and budgetary situation in Ireland and particularly in Greece risked threatening to undermine the future of the euro. As markets started to downgrade eurozone economies, beginning with the lowering of Greece's credit rating by the Standard & Poor's rating agency in October 2009, the risk that the debt crisis would affect further eurozone countries became obvious. As a result Merkel started to warm towards collective European action which followed in a gradual process from the *Europe 2020* Strategy in 2010 towards the *Fiscal Compact* in 2012. This slow adaptation by Angela Merkel to the expectation that Germany was expected to take leadership was widely described as a 'reluctant hegemon' approach (Paterson, 2011, p. 73). The Polish foreign minister Radek Sikorski aptly hinted at this when he reminded Merkel during his visit in Berlin in November 2011 that particularly Germany's partners in the Eastern part of the EU expected an active German role under the crisis conditions. In Sikorski's own words: 'I fear German power less than I am beginning to fear German inactivity. You have become Europe's indispensable nation' (Sikorski, 2011, p. 9).

The Fiscal Compact which emerged from the ongoing negotiations on the reform of the eurozone SGP since 2010, illustrates that the EU has been affected by a new and unprecedented wave of functionalist *spillover* as a result of unprecedented and severe external circumstances. In this respect it has to be emphasised that the *spillover* which occurred since the onset of the sovereign debt crisis is different from previous waves in two ways. Firstly it is caused by external pressures which empowered non-governmental actors at the expense of governing elites. Secondly the spillover that occurred signifies a break with the classic Community method of integration which was orientated towards the goal of collectivising increasing policy areas.

I will address each of these characteristics individually. The first characteristic of the new wave of *spillover* is that its main driver was an exceptional external event in the form of the global financial crisis, which subsequently strengthened market forces at the expense of political decision-makers. This caused the, albeit reluctant, realisation amongst EU leaders that they had to rectify their initial failure to accompany monetary union with fiscal and economic policy coordination in order to regain market confidence and to re-establish at least a certain degree of political control over emerging events. This is in line with what revised neofunctionalist approaches considered to be one of the likely causes of integrative pressures towards political spillover, namely 'internationally induced incentives drive or reinforce the rationale for seeking supranational solutions' (Niemann & Schmitter, 2009, p. 59). With the onset of the sovereign debt crisis in individual eurozone economies, bond markets and rating agencies started to become the key players in determining the prospects for economic recovery in the eurozone. Germany as the strongest economic and political player in the EU therefore reluctantly accepted the need to push towards binding policy coordination with the purpose of restoring market confidence and regaining political control in the eurozone. The crisis forced political leaders in the eurozone to abandon the informal consensus upon which they had operated the Eurozone since its creation in 2002. This consensus rested on the assumption that the completion of monetary union with the transfer of monetary sovereignty to the European Central Bank would not require further steps towards binding policy coordination or even harmonisation. In practice this was reflected by the reform of the SGP towards greater flexibility in 2005, only two years before the financial crisis harshly revealed the inefficiencies of the pact. Under the reforms the eurozone members allowed significantly more room for member states to put forward political reasons for breaking the budgetary limits and in essence therefore contributed towards a '(re)politicisation of fiscal relations' (Paudyn, 2011, p. 2207). The *Fiscal Compact* represents a first significant step in moving away from the coordinative practical operation of the SGP and to introduce a system of binding budgetary supervision and fiscal responsibility. This was clearly Merkel's priority who rejected proposals to swiftly move towards further policy harmonisation in the eurozone. The prime example for this was Merkel's refusal to accept the introduction of Eurobonds which would naturally come with a more political role for the European Central Bank in independently supporting crisis economies (Hübner, 2012, p. 174). Merkel considers the Fiscal Compact as a move towards restoring market confidence in the eurozone and ensuring the long-term stability of the European Union by turning it into a 'stability union'. In her official declaration on the Fiscal Compact in the German parliament on 29 June 2012 Merkel emphasised that the purpose of the treaty was to learn the lessons from the failure to exercise efficient supervision and control over national budgets under the pre-crisis SGP:

> If the European sovereign debt crisis has shown us something than it is that the irresponsible fiscal policy of one euro country can endanger the financial stability of the whole eurozone. We have to put a halt to this (… .) With the Fiscal Compact national governments and national parliaments connect themselves in an unprecedented fashion in order to transform Economic and Monetary Union into a stability union. (Merkel, 2012, http://www.bundeskanzlerin.de/ContentArchiv/DE/Archiv17/ Regierung serklaerung/2012/2012–06–29–merkel.html)

The fact that Merkel speaks of a 'stability union' rather than a federal union illustrates that she pursues a strategy of deepening intergovernmental policy coordination rather than to advocate the complete supranationalisation of further policy areas which would inevitably result in substantially enhanced independent regulatory powers for the EU institutional level. In spite of the British veto Merkel clearly has not abandoned her ambition to make the provisions of the *Fiscal Compact* binding for all 28 EU member states. Merkel emphasised in her address to the German *Bundestag* that this should happen 'whenever it becomes possible' (Merkel, 2012). This shows that she is adamant to ensure that budgetary stability is instilled not just in the eurozone but in the economies across the whole of the Single

European Market. In terms of the future institutional shape of the EU and the eurozone Merkel however adopts a far more cautious approach and does not advocate the supranationalisation of further policy areas for now. Instead she promotes the deepening of binding intergovernmental policy coordination in further core economic policy areas. In an interview with the German weekly *DER SPIEGEL* which accompanied the ratification of the *Fiscal Compact* in the German parliament, Merkel laid out her rather pragmatic approach towards the future shape of the EU which she presented as a shared Franco-German vision:

> At this stage I do not see the necessity to transfer further competences to the Commission in Brussels. President François Hollande and I rather want a better coordination of policy areas which are crucial for our competitiveness. We are for example thinking of employment and pension policy but also taxation and social policy. Economic policy coordination in Europe is far too weak, it needs to be strengthened, which is different from giving more competences to the Commission. (Merkel, 2013, p. 30)

This shows that the political *spillover* that has occurred in the EU since the onset of the crisis leads to a more differentiated outcome in terms of both vertical and horizontal integration than previous developments, where binding supranationalisation for all member states was usually the desired outcome. The pressures exercised by financial markets on political actors have to this date resulted in only limited institutionalisation and creation of new supranational bodies such as the *European Stability Mechanism*. Instead member states governments have in effect continued to pursue a slight modification of a strategy which Schmitter characterised as 'encapsulation' in his early revision of Haas's original neofunctionalist approach. Schmitter defined this as a strategy by political elites 'to respond to crisis by marginal modifications within the zone of indifference' (Schmitter, 1970, p. 846). 'Encapsulation' is essentially the reluctance to radically alter the existing institutional setup in a given policy area beyond a certain integrative point. Schmitter considered this to be generally the default approach, especially in areas where 'actors adopt ever more divergent policies' and 'new initiatives in scope and level are likely to be very risky and contentious' (Schmitter, 1970, p. 867). This approach was very obvious in the design of the eurozone before the crisis, where member states prioritised the protection of the competitive advantage of their domestic economies over the stability of the single currency. The resulting regulatory framework consequently favoured preserving national policy-making autonomy (Hall, 2012, p. 357). Encapsulation was less visible in the horizontal dimension as even during the crisis period the eurozone has continued to enlarge to new member states. Between 2007 and 2014 the eurozone adopted six new member states (Slovenia, Cyprus, Malta, Slovakia, Estonia and most recently Latvia).

The essential question is to what extent the new policy mechanisms in the EU and the eurozone will remain within or alternatively move beyond a state of relative encapsulation, i.e. the pursuing a strategy of 'stable self-maintenance' (Schmitter, 1970, p. 844), both in vertical and horizontal terms. The Fiscal Compact signifies a crucial development in this respect. At least to a certain extent the treaty shows the political willingness to move beyond encapsulation by deepening vertical policy coordination within the eurozone while at the same time attempting to maintain its horizontal openness towards the ten outsiders.

The Compact nevertheless also significantly reflects the current political reality within the EU, where even the external pressures under crisis conditions have not substantially weakened member state resistance against giving up their sovereignty in key policy areas. The treaty hence pursues the twofold ambition of combining 'ever-closer policy coordination in the euro area' with the promotion of 'conditions for stronger economic growth' in the EU as a whole (European Council, 2012, p. 1). The overall purpose is to ensure the long-term stability of the eurozone by instilling fiscal responsibility amongst the participating member states. This is reflected by the fact that the 'balanced budget rule' in article 3 of the treaty of limiting the structural deficit to 0.5 per cent of the national GDP at market prices (European Council, 2012, p. 11), which all signatories are expected to implement in their domestic constitutional legal framework, is practically only binding for the eurozone countries. Under the provisions of the treaty the latter are subjected to the new system of reverse qualified majority. The Commission is therefore permitted to initiate an excessive deficit procedure against any eurozone country who is considered to be in breach of the golden budget rule and the SGP limits without having to consult the Council first. The Council can only stop this process by a qualified majority. It is only eurozone countries who eventually face a potential financial penalty of a maximum of 0.1 per cent of the national GDP if the European Court of Justice agrees with the Commission that a case of non-compliance exists (European Council, 2012, article 8, paragraph 2, p. 16). In spite of the strengthening of the Commission's independent supervisory powers under the provisions of the treaty, it also sets clear limitations and stops far short from equipping the Commission with executive competences beyond ensuring the compliance with the budgetary rules in the eurozone. The treaty emphasises that any corrective measures for member states deemed in breached of these rules by the Commission 'shall fully respect the prerogatives of national parliaments' (European Council, 2012, article 3, paragraph 2, p. 12).

The treaty provides the legal basis for the intended compulsory supervision and coordination of national policies within the eurozone and also amongst the aspiring members on the outside. It remains vague on which policy areas should fall under this coordination other than to state that economic policy coordination should take place in 'all the areas which are essential to the proper functioning of the euro area in pursuit of the objectives of fostering competitiveness, promoting employment, contributing further to the sustainability of public finances and reinforcing financial stability' (European Council, 2012, article 9, p. 17). The intention to improve the horizontal link between the eurozone core and the outside periphery is clearly visible in the fact that the treaty is deliberately open towards the inclusion of new signatories (European Council, 2012, article 15, p. 23). Most importantly the treaty also guarantees all signatories who are currently not in the eurozone full participation in the euro summit meetings and the right to contribute to the institutional design of the eurozone (European Council, 2012, article 12, p. 20).

Beyond the *Fiscal Compact*: Towards Differentiated *Encapsulation* or Further *Spillover*?

Until the plans for a eurozone banking union are put into concrete action, the Fiscal Compact remains the temporarily final step towards deeper policy coordination in response to the effects of the global financial crisis. In spite of the rather limited provisions of the treaty when it comes to constraining national policy autonomy, it has pushed two member states, who refused to subject themselves to its rules, into an outer periphery position. Both the British and Czech governments opted out of the treaty due to concerns about of it potentially representing a first step towards the federalisation of the EU. Former Czech Prime Minister Petr Nečas, who was under significant pressure from the Eurosceptic Czech president Václav Klaus not to sign the treaty in 2011, defended his decision to opt out by arguing that the treaty expanded policy cooperation beyond the desired focus on internal market liberalisation. Like David Cameron, Nečas argued that his opt out represented the new reality of differentiated integration in the EU, where individual member states would want to choose in which policy areas they are willing to agree to deeper cooperation (Nečas, 2012). David Cameron spoke of the need to protect Britain from the vision of 'ever closer union' which the member states of the eurozone wanted to pursue and which was not the same flexible agenda he would like to see being implemented in the EU: 'This vision of flexibility and co-operation is not the same as those who want to build an ever closer political union – but it is just as valid' (Cameron, 2013).

The treaty therefore represents a crucial cornerstone for the EU whose leaders are currently unsure about which direction its future development should take. The Fiscal Compact reflects a definite chance towards differentiated integration between the eurozone core group and the periphery. The current division between a semi-periphery group of predominantly aspiring eurozone members and the relatively small outer periphery, which at present is represented only by the UK and the Czech Republic is likely to be only a temporary setup. Even if the eurozone core remains open towards horizontal expansion it is certain that not all countries who are at present on the outside will eventually want to join. More sceptical countries such as the Sweden, Denmark, the Czech Republic and most of all the UK are likely to reject eurozone entry on the basis that it would significantly constrain their national policy autonomy. The essential core–periphery division between the eurozone and the outsiders is therefore likely to remain in the future, even though existing member states will make attempts to avoid a horizontal encapsulation of the euro core. The level of horizontal encapsulation inside the eurozone will substantially depend on to what extent the new policy mechanisms are equipped to once again create the perception of what Schmitter has called 'equitable returns', i.e. beneficial outcomes from monetary integration in the form of boosting economic growth and supporting competitiveness. If the latter occur on the basis of the limited policy coordination adopted under the new mechanisms the willingness to move towards deeper policy coordination in further areas is likely to wane amongst eurozone. Renewed horizontal encapsulation of the new status quo or at best limited change by granting 'central decision-makers with more resources or authority to redistribute returns' (Schmitter, 1970, p. 858) is therefore a realistic prospect under conditions of medium-term recovery of the eurozone from the sovereign debt crisis. Support for a political federalisation of the eurozone remains limited, even amongst the central players France and Germany. Many other countries in the eurozone show an increasingly sceptical attitude towards what they perceive as a German attempt to narrow the purpose of the eurozone to that of a fiscal austerity union (Lane, 2012, p. 64). This perception of the future of the EU being determined on the basis of German economic hegemony (Bulmer & Paterson, 2013, p. 1388) is likely to be a substantial factor which will keep the EU on the path towards increasingly differentiated integration. Even in the current *Euro Plus Pact* group countries like Denmark and Hungary remain sceptical of the emerging policy framework (Schweiger, 2013). For the foreseeable future the EU is therefore likely to waver between the option of encapsulation in a dichotomy between the eurozone core and the external periphery on the one hand and a more transparent differentiated integration between the now 28 membership base on the other hand. An increasingly differentiated encapsulation between multiple groupings of member states currently looks like the most likely and viable option to accommodate the increasing variety of national economic and political interests in the EU-28. The Fiscal Compact has created a flexible framework for the eurozone and rest of the EU to determine the right balance between encapsulation and further selective *spillover*.

References

Borrás, S. & Jacobsson, K. (2004) The open method of co-ordination and new governance patterns in the EU, *Journal of European Public Policy*, 11(2), pp. 185–208.

Börzel, T. A. (2006) Mind the gap! European integration between level and scope, *Journal of European Public Policy*, 12(2), pp. 217–236.

Brown, G. (2010) *Beyond the Crash: Overcoming the First Crisis of Globalisation* (London: Simon and Schuster).

Bulmer, S & Paterson, W. E. (2013) Germany as the EU's reluctant hegemon? Of economic strength and political constraints, *Journal of European Public Policy*, 20(10), pp. 1387–1405.

Cameron, D. (2013, 23 January) EU Speech at Bloomberg. Available at https://www.gov.uk/government/speeches/eu-speech-at-bloomberg (accessed 1 March 2013).

European Council. (2012) Treaty on Stability Coordination and Governance in the Economic and Monetary Union. Available at http://europeancouncil.europa.eu/media/639235/st00tscg26_en12.pdf (accessed 1 March 2014).

Grant, C. (2011) *Britain on the Edge of Europe* (London: Centre for European Reform). Available at http://centreforeuropeanreform.blogspot.co.uk/2011/12/britain-on-edge-of-europe.html (accessed 26 February 2014).

Haas, E. B. (1970) The study of regional integration: Reflections on the joy and anguish of pretheorizing, *International Organization*, 24(4), pp. 606–646.

Hall, P. A. (2012) The economics and politics of the euro crisis, *German Politics*, 21(4), pp. 355–371.

Hantrais, L. (2007) *Social policy in the European Union* (3rd ed.). (Basingstoke: Palgrave MacMillan.

Hay, C. & Wincott, D. (2012) *The Political Economy of Welfare Capitalism* (Basingstoke: Palgrave MacMillan).

Hodson, D. (2010) Economic and monetary union: An experiment in new modes of EU policy-making, in: H. Wallace, M. A. Pollack, & A. R. Young (Eds) *Policy-Making in the European Union*, pp. 157–180 (Oxford: University Press).

Hübner, K. (2012) German crisis management and leadership – from ignorance to procrastination to action, *Asia Europe Journal*, 9(2–4), pp. 159–177.

Lane, P. (2012) The european sovereign debt crisis, *Journal of Economic Perspectives*, 26(3), pp. 49–67.

McCann, D. (2010) *The Political Economy of the European Union* (Cambridge: Polity).

Merkel, A. (2012, 29 June) Regierungserklärung zu Stabilitätsunion Fiskalvertrag und Europäischer Stabilitätsmechanisms. Available at http://www.bundeskanzlerin.de/ContentArchiv/DE/Archiv17/Regierung serklaerung/2012/2012–06–29-merkel.html (accessed 1 March 2014).

Merkel, A. (2013) Wir sitzen in einem Boot, DER SPIEGEL, 23, 3 June, pp. 29–31.

Merkel, A. & Sarkozy, N. (2011, 16 August) Joint press conference, Paris.

Nečas, P. (2012, 3 April) Lecture by Czech Prime Minister Petr Nečas on the occasion of his joint appearance with Federal Chancellor Angela Merkel at the Law Faculty of Charles University.

Niemann, A. & Schmitter, P. C. (2009) Neofunctionalism, in: A. Wiener & T. Diez (Eds) *European Integration Theory*, pp. 45–66 (Oxford: University Press).

Osborn, A. (2002) Prodi disowns 'stupid' stability pact. *The Guardian*, 18 October. Available at http://www.theguardian.com/business/2002/oct/18/theeuro.europeanunion (accessed 1 March 2014).

Paterson, W. E. (2011) The reluctant hegemon? Germany moves centre stage in the European Union, *Journal of Common Market Studies*, 49(Annual Review), pp. 55–75.

Paudyn, B. (2011) The uncertain (re)politicisation of fiscal relations in Europe: A shift in EMU's modes of governance, *Review of International Studies*, 37(5), pp. 2201–2220.

Sarkozy, N. & Merkel, A. (2008, 24 November) Joint Press Conference at the 10th Franco-German Council of Ministers, Paris. Available at http://www.ambafrance-uk.org/10th-franco-german-council-of (accessed 14 January 2014).

Schmitter, P. (1996a) Examining the present Euro-Polity with the help of past theories, in: G. Marks, Fritz W. Scharpf, Philippe Schmitter, & Wolfgang Streeck (Eds) *Governance in the European Union*, pp. 1–14 (London: Sage Publications).

Schmitter, P. (1996b) Imagining the future of the Euro-Polity with the help of new concepts, in: G. Marks, Fritz W. Scharpf, Philippe Schmitter, & Wolfgang Streeck (Eds) *Governance in the European Union*, pp. 121–150 (London: Sage Publications).

Schmitter, P. C. (1970) A revised theory of regional integration, *International Organization*, 24(4), pp. 836–868.

Schweiger, C. (2013) The EU's multiple cores and the CEEs: A threat or an opportunity? *Yearbook of the Institute of East-Central Europe*, 11(3), pp. 27–46.

Sikorski, R. (2011, 28 November) Poland and the Future of the European Union: Address at the German Council of Foreign Relations, Berlin. Available at http://www.mfa.gov.pl/resource/33ce6061-ec12–4da1-a145–01e2995c6302:JCR. (accessed 1 March 2014).

Traynor, I., Watt, N., Gow, D. & Wintour, P. (2011) David Cameron blocks EU treaty with veto casting Britain adrift in Europe. *The Guardian*, 9 December 2011. Available at http://www.theguardian.com/world/2011/dec/09/david-cameron-blocks-eu-treaty (accessed 1 March 2014).

Wyplosz, C., Nickell, S. & Wolf, M. (2006) European monetary union: The dark side of a major success, *Economic Policy*, 21(46), pp. 207–261.

Why has the German Job Market Done Astonishingly Well Despite the 2008–2009 'Great Recession'? New Economic Miracle, Institutional Transformation or Beggar-thy-Neighbour Policies?

LOTHAR FUNK

Department of Business Studies, Duesseldorf University of Applied Sciences, International Economic Relations, Duesseldorf, Germany

ABSTRACT   *Since the early 2000s, the German labour market has undergone a sweeping institutional transformation. While during the 1990s and early 2000s, Germany was usually regarded as the 'sick man of Europe', the country's economy has recently been described in many respects as an international role model. Around a decade ago, a reform package was introduced that resulted in the unemployment rate being almost cut in half, in spite of the difficult economic climate due to the financial crisis and the succeeding and still ongoing problems in the Eurozone. However, the success has also been challenged due to its alleged internal and external unpleasant side-effects by critics. After having explained the essence of the German social market economy and its development prior to the deep downswing of 2008/2009 which was coined the 'Great Recession' by leading US economists, the paper summarises the key aspects of the rather unexpected German labour market successes since 2009 and addresses claims of related distributional injustice of these reforms within the country as well as assertions that the German success of ongoing high exports and current account surpluses is based on beggar-thy-neighbour policies. Finally, the paper briefly asks whether Germany has faced up to its responsibilities during the crisis in the Eurozone since the end of 2009.*

1. Introduction

Nowadays, Germany's achievement of economic goals in large parts appears to resemble the ones desired for the European Union (EU) as a whole, whose economic order is supposed to be a 'highly competitive social market economy (SME)' since the Treaty of

Lisbon entered in force on 1 December 2009. In contrast to these goals, however, deep divisions with respect to economic performance exist among the member states of the E(M)U, that is the EU and the European Monetary Union (EMU) or Eurozone. A divergence of national competitiveness became very visible since the outbreak of an acute crisis in EMU since the end of 2009. Also contrary to just a decade ago when Germany was still seen as the 'sick man of Europe' (a catchword often used during the 1990s outside the country due to – possibly partially alleged – notorious overregulation and bureaucracy), the country is now often regarded as E(M)U's dominant economy among the now 18 EMU and 28 EU member states and the clear number one economic nation (*primus inter pares*) whose economic and financial policies and plans other EU countries nowadays always (have to) take into account in contrast to just a decade ago (Garton Ash, 2013; John, 2007; Paterson, 2011). Currently, quite a few countries particularly in the Eurozone can hardly be assessed as lastingly healthy in spite of the repeated and ongoing efforts to resolve the diseases of overspending and low competitiveness in the last four years (EEAG, 2014, p. 23). Nevertheless, this chapter focuses foremost on labour market-related issues of Germany and potential lessons for other countries (cf. the other EMU issues Funk, 2014). The chapter will highlight the following questions in some depth after a tour d'horizon into the economic history of the German SME (*Soziale Marktwirtschaft*): Does a new German Jobs miracle really exist? What are the 'secrets' or drivers of the definitely better performance compared to a few years before? Will this improved performance survive? Does it have very unpleasant distributional side-effects within Germany? Is this performance at the expense of other countries? Can we learn lessons from the German labour market experience and has Germany acted sufficiently responsibly during the crisis in the Eurozone?

2. A Sketch of the Social Market Economy Prior to the Great Recession

The economy of the Federal Republic of Germany (FRG or West Germany and after unification Germany and FRG) was established on the principles of the SME. The (West) German SME has been trying to merge an approach to pursue open markets with functioning competition wherever possible with a concern to preserve price stability and social justice in society (Funk, 2000, p. 16). In other words, SME defines a policy concept of economic order or *Ordnungspolitik* which is based on open markets but, at the same time, includes elements of social balancing (John, 2007, p. 143). On the one hand, the SME label has been attached to a theoretical normative framework to guide economic policy which was developed by several German economists and law academics. On the other hand, the label has been used as a name for the (West) German economic order as well as the German economic policy conduct in practice. Beyond that, the interpretations of the normative content of the concept were by no means uniform. Therefore, enduring conflicts among alternative interpretations proved inevitable and can explain by and large the German post-war experience that will be sketched now.

The remarkable West German early post-war economic success – popularly coined *Wirtschaftswunder* (economic miracle) – was partly attributed to temporary factors (positive supply-side factors such as a pool of motivated and skilled workers) and the incentives set by the early SME economic order conducive to catching up. This includes foremost the introduction of a stable currency based on an independent central bank as well as the lifting of most price controls in 1948.

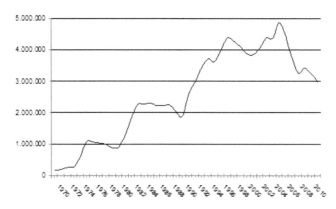

Figure 1. Registered unemployment stocks in the FRG since 1970 (until 1990, West Germany only)
Source: Own Compilation based on figures by the German Federal Labour Agency.

Starting already in the mid-1970s and increasingly after the 1980s, however, the German model performed worse arguably because its traditional institutions proved to be rather inflexible. The fact of a falling trend rate of real economic growth in the longer term hinted in that direction: the average growth of real gross domestic product (GDP) in per cent amounted to 8.3 in the 1950s, 4.3 in the 1960s, 2.8 in the 1970s, 2.3 in the 1980s, 2.1 in the 1990s and 1.5 per cent in the period 2001 until 2008. At the same time, a stepwise increase in seemingly ever-rising (mostly non-cyclical) unemployment since the mid-1970s (Figure 1) until the financial crisis – autumn 2008 when it became a problem for many countries – that resulted in the Great Recession among most highly industrialised countries appeared to have become structural in the FRG. Both facts support the hypothesis of a decreasing steam of the German power engine over time (Funk, 2012, pp. 7–10) while the inflation performance remained better than in almost all other countries over time prior to and after the adoption of the Euro.

Many economists certainly in Germany regard as an important reason for these develop-ments the change of the early SME towards an increasingly inflexible system as a result of growing regulation and a rising wedge of compulsory social security contributions and taxes since the late 1950s and particularly after the mid-1960s. In other words, the German institutions did not adapt sufficiently to the new challenges of structural changes, globalisation and reunification for quite a while. Partly, their former capacity to cope with challenges was decreased by new legislation (Funk, 2007b).

> In this view, the retardation of economic growth experienced by West Germany after the first oil price crisis in 1973 as well as rising unemployment are the consequences of institutional changes that have focused too much on the word "social" and that have hampered economic activity. (Funk, 2002, p. 149)

After all, a fact that academic admirers of *Modell Deutschland* (Funk, 2000) have neglected for a long time is that Germany has suffered from endemic structural unemployment and high numbers of long-term unemployed. In particular, despite its supposed consensus culture and consensus-building institutions developed during the economic miracle of West German industrialism, it was especially difficult for unskilled workers to find employment due to significant barriers that prevented them from entering the labour market as a result of prevailing insider–outsider problems, especially since the mid-1970s. Key to these problems are turnover costs to firms. As Annesley *et al.* (2004, p. 85 and p. 87) explain

> These refer to the costs of recruiting and training employees, as well as to dismissal costs. Labour turnover gives market power to experienced incumbent employees – insiders – because they know that their employers find it costly to replace them. Insiders use their power to improve their wages. Employers concede wages above market-clearing rates, because the costs of dismissing and replacing existing workers – even if this were legally possible – make it unprofitable to hire outsiders.

In other words, insider–outsider problems have particularly bad side-effects especially on the weakest groups in the labour market. These effects become worse in economies with stricter regulations, higher payroll taxes and rather strong trade unions which favour 'solidaristic' policies (a policy that results in a compressed and rigid wage structure which leads to a substitution especially of unskilled labour by capital and a relocation of production abroad which needs a lot of unskilled labour) that support insiders at the expense of persons that want to enter the labour market. Also, it must not be forgotten that high marginal taxes at the bottom end of pay scales may also reflect the political lobbying of the insiders and their representatives in the labour market in favour of such regulations to shield themselves against competition (cf. Funk, 2000, pp. 21–27; cf. also Funk, 2001 on the need of a strategic response to overcome such entrenched problems).

Starting in 1982, the Christian Democratic Union/Christian Social Union-Free Democratic Party (CDU/CSU-FDP) government led by Chancellor Helmut Kohl implemented policies that have reshaped the German economy in the longer term away from the previously inflexible system at least to some extent. This happened because of the decisions on how to conduct the economic restructuring of eastern Germany (later contributing to pressures on governments to deregulate labour and product markets) and to give up the Deutsche Mark (DM) (cf. details on this Funk, 2007a, pp. 23–134 and Funk, 2010, pp. 85–94).

If successfully implemented, the controversial adoption of the Euro was regarded by its political proponents as beneficial for Germany as a whole at least in the longer term. In the view of many of its academic and political proponents,

> Germany accepted the euro to avoid a repetition of the situation in the 1990s when, after reunification and the break-up of the European Monetary System, the real appreciation of the mark had disastrous consequences … on industrial production, manufacturing employment, growth, foreign trade and wages, which had to be squeezed for 15 years to restore competitiveness. (Artus, 2010, p. 7)

Moreover, both the opportunities of globalisation (new markets and lower cost abroad due to further opening up of borders) as well as improved transportation and information and communication opportunities first of all challenged and, after a period of adjustment, benefited the many world-open German companies. The benefits materialised by taking advantage of diversifying and cheapening the supply chains as well as opening up new export and production markets in Eastern Europe and Asia (Hamilton & Quinlan, 2008, pp. 156–158).

Additionally and complementary to these changes, sweeping reforms were implemented also by the Social Democrat/Green-Party government led by Chancellor Gerhard Schröder. Prior to this, however, a period of zig-zagging in domestic economic policy had occurred which was accompanied by an increasing feeling of lagging behind the rest of Europe (Funk, 2000, pp. 27–35). Indeed, as mentioned before Germany's economic record at the time was at the lower end of the league of tables for quite a few years, first, due to difficulties in transition from central planning in the East to a market-based economy after unification and, second, due to adjustment difficulties when the Euro had been introduced.

The courageous political efforts to improve Germany as a business location by the Agenda 2010 reforms of the second Schröder government changed the German economy's adjustment trajectory considerably after 2003 (Funk, 2003a, 2003b). The package was an extremely controversial reform programme which cut supposed entitlements of quite a few people hitherto (almost) entirely depending on the German welfare state. The reforms aimed particularly at improving the incentives to supply labour and more generally at increasing the flexibility of the labour market as well as product markets. Above all, one may argue that the measures jointly implemented under the name of 'Hartz reforms' created a new labour market regime of 'promote and demand' (*Fördern und Fordern*) with a stronger emphasis on the component to create market incentives to work (Koch & Rees, 2010). The reform package earned much praise by international institutions such as the OECD (Table 1) and other analysts because it helped to break up the much damaging insider–outsider problems in Germany. For example, liberalising temporary jobs in early 2004 has proved to be very effective as it enabled the outsiders to circumvent still comparatively rigid dismissal protection laws in Germany. At the same time, the crumbling of the collective bargaining system – a drop of the share tied to collective bargaining agreements from 70 per cent in 1996 to 56 per cent in the west under the pressure of globalisation – also contributed to more flexibility at the company level. In the eastern part of the FRG, the level dropped from 56 to 37 per cent in the same period (cf. Rees, 2011 and for more details also IMF, 2013 and Lesch, 2010).

These and further policy measures (e.g. the gradual increase in the retirement age and the implementation of a debt brake; Funk & Allen, 2012) combined with the other trends affected mainly the supply side of the economy and contributed to a prolonged period of very modest increases in unit labour costs (Funk, 2013b, p. 207) and the accompanying comparatively strong performance of the labour market and economic growth since 2005. On the demand side, however, Germany's economic performance has been helped by strong exports – a feature of the German economy which is well known. The latter fact, however, also contributed to persistent controversies with respect to Germany's allegedly insufficient domestic demand performance to be addressed in more detail.

3. The German Job Market-Related Policy Mix During the Crisis

As opposed to many other countries and in spite of the largest fall of real GDP in the country since the second World War (minus 5.1 per cent of real GDP in 2009, cf. Table 2), the German economy proved particularly resistant to recent crisis pressures. Obviously, above all the supply-side reforms during the last decade combined with more traditional elements of its SME are responsible for Germany's continuing positive economic growth in terms of annual average figures while much of the Euro area's periphery sinks back into recession or stagnation. Such a situation was regarded as hardly possible

Table 1. Important employment-related reforms in Germany prior to the financial crisis

Main reform acts	Measures taken	Effects to be expected
Job-AQTIV (2002)	• More efficient use of active labour market policies • Introduction of qualitative profiling of jobseekers • Changes in benefit claim during and after participation in training	Improves efficiency of job search
Hartz I (January 2003)	• Deregulation and liberalisation of temporary agency work • Tightened conditions for acceptability of jobs and introduction of sanctions for unemployment benefit recipients • Enlisted private firms are allowed to help workers search for jobs	Improves job search efficiency and raises incentives for taking up a job
Hartz II (January 2003)	• Reform of minor jobs with limited social security contributions • Subsidies for unemployed who become self-employed	Raises incentives for taking up a job
Hartz III (January 2004)	• Federal employment office re-organised to an Agency which becomes a more efficient service provider • Simplification of active and passive policy measures	Improves job search efficiency
Hartz IV (January 2005)	• Merging unemployment assistance and social assistance into the means-tested unemployment benefit II • Introduction of One-Euro-Jobs	Raises incentives to work for welfare recipients due to reduced reservation wages
Further measures prior to the crisis	• Increase in age threshold for the early pension for unemployed from age 60 to age 63 from 2006 to 2008 • Raising normal VAT rate by 3 percentage points to 19 per cent and at the same time lowering contributions to unemployment insurance • Phasing out the regulation that unemployed persons aged 58 can receive benefits without actively searching for jobs in January 2008	Improves incentives to work especially for older persons and in general

Source: With slight amendments mainly OECD (2012, p. 43) and cf. also IMF (2012, pp. 14 and 43).

only a few years before the great financial crisis started to have world-wide repercussions in 2008 and particularly led to the recessions in 2009 and after in many countries.

While consumer prices remained rather stable, Germany could recoup the losses sustained during the recession which was limited in Germany mainly to 2009 during the succeeding process of strong recovery (increase in real GDP by 4.2 per cent in 2010 and 3.3 per cent in 2011). Total employment reached record levels in 2010 with the highest level of persons employed since unification (with even higher figures thereafter). The registered

Table 2. Development of consumer prices and real GDP since the 1990s, selected figures

Years	1990–2000	2000–2010	2009	2010	2011	2012	2013
	Growth rates, annual averages		Percentage change to previous year				
Consumer prices	2.4	1.6	0.4	1.2	2.1	2.0	1.5
Real GDP	1.8	0.9	−5.1	4.2	3.3	0.7	0.4

Source: Funk (2012, p. 14) and German Council of Economic Experts (2014).

Table 3. Additional key indicators for Germany

Year Indicators	2009	2010	2011	2012	2013
Persons employed (domestic), in million (mn.)	40.37	40.60	41.15	41.6	41.8
Total hours worked (percentage change to previous year)	−2.7	2.2	1.5	0.2	0.2[a]
Persons employed, covered by social security, mn.	27.49	27.76	28.44	29.0	29.35
Registered unemployment stocks, mn.	3.42	3.24	2.98	2.90	2.95
General government balance	−3.2	−4.1	−0.8	0.1	0.0

[a]Preliminary.
Source: Fuchs *et al.* (2013), Funk (2012) and German Council of Economic Experts (2014).

unemployment level fell to new lows not reached since 1991 just after unification while simultaneously the number of jobs fully subject to social contributions rose at a figure of 28.4 million in 2011 to the highest level within the last 15 years and was in 2013 almost 1 million higher again (Table 3). This figure is highly important since Germany is still a country with a welfare system dominated by pay-as-you-go. When this figure goes up, there is an increase in the number of employed persons who earn enough money to contribute to financing the system and thus can decrease the pressure on governmental budget which improved during the crisis in Germany as Table 3 demonstrates as well. The Council of Economic Advisers particularly emphasises the 'remarkable … almost continuous rise in employment since the middle of the past decade and … the fact that the situation is actually better than before the crisis.' (German Council of Economic Experts, 2011, p. 19). The path of enduringly rising structural unemployment was thus broken for the first time within decades when many other countries also suffered a crisis not only in growth but also in their labour market

However, the upturn slowed down in 2013 due to external cooling factors including the sovereign debt crisis in the Euro area and the accompanying tensions in the financial markets as well as the consolidation efforts in many countries before growth is due to return again in Germany at a higher rate in 2014 (IMF, 2013; Federal Ministry for Economic Affairs and Energy, 2014). Despite risks due to potential future problems of instability in some of the emerging economies such as China and looming risks due to the reversal of German energy policy, Germany appears to be well-placed compared to other countries – at least if no major further crisis related to the Euro or as a result of previously other rather unexpected factors occurs. The main reason is a production base which depends still more on manufacturing goods than in other highly industrialised countries. At the same time, the demand in emerging economies is focused still rather strongly on German reliable, high-quality investment products as well as luxury cars, for example. If emerging countries will continue to expand as they are increasingly the destination countries of German exports, Germany is likely to prosper as a result.

What have been the main drivers of the surprisingly stable labour market developments in Germany despite the sharp fall of GDP and the other external challenges? The stable labour market and its further recovery after the financial crisis is based on an interaction of several factors including – apart from certain direct fiscal policy measures (car scrapping subsidies) – a large amount of labour hoarding and the use of short-time work (an instrument traditionally used for labour market adjustment in Germany) that was previously unseen in Germany (cf. details Funk, 2013b). The approach worked well because it was based on expectations by employers of a short recession only and to have a fundamentally appropriate structure of their products to meet the future demand in global markets as well as within Europe and Germany.

One may summarise that the current labour market in Germany goes along with a mix of more external flexibility due to labour market reforms and more firm-specific internal flexibility during the successful management of the crisis. Foremost these factors can explain the resilience of the labour market in spite of the fact that Germany was heavily affected, above all, by the steep decline in international trade due to the great financial crisis which affected especially German exports in the core area of the Germen production model, i.e. machinery and auto-mobile manufacturing. However, the previous upswing between 2005 and 2008, combined with the accompanying wage moderation and increased flexibility as well as the resulting high profits in these sectors before the breakdown of demand, allowed for this rather unique German way of adjustment to the Great Recession. After all, the structural changes in German output have been relatively small and employment structures in terms of distribution among sectors in Germany changed very little since 2008 (Havlik, 2014).

What is more, however, is the fact that the German labour market has become more resilient according to several studies that the German Central Bank summarises in its January 2014 Monthly Report as 'the fall in the unemployment rate was due principally to the more efficient operation of job placement processes in the labour market and the fact that unemployed persons stepped up their efforts to find work'. The German Central Bank adds a few sentences later that in the staff's assessment a structural improvement of the German labour market as a result of the reform package adopted and thus a structural transformation of the German labour market performance can be detected:

> If the transition rate from unemployment to employment since 2005 had remained at the same low level as before the Hartz reforms, the structural unemployment rate would not have moderated substantially by 2010. It would have been virtually just as high in 2012 as in the middle of the past decade. (*Deutsche Bundesbank*, 2014, p. 35; Funk, 2012, pp. 16–18)

Also, the most recent assessment by the OECD's Secretary-General demonstrates high recognition for the German achievements:

> Unemployment is at an impressive low. Although job losses are still mounting across Europe, in Germany, unemployment is at 5.1 per cent, which is almost half the rate of nearly 10 years ago. And the German "dual" system of vocational training and

professional education has also become a reference model for combating high youth unemployment in other countries. (Gurria, 2014)

In its report on 'Keeping the edge: Competitiveness for Inclusive Growth' published in February 2014 the assessment appears to be unequivocal at first sight (pp. 14):

> The outstanding performance of the German labour market during the crisis illustrates the benefits of past labour market reforms in strengthening work incentives, improving job matching and increasing flexibility in working hours. Germany's unemployment rate is one of the lowest in the OECD, and its employment rate is among the highest.

Indeed, the record of total employment rates in selected OECD countries shows significant differences among different countries and over time. While the employment rate has increased by almost 8 (4) percentage points from 2000 (2007) to 2011 and stood at 74 per cent in 2011, the situation especially in some of the EMU countries in crisis demonstrates considerable lagging behind with countries such as Spain, Italy and Ireland having employment rates at 60 per cent or lower – partly as a result of the recession, but partly also persistently as in Italy (Artus & Caffet, 2014, p. 3).

To conclude this section, one may say that the specific experience of Germany is that controversial structural reforms within say the last dozen years finally paid off by shortening crisis situations and strengthening the economy. More generally, this may explain why many Germans usually think that at least some of the basic lessons of the German experience of having successfully pursued supply-side-orientated measures can serve as a guideline for national reform efforts in the crisis countries of the Euro area. Some commentators even spoke of a 'new German miracle' (Koch & Rees, 2010) and regarded 'German reform success as blueprint for Europe' (Rees, 2011). They have suggested that the German success even may have structural policy lessons also for laggards. It has to be noted, however, also that both the Bundesbank and the OECD see room to manoeuvre for further improving the German labour market record rather considerably in the future (*Deutsche Bundesbank*, 2014, p. 36 and OECD, 2014, p. 14). Indeed, using this leeway may be important to counter future demographic problems as well as some of the criticisms against the praise of German labour market successes.

4. Controversies on Internal and External Side-Effects of Germany's Labour Market Transformation

In contrast to the positive assessment until now, some critics highlight potential negative internal and external side-effects of the approach adopted in Germany since the early 2000s. Some left-leaning heterodox critics foremost emphasise that in their view the structural labour market reforms adopted in Germany have to be regarded more as parts of the current problems, e.g. in EMU rather than parts of their solutions (Lehndorff, 2012). On the one hand, is it really true that from a domestic perspective 'the German approach to create a favourable competitive position for its producers by very low wage growth in relation to the progress of productivity has not been successful' (Flassbeck, 2013, p. 69)? On the other hand, should we really regard German wage policy as 'uncooperative' against other EMU member states (Artus, 2013a)?

The analysis of the characteristics of the German adjustment process shows that on average the rate of labour productivity growth was relatively high at 1.1 per cent annually between 2000 and 2012. As the respective per cent figures for the Netherlands, Denmark and the United States are rather similar at 0.9, 1.3 and 1.5 (OECD, 2014, p. 3), this can be seen positively as the inclusion of former 'outsiders' (often with skills gaps) in jobs (Funk, 2013d) succeeded simultaneously. Furthermore, the development of total hours worked (Table 3) has to be seen against foremost voluntary decisions of employees to supply less working time on average. Taking that into account, the expected figure of total hours worked of all persons employed amounts to 58.67 bn. hours in 2014 – 'the highest value since 1992' (Fuchs *et al.*, 2013, p. 9) and an increase of 1 per cent compared to 2013. Moreover, the considerable fall in total hours worked of −2.7 per cent in 2009 as a result of mutually beneficial short-time work can foremost explain why a decrease in employment in terms of persons could be avoided even if simultaneously productivity fell and unit labour costs increased briefly (Funk, 2012, pp. 22–23).

Furthermore, empirical evidence refutes most of the alleged negative domestic side-effects. The increase in new forms of gainful employment such as temporary agency and minor jobs is usually additional to the traditional regular employment which is fully integrated into the social security system. If other socio-economic factors are taken into account these additional jobs are neither accompanied by vast pay gaps as critics often claim nor is the prevalence of temporary work at 2 per cent in terms of whole-time equivalents higher than in similar countries such as the Netherlands or Britain (Funk 2013b, pp. 215–220; Peters, 2012). It has to be noted also that the amount of permanent full-time employment increased in 2012 slightly to the level of 41 per cent of the working-age population as in 2001 while the amount of the inactive working-age population fell from 25 to 19 per cent in the same period (Table 4).

Moreover, attacks against negative distributional side-effects of the structural reforms implemented in Germany have to be put into perspective since the German income distribution has risen only moderately since 1991 and the size of the middle class has hardly changed since then (German Council of Economic Experts, 2013, p. 7). Nevertheless, German inequality has risen steadily in early 2000, while 'this trend appears to have moderated in recent years, and the country remains more equal than the OECD average'

Table 4. Working-age population by employment status – no crowding out of permanent full-time employment by atypical jobs

Year	1992	1996	2001	2004	2008	2012
100 per cent of which … (in per cent)						
inactive	26	26	25	24	20	19
unemployed	6	7	6	8	6	6
self-employed	6	6	7	7	6	7
marginal/irregular	1	2	3	3	5	4
agency work	–	–	1	2	2	2
fixed-term contract	5	4	4	4	6	7
vocational education	4	3	3	3	3	3
permanent part-time	8	8	9	10	10	11
permanent full-time	45	43	41	38	40	41

Source: IZA (2013).

Table 5. Low-wage employees in Germany in per cent of respective groups

Low-wage paid (per hour) Categories	Less than € 8.50 (in per cent of …)	Less than € 10 (in per cent of …)
Employment status		
Total employees	17	26
Full-time employees	10	18
Part-time employees	18	28
Marginally employed	54	73
Pupils, students, pensioners and unemployed	43	54
Qualification required		
None, on-the-job-training, courses	40	54
Apprenticeship or vocational degree	12	22
University degree	4	6
Age		
Up to 24 years	4	6
25–60 years	44	62
60 years and older	21	31

Notes: The figures above exclude apprentices and persons in active labour market programmes. The percentages refer to the total number of persons employed in the respective group. E.g. of all employed persons, 17 per cent receive hourly wages of less than € 8.50, while 26 per cent earn less than € 10. Among part-time employees, these shares are 18 and 28 per cent.
Source: Table based on diagram of Zimmermann (2013, p. 8).

(OECD, 2014, p. 9). At the same time, the progress with respect to jobs creation 'since 2005 has not been accompanied by a significant decline in poverty' (OECD, 2014, p. 9; cf. also Artus, 2013b; Gräf, B. & Grewenig, E. 2014).

The announced implementation of statutory minimum wages within the next three years in Germany at €8.50 by the new CDU/CSU-Social Democrat (SPD) government led by Chancellor Angela Merkel will hardly lead to a more equal income distribution as only a small fraction of full-time employees will be directly affected while larger fractions of atypical workers would be affected (Table 5). The distributional effect is, however, expected to be minimal: 'As a result, even a relatively high minimum wage of €10 would reduce income inequality only by 1 per cent' (Zimmermann, 2013, p. 7). This, and the fear of negative employment effects, explains why the German Council of Economic Experts (2013, p. 4) has rejected encompassing minimum wages outright in its annual report of November 2013 and rejects also all other measures that water down the economically successful Hartz reform that helped to overcome persistent German problems. Other analysts are, however, less pessimistic (Broyer & Gareis 2013, p. 3; OECD, 2014, pp. 14–16) but nevertheless ask for caution with this instrument. It must not undermine German employment prospects.

Critics often argue that Germany's rising export surpluses since Euro's adoption have to be regarded as most important drivers of Germany's improved (un)employment performance. They often assert that the German moderate wage and labour cost growth during the last decade have caused to a large extent the high current account imbalances in the EU. In other words, they often blame the alleged deflationary wage policy in Germany as beggarthy-neighbour policy. Nevertheless, counter-critics claim that the attacks on German export surpluses as well as structural reforms and related moderate wage policies are largely unjustified as German mercantilism is seen as only a 'myth' (Krauss, 2013; Meier, 2012).[1] Rather, according to these critics as well as from the point of view of different German governments led by Chancellor Merkel since the start of the financial crisis the reforms within Germany should serve at least in parts as guidelines also for other nations as they contributed to these successes.

The background for this view is the basic idea that it is by no means necessarily at the expense of other countries if one country is doing well. Indeed the former CDU/CSU-FDP government led by Chancellor Merkel regarded its role as actively helping to determine the route to greater stability in Europe by actively promoting the principles of its original rule-based SME. In other words, bad governance has, to a large extent, been responsible for the current crisis largely also at the national levels in the countries in crisis. Indeed, according to an independent academic outside of Germany: 'The crisis of the southern European Euro is not simply a sovereign debt crisis: it is also a growth and competitiveness crisis resulting from insider power' (Iversen, 2013, p. 77). In other words, the situation in these countries mirrors the German situation when it was the overregulated 'sick man of Europe' to a notable extent (Heinen, 2010).

Therefore, rules of governance have to change considerably and lastingly according to the '2013 Annual Economic Report' of the Government of January 2013:

> In order to restore political credibility and to overcome the European crisis of confidence on a lasting basis, Europe needs a reliable regulatory framework which imposes – and enforces – common rules. …. Europe has improved its rules. It is now important for all countries to work hard – chiefly on their own responsibility – to ensure disciplined reforms, growth and high competitiveness. (Federal Ministry for Economic Affairs, 2013)

Despite recent successes in fighting the crisis (*Deutsche Bundesbank*, 2014, pp. 13–18) which were also made possible by the unconventional monetary and fiscal actions taken (cf. details Funk, 2013c, 2014), the German-inspired consensus that fiscal consolidation and structural reforms according to the slogan 'solidity in exchange for solidarity' should be the central pillar of future success has crumbled to some extent outside Germany.[2] More serious, perhaps, is the impression, which is spreading in Germany, that quite a few of the countries in crisis are tending to regard their consolidation and reform efforts as sacrifices ('unjustified imposed austerity') that are necessary to receive further support rather than being inherently correct and prudent from an economic point of view. In order to support even more vigorously the reform efforts in EMU countries in crisis the new German federal government in its coalition agreement and particularly the SPD-led Ministry of Economic Affairs and Energy (2014) decided to change its economic position with respect to rebalancing at least to some extent towards the position taken at the European Commission (Funk, 2013a) also in order to take into account potential problems related to unwanted side-effects of ongoing low growth. The more nuanced position taken by the European Commission (Buti, 2014), which is also controversially debated in Germany (Fuest, 2013), tries to turn Germany's surplus into a win-win for the Eurozone by facilitating a mutually beneficial rebalancing rather than concentrating on measures that impose the burden of adjustment foremost on Germany and its tax payers (while pretending that Germany has hardly contributed to rebalancing until now as critics often do).[3]

Nevertheless, it remains somewhat mistaken to pretend that Germany's current account surpluses only put pressure on demand in other EMU countries and suggesting that Germany thereby contributed to the Eurozone's crisis for at least two reasons: First, Germany's trade balance with the Eurozone fell considerably in recent years and almost halved since 2006 (when it stood at 4 per cent) to 2.5 per cent of GDP in 2012. Second, Germany's strong export performance against the countries beyond the Euro area benefits the EMU countries from which the Germans import a large share of capital and intermediate goods (especially as the import content of German exports is high compared to many other countries). Aiming at decreasing the German trade surplus could thus end up in hurting the other Euro area's exports to Germany. All in all, Germany's external account surpluses are a much smaller problem for the Eurozone than is often stated. In other words, up until now Germany has not idly left the task of adjustment and rebalancing to others, but obviously reduced its export surpluses in inner-European trade. Additionally previously persistently weak growth in unit labour costs has been stalled. Since 2010, German unit labour costs have been rising more than the EMU's average. These facts contributed directly or indirectly to stabilising aggregate demand in the EMU countries particularly affected by the crisis (Artus, 2013a, Artus, 2013b; cf. Garreis & Lefebvre, 2013, p. 2).

Nevertheless, there is further leeway to improve German policies since the export surpluses to some extent reflect – apart from population ageing (which helps in explaining German savings efforts and investments of capital abroad) – structural weaknesses in the German economy's markets (*Deutsche Bundesbank*, 2014, p. 36; OECD, 2014). For example, focusing on infrastructure spending to ensure a greener growth or energy transformation is particularly important in order to counter particularly low German domestic investment and to increase future potential growth which will be hit by the ageing population. Contributing to this will be also a further stimulus of competition in services jobs (e.g. professional services, certain crafts, construction, network industries) as well as lower (payroll) taxes for low-paid workers in order to boost further domestic sources of economic growth.

Germany will nonetheless probably accept further pressures from abroad only to a very limited extent as the country risks being overburdened (Das, 2013; Sinn, 2013) and because the new plans of implementing a national minimum wage by the new coalition and measures to increase public and private investments will likely help further stimulate domestic German demand.[4] What will not occur, however, is the implementation of a traditional Keynesian stimulus programme that would be incompatible with Germany's budgetary rules and population ageing. Rather the duty for the countries still in crisis will be to create a viable new 'national business model', e.g. by making themselves attractive as part of the German supply chain of exports. Furthermore, if there is a rise in German domestic demand as a result of implementing the new measures such as statutory minimum wages this will likely increase somewhat the still very low German inflation and may contribute to the Euro's depreciation. This would ease the access to global markets for exporters in the periphery and contribute to less competition from outside the EMU and higher profit margins for them in their domestic markets. Beneficiaries could also include France and Italy.

5. Conclusions

In contrast to other countries and in spite of its large negative growth rate due to massive export losses in 2009, Germany's labour market proved stable. Despite of the twin crises of the Great Recession in 2009 and the still ongoing critical situation in EMU, structural changes in German output have been relatively small and employment structures in Germany changed very little since 2008. Focusing on its recently reformed labour market-related institutions and supplementary emergency policies, after the recession Germany proved to be better placed than most economies.

As Germany has benefited all-in-all from the creation of the Euro, Germany has shown solidarity with countries in crisis. For obvious reasons such solidarity has to be limited, however, to emergency aid in order to ensure that self-sustainable new structures can develop in the countries in crisis. Representatives of receiving countries sometimes seem to forget that Germany has already accepted, among other issues, exceptional monetary policy measures that entail substantial risks. This is especially true since too many unconventional measures for too long may reduce national incentives to initiate urgently required structural reforms in the countries in crisis.

The still ongoing German success does not mean that it can simply be transferred to other nations without amendments. However, the German experience is basically in line with the causal relationships highlighted in mainstream economics textbooks. The reforms taken in Germany (as well as case studies of other countries) and cross-country evidence can certainly help the countries currently in crisis to learn from the reform measures and processes in their own national labour markets.

It is not entirely certain that – everything else being the same – the announced German government plans to stimulate investment will lead to a fall in the export surplus since it may even stimulate further German exports due to the increased productivity of the German supply-side. Nevertheless, this in turn will increase the German demand for foreign inputs and thus stimulate the exports of countries that are parts of the German supply-chain as some of the Central and Eastern European Member States. The Southern countries currently in crisis may thus take them as a potential role model for their future 'national business model'. Their success thus depends to a much larger extent on doing their national homework of much needed structural reforms than on German efforts to stimulate its own economy.

Notes

[1] Indeed, there has been an ongoing controversial debate on the recently steadily rising German export surpluses for some time. Especially, US economists such as Paul Krugman (2013) have attacked with sentences such as 'Germany failed to make any adjustment at all', that 'Germany's failure to adjust magnified the cost austerity' and that it beggars its neighbours and the world. Moreover, he states that German officials 'consider their country a shining role model, to be emulated by all'. These criticisms, which are to some extent wrong (Krauss, 2013), are hardly justified similar to the ones by US treasury. However, other nobel-prize-winning US economists, such as Michael Spence (2012) and Edmund S. Phelps (2012), have supported, in principle, the response taken within the EU inspired to a noteworthy extent by German economic thinking. This academic support of the German official position has been often entirely neglected or at least downplayed in the public debate (Funk & Allen, 2012).

[2] This is despite of the concessions that have been agreed by creditor countries governments such as, amongst other things, extensions of pay-back periods of public loans to countries in crisis.

[3] Recent consultations by experts to the House of Lords have demonstrated that the approach supported by Germany officially is by no means necessarily flawed, as some commentators claim. This is true especially when taking into account Germany's 'need to secure parliamentary and public support for its position' (House of Lords European Union Committee, 2014, p. 13).

[4] Amongst other things, this depends on the net effect of governmental policies which may on net increase the burden on German business and parts of consumers to such an extent that the entire growth effect may be negative in the medium term.

References

Annesley, C., Pugh, G. & Tyrall, D. (2004) The German economic model: Consensus, stability, productivity and the implications for reform, in: J. Perraton & B. Clift (Eds) *Where are National Capitalisms Now?* pp. 70–90 (Basingstoke: Palgrave Macmillan).

Artus, P. (2010, 28 October) Germany is different from the rest of the euro zone, but in reality it is not in a position of strength to impose its views. *Flash Economics Economic Research*, No. 580, *Natixis*.

Artus, P. (2013a, 27 November) Can Germany be criticised for its external surplus? *Flash Economics Economic Research*, No. 837, *Natixis*.

Artus, P. (2013b, 3 May) Three questions about the German "model". *Flash Economics Economic Research*, No. 333, *Natixis*.

Artus, P. & Caffet, J.-C. (2014, 28 February) Is it possible to cut government spending? *Flash Economics Economic Research*, No, 165, *Natixis*.

BMWI – Federal Ministry for Economic Affairs and Energy (2014) *2014 Annual Economic Report – The Social Market Economy Today – Stimulating Growth and Cohesion* (Berlin: BMWI). Available at http://www.bmwi. de/English/Redaktion/Pdf/2014-annual-economic-report,property=pdf,bereich=bmwi2012,sprache=en,rwb= true.pdf (accessed 29 February 2014).

Broyer, S. & Gareis, J. (2013, 28 November) Germany to introduce statutory minimum wage: Good news? *Economic Research Special Report*, No. 183, *Natixis*.

Buti, M. (2014, 9 January) A consistent trinity for the Eurozone. VoxEU.org. Available at http://www.voxeu.org/ article/consistent-trinity-eurozone (accessed 10 January 2014).

Das, S. (2013, 5 November) Debt crisis has left Germany vulnerable. *Financial Times*, p. 26.

Deutsche Bundesbank (2014) Monthly Report, Vol. 66, No. 1. Available at http://www.bundesbank.de/Redaktion/ EN/Downloads/Publications/Monthly_Report/2014/2014_01_monthly_report.pdf?__blob=publicationFile (accessed 29 February 2013).

EEAG – European Economic Advisory Group (2014) *The EEAG Report on the European Economy 2014* (Munich: Cesifo Group). Available at http://www.cesifo-group.de/de/ifoHome/policy/EEAG-Report/Archive/ EEAG_Report_2014/eeag_2014_report.html (accessed 29 February 2013).

Federal Ministry for Economic Affairs (2013) *2013 Annual Economic Report – The Key to Growth and Jobs in Germany and Europe* (Berlin: BMWI). Available at http://www.bmwi.de/English/Redaktion/Pdf/2013-annual-economic-report-competitiveness-_20key-to-growth,property=pdf,bereich=bmwi,sprache=en,rwb=true.pdf (accessed 20 January 2014).

Flassbeck, H. (2013) Labor markets and economic development, in: H. Flassbeck, P. Davidson, J.K. Galbraith, R. Koo & J. Ghosh (Eds) *Economic Reform Now*, pp. 55–83 (Frankfurt am Main: Westend Verlag).

Fuchs, J., *et al.* (2013) Arbeitslosigkeit sinkt trotz Beschäftigungsrekord nur wenig, *IAB-Kurzbericht 23 (18)*. Available at http://doku.iab.de/kurzber/2013/kb1813.pdf (accessed 29 February 2014).

Fuest, C. (2013) Germany's Trade Surplus: A Cause for Concern? *ZEW News*, November–December, Centre for European Economic Research, p. 12. Available at http//:www.zew.de/en (accessed 10 December 2013).

Funk, L. (2000) Economic reform of *Modell Deutschland*, in: R. Harding & W. E. Paterson (Eds) *The Future of the German Economy – An End to the Miracle?* pp. 16–35 (Manchester: Manchester University Press).

Funk, L. (2001) Strategic policy to fight Germany's unemployment problem, *International Journal of Manpower*, 22(6), pp. 508–525.

Funk, L. (2002) *Wirtschaftswunder*, in: H. Briel (Ed) *German Culture and Society*, pp. 148–149 (London: Arnold).

Funk, L. (2003a) Chancellor proposes Agenda 2010 to Revive Economy. *Eironline*. Available at http://www. eurofound.europa.eu/eiro/2003/03/feature/de0303105f.htm (accessed 20 February 2014).

Funk, L. (2003b) Lower house approves key elements of Agenda 2010 reforms. *Eironline*. Available at http:// www.eurofound.europa.eu/eiro/2003/11/inbrief/de0311101n.htm (accessed 20 February 2014).

Funk, L. (2007a) Convergence in employment-related public policies? A British-German comparison, *German Politics*, 16(1), pp. 116–136.

Funk, L. (2007b) New structural changes: Challenges for the German labour market and collective bargaining, in: J. Hölscher (Ed) *Germany's Economic Performance. From Unification to Euroisation*, pp. 175–195 (London: Palgrave).

Funk, L. (2010) Social market economy at sixty: Path dependence and path changes, in: C. L. Glossner & D. Gregosz (Eds) *Sixty Years of Social Market Economy: Formation, Development and Perspectives of a Peacemaking Formula*, pp. 85–103 (Berlin: Konrad-Adenauer Foundation). Available at http://www.kas.de/ upload/dokumente/2010/06/60_Years_SME/funk.pdf (accessed 10 December 2013).

Funk, L. (2012) *The German Economy During the Financial and Economic Crisis since 2008/2009: An Unexpected Success Story Revisited* (Berlin: Konrad-Adenauer Foundation). Available at http://www.kas.de/wf/doc/kas_33244-1522-23-30.pdf?130110040349 (accessed 10 December 2013).

Funk, L. (2013a, 28 November) Germany's return to a two-sided economic policy (letter*). Financial Times*, p. 8. Available at http://www.ft.com/intl/cms/s/0/a19007c8-52cb-11e3-a73e-00144feabdc0.html#axzz2v4hQ6UXC (accessed 10 December 2013).

Funk, L. (2013b) Germany: Sweeping structural reforms can work, in: V. Novotný (Ed) *From Reform to Growth – Managing the Economic Crisis in Europe*, pp. 201–233 (Brussels: Centre for European Studies).

Funk, L. (2013c) Getting the Eurozone back on its feet, *European Voice*, 19(9), p. 11. Available at http://www.europeanvoice.com/article/imported/getting-the-eurozone-back-on-its-feet/76597.aspx (accessed 10 December 2013).

Funk, L. (2013d, 13 April) Von Deutschland lernen – ja, aber anders. Finanz und Wirtschaft, No. 29, p. 2.

Funk, L. (2014) The German approach to finance in the European Context, in: S. Colvin (Ed) *Handbook of Contemporary German Politics and Culture*, Chapter 22, (London: Routledge). In print.

Funk, L. & Allen, M. (2012) Germany – Economy', in: Europa Publications (Ed) *Western Europe 2013*, pp. 308–322 (London: Routledge).

Garreis, J. & Lefebvre, J. M. (2013) Understanding Germany's current account surplus, *Special Report Economic Research*, No. 190, *Natixis*.

Garton Ash, T. (2013) The New German question. *The New York Review of Books*, 15 August 2014. Available at http://www.nybooks.com/articles/archives/2013/aug/15/new-german-question/?pagination=false (accessed 12 February 2014).

German Council of Economic Experts (2011) Assume responsibility for Europe – Annual Report 2011/2012 Chapter 1, Wiesbaden & Paderborn: Sachverständigenrat zur Begutachtung der Gesamtwirtschaftlichen Entwicklung. Available at www.sachverstaendigenrat-wirtschaft.de (accessed 12 December 2013).

German Council of Economic Experts (2013) Against a backward-looking economic policy – Annual Report Chapter 1, Wiesbaden & Paderborn: Sachverständigenrat zur Begutachtung der Gesamtwirtschaftlichen Entwicklung. Available at www.sachverstaendigenrat-wirtschaft.de (accessed 12 December 2013).

German Council of Economic Experts (2014, 20 March) Press release: Updated economic forecast, Wiesbaden & Paderborn: Sachverständigenrat zur Begutachtung der Gesamtwirtschaftlichen Entwicklung. Available at www.sachverstaendigenrat-wirtschaft.de (accessed 12 April 2014).

Gräf, B. & Grewenig, E. (2014, 28 February) Temporary work: Success story with an uncertain outcome, *Current Issues*, Deutsche Bank Research, pp. 10–15.

Gurria, A. (2014) Visit to the OECD by Angela Merkel, Federal Chancellor of Germany – Introductory Remarks. Available at http://www.oecd.org/about/secretary-general/visit-to-the-oecd-by-angela-merkel-remarks-by-angel-gurria.htm (accessed 25 February 2014).

Hamilton, D. S. & Quinlan, J. P. (2008) *Globalization & Europe: Prospering in the New Whirled Order* (Washington, DC: The Johns Hopkins University).

Havlik, P. (2014, January) Structural change in Europe during the crisis, FIW Policy Brief No. 22 (Austrian Ministry for the Economy, Family and Youth). Available at http://www.fiw.ac.at/fileadmin/Documents/Publikationen/Policy_Briefs/22.FIW_PolicyBrief_Havlik.pdf (accessed 10 February 2014).

Heinen, N. (2010, 18 February) EMU countries in systems competition: Winners and Losers, *Deutsche Bank Research*.

House of Lords European Union Committee (2014) *Euro Area Crisis: An Update*, 11th Report of Session 2013-14 (London: The Stationery Office Limited). Available at http://www.publications.parliament.uk/pa/ld201314/ldselect/ldeucom/163/163.pdf (accessed 12 April 2014).

IMF – International Monetary Fund (2012) Fostering Growth in Europe now, IMF Staff Discussion Note, Washington, DC. Available at http://www.imf.org/external/pubs/ft/sdn/2012/sdn1207.pdf (accessed 10 December 2013).

IMF – International Monetary Fund (2013) Germany – 2013 Article IV Consultation, IMF Country Report No. 13/255, Washington, DC. Available at http://www.imf.org/external/pubs/ft/scr/2013/cr13255.pdf (accessed 10 December 2013).

Iversen, T. (2013) Combining competitiveness, growth, and solidarity, in: Global Progress –Policy network (Ed) *The Politics of Growth, Stability and Reform, Policy network*, pp. 75–78 (London). Available at http://www.policy-network.net/publications/4361/The-Politics-of-Growth-Stability-and-Reform (accessed 23 October 2014).

IZA – Institute for the Study of Labor (2013, December) Flexible Arbeitswelt: Atypische Beschäftigung wächst nicht zu Lasten des Normalarbeitsverhältnisses, IZA Compact, pp. 6–8. Available at http://ftp.iza.org/compacts/iza_compact_de_45.pdf (accessed 10 December 2013).

John, K.-D. (2007) Die Soziale Marktwirtschaft im Kontext der Europäischen Integration. Befund und Perspektiven, in: M. von Hauff (Ed) *Die Zukunftsfähigkeit der sozialen Marktwirtschaft*, pp. 143–191 (Marburg: Metropolis).

Koch, A. & Rees, A. (2010, 12 November) The New German miracle, *The Wall Street Journal Europe*, p. 13.

Krauss, M. (2013) Treasury and Krugman are wrong about Germany. *Bloomberg View*. Available at http://www.bloombergview.com/articles/2013-11-07/treasury-and-krugman-are-wrong-about-germany (accessed 12 January 2014).

Krugman, P. (2013, 5 November) Those depressing Germans. *International New York Times*, p. 7. Available at http://www.nytimes.com/2013/11/04/opinion/krugman-those-depressing-germans.html (accessed 20 January 2014).

Lesch, H. (2010) Free Collective Bargaining: Support Column or Crumbling Pillar of the Social Market Economy, in: C. L. Glossner & D. Gregosz (Eds) *Sixty Years of Social Market Economy: Formation, Development and Perspectives of a Peacemaking Formula*, pp. 104–126 (Berlin: Konrad-Adenauer Foundation). Available at http://www.kas.de/wf/en/33.20040/ (accessed 10 December 2013).

Lehndorff, S. (2012) German capitalism and the European crisis – Part of the solution or part of the problem? in: S. Lehndorff (Ed) *A Triumph of Failed Ideas – European Models of Capitalism in Crisis*, pp. 79–102. Available at http://www.etui.org/Publications2/Books/A-triumph-of-failed-ideas-European-models-of-capitalism-in-the-crisis (accessed 25 February 2014).

Meier, C.-P. (2012, 4 October) Myth of German mercantilism (letter). *Financial Times*, p. 10.

OECD (2012) *OECD Economic Surveys: Germany* (Paris: OECD).

OECD (2014) Keeping the edge – competitiveness for inclusive growth, Paris. Available at http://www.oecd.org/economy/Better-policies-germany.pdf (accessed 28 February 2014).

Paterson, W. E. (2011) The Reluctant Hegemon? Germany Moves Centre Stage in the European Union, *Journal of Common Market Studies*, 49 (Issue Supplement s1), pp. 57–75.

Peters, H. (2012) Pluralisation of forms of employment yielding positive effects on labour markets, *Current Issues*, May, 9, 2012, Deutsche Bank Research, pp. 9–13.

Phelps, E. S. (2012, 20 July) Germany is right to ask for austerity before any more union. *Financial Times*, p. 7.

Rees, A. (2011, 4 November) German reform success as blueprint for Europe. *Friday Notes*, UniCredit, 6–8.

Sinn, H.-W. (2013) Relaunching Europe: Problems, reform strategies and future options, *CESifo Forum*, 14(3), pp. 8–13.

Spence, M. (2012, 19 June) Clarity about Austerity. Available at http://www.project-syndicate.org/commentary/clarity-about-austerity (accessed 20 September 2012).

Zimmermann, K. F. (2013) Labor market reforms and the Great Recession December. *IZA Policy Paper No. 75*.

The Limits of Transnational Solidarity and the Eurozone Crisis in Germany, Ireland and Slovakia

STEFAN AUER

School of Modern Languages and Culture, University of Hong Kong, Hong Kong

ABSTRACT   *This paper presents contrasting stories of three pro-EU nations, Germany, Ireland and Slovakia, which have seen their European projects put on a collision course with their political traditions, expectations and material interests. Slovaks can no longer be confident in strengthening their post-communist democracy through its engagement with Europe. In Germany, people are concerned that they can no longer trust their currency, the euro, let alone see it as the bedrock of economic and political stability. Germans are also profoundly worried about the erosion of the rule of law, the Rechtsstaat, through euro rescue measures, which are yet to prove their effectiveness. In Ireland too, people who had experienced European integration as hugely beneficial, both economically and politically, have been forced to question their commitments. To sum up, many German, Slovak and Irish citizens have seen their EU-integration goals severely undermined by the crisis. What is more, the strategies that have been employed to safeguard the single currency have resulted in increased scepticism towards the European project as such. Instead of differentiated integration, the conflicting goals may well be pointing towards Europe's disintegration.*

The single European currency has significantly contributed to the EU's fragmentation, accelerating the process of differentiated integration. Instead of equalising economic conditions across the continent, the euro crisis appears to have entrenched, or even increased, the disparities between its member states. This seriously erodes feelings of transnational solidarity, which are a prerequisite for any lasting solutions to the crisis. Consequently, many scenarios advanced both by policy-makers and EU scholars, which seek to address the crisis by reinforcing Europe's commitment towards an ever closer union, have little chance of succeeding.

This paper focuses on three traditionally pro-integration eurozone members. For a variety of reasons, German, Irish and Slovak citizens tended to see themselves as beneficiaries of European integration and their political elites have been largely supportive of moves towards further integration, including the introduction of the single European currency. The reasons for such a pro-EU consensus are familiar, but worth restating. From the outset, German elites rightly perceived the European project as a vehicle for their country to regain credibility as a decent, dependable and trustworthy nation. For Ireland, European integration was crucial in helping the small nation to gain control over its destiny. To be truly sovereign and no longer dependent on Britain, it appeared beneficial for the Irish to share sovereignty with their European partners. Slovakia shared similar goals and pursued them by strikingly similar means. Like the Irish, Slovaks remain anxious about their national independence, but have sought to strengthen it by becoming truly European, which was in their eyes equated with being prosperous, democratic and embedded firmly in EU institutions. All three nations have seen their EU-integration goals severely undermined by the crisis. What is more, the strategies that have so far been employed to safeguard the single currency have resulted in increased scepticism towards the European project as such.[1] Instead of differentiated integration, the conflicting goals may well be pointing towards Europe's disintegration.

This paper takes as a point of departure the provocative proposition by David Marsh that the EU crisis can no longer be solved: 'The eurozone and its institutions have enough means to manage paralysis, but they can do no more' (Marsh, 2013, p. 14). This is caused by both the conflicting material interests of the participating members as well as their differing political cultures, which shape their expectations with respect to the appropriate means of dealing with the crisis (Guiso et al., 2013). The three countries at the heart of this analysis exemplify these dilemmas, which have no obvious answers. To cite Marsh again, 'the escape route from the labyrinth cannot be located because it doesn't exist' (Marsh, 2013, p. 24).

The EU system of governance is confused and confusing. The euro crisis brought into stark relief how little we understand of the way in which Europe is ruled. This is partly owing to the fact that the dominant approaches in EU scholarship tended to reject questions about power and the location of sovereignty as antiquated. To ask, 'Who is in charge of Europe?' is to misunderstand the unique nature of this experimental polity and its intricate governing structures, or so the argumentation went. Yet, Europe's new problems compel us to re-state old questions of politics, which can be grouped around three key concepts: sovereignty, the rule of law and solidarity.

As will become clear, the three nations considered in this article have differing expectations with respect to these key concepts, reflecting their varied historical experiences.

Sovereignty

'Sovereign is he who decides on the exception' (Schmitt, 1985, p. 5), as the controversial German thinker, Carl Schmitt, pithily observed. There are two aspects to this definition, and both are highly pertinent to Europe's current predicament. First, the sovereign is endowed with the authority (or usurps the authority) to ascertain what constitutes exceptional circumstances in demand of a solution. Second, the sovereign claims the authority to propose a suitable course of action to solve the problems identified as exceptional. It is ironic then that the very same nation that has been the least concerned about its sovereignty in post-war Europe is also the one that appears to be still largely in control of its destiny (and indeed, by extension, Europe's destiny): Germany.

Without their wanting it, leadership of the crisis management fell into the hands of the German ruling elite, creating a new power-constellation in Europe, which threatens to undo the decades-long process of post-war reconciliation. As the prominent Irish writer and commentator, Colm Tóibín, wryly observed:

> For the third time in a century, Germany has come to dominate Europe. The first and second time this led to unbearable tragedy and came close to destroying the continent. The third time it comes in the guise of dullness, lack of political flair or any sense of social solidarity. (Tóibín, 2013)

Revealingly, the success of the Christian Democratic Party in September 2013 German national elections was greeted by a major Spanish newspaper, *El Mundo*, with the front page headline, 'Merkel, Merkel über alles' (23 September 2013), echoing similar responses in other EU member states concerned about Germany's preponderance. Whatever course of action the German government pursues, it appears to lead to an increase in anti-German sentiments across Europe. Such sentiments may not (yet?) be all that pronounced in Slovakia and Ireland. However, in contrast to Germany, both countries share a concern for their national sovereignty.

In Slovakia, resentment against bailouts for indebted nations of the eurozone, particularly Greece, led to the collapse of the pro-EU, centre-right coalition government, which was replaced by the populist leader, Robert Fico – who emerged as the main beneficiary of the crisis following the March 2012 national elections. In Ireland, the crisis has constrained the choices of the government to such an extent that the nation's fate appeared to be shaped by the decisions taken in Brussels, in Frankfurt or in Berlin, rather than those taken by the *Taoiseach* (the prime minister) or the *Dáil Éireann* (the lower house) in Dublin. In this vein, the *Irish Times* editorialised after the bailout:

> [Is this] what the men of 1916 died for: a bailout from the German chancellor with a few shillings of sympathy from the British chancellor on the side. There is the shame of it all. Having obtained our political independence from Britain to be the masters of our own affairs, we have now surrendered our sovereignty to the European Commission, the European Central Bank, and the International Monetary Fund. (19 November 2010)

This sentiment and the image of past national traumas was echoed by the leader of the Irish Confederation of Trade Unions, Mr David Begg, who was quoted as saying in 2013 that 'the Troika has done more damage to Ireland than Britain ever did in 800 years' (Evans-Pritchard, 2013). As is to be expected from a political actor, Mr Begg may well have overstated his point. In fact, in December 2013 Ireland became the first country to leave its EU-managed bailout programme. Yet, this is unlikely to translate into a significant increase in support for the EU, particularly with massive political and economic challenges ahead.[2]

However successful Ireland's departure from the bailout programme is going to be, it will not change the way in which the European Union has been ruled since the outbreak of the crisis. Whether this is described as 'executive federalism' (Habermas, 2013, p. 20), 'EU2' (Giddens, 2013, p. 6), 'authoritarian managerialism' (Everson & Joerges, 2013, p. 20) or 'Merkiavellism' (Beck, 2012, 2013), what has characterised EU governing methods since 2010 are ad hoc decisions taken by the key actors within the governments of the most powerful member state(s) (particularly Germany, to a lesser extent France) and the European Central Bank (ECB). As Habermas (2013, p. 21) put it, 'as national citizens see it, their political fate is determined by foreign governments who represent the interests of other nations, rather than by a government that is bound only by their own democratic vote'.

Exemplary in this respect was the way in which the extension of the first bailout fund was negotiated and implemented. While the agreement brokered primarily between Germany and France (under the leadership of their respective leaders, Angela Merkel and Nicolas Sarkozy, dubbed in popular media 'Merkozy') received reluctant endorsement by all 17 eurozone member states, the Slovak government had to deal with an internal rebellion, when a junior coalition partner, Richard Sulík's party *Sloboda a Solidarita* (SaS, Freedom and Solidarity), refused to support the measure. This led to the collapse of the Slovak coalition government in October 2011 and a series of recriminations directed at Sulík. EU Commission President José Manuel Barroso argued, for instance: 'sovereignty is fine, but you cannot allow a small stakeholder in the community [Slovakia] to slow down all the others' (*Financial Times*, 28 September 2011, see also Auer, 2013b).

Paradoxically, the leader of the current ruling party *Smer – Sociálna demokracia* (Direction – Social democracy), Prime Minister Robert Fico, was far more prone to voicing concerns about Slovak national sovereignty than the SaS leader Sulík. In fact, in 2006 Fico did not shy away from entering into a coalition with the extreme right *Slovenská národná strana* (SNS, Slovak National Party), very much to the consternation of his European partners. For scholars of European integration, the 2006 Slovak elections were exemplary of the limits of conditionality on strengthening democracy in post-communist Europe.[3] Though anxious to present itself as a mainstream, social democratic party, *Smer* and its leader, Fico, continued to appeal to nationalist sentiments in the electorate, particularly with respect to the Hungarian and Roma minorities (Buraj, 2013; Pytlas, 2013). In relation to the European Union, however, Fico's post-2012 government became unambiguously favourable towards all major initiatives that sought to strengthen the viability of the eurozone, such as the banking union and fiscal union. As his opponent, Sulík, pointed out, this was incompatible with Fico's professed commitment to defend Slovak national interests:

> I challenge Robert Fico, the premier of our country who pledged that he will fulfil his duties in the best interests of Slovak citizens and not in the interests of a handful of unelected officials in Brussels, to reject the Treaty about the European Stability Mechanism from his position of the Prime Minister. Mr Fico, it is your moral duty to protect Slovak national interests and not to damage them. To be a statesman does not mean that one simply obediently follows the instructions from Brussels, in order to be popular there. To be a statesman means to act in one's country's interest.[4]

Such language might sound antiquated in Germany, where the ideal of shared sovereignty has remained attractive amongst both intellectuals and political leaders, regardless of their ideological persuasion.[5] Yet, shared sovereignty can only be credible in a situation in which all member states enjoy – at a minimum – formal equality guaranteed by the existence of a supranational rule of law. This is what underpins traditional arguments in favour of a true European federation, ever since Walter Hallstein, the first president of the European Commission, articulated a vision of the United States of Europe as 'a community of law'. Dr Hallstein, a German jurist, tapped into the tradition of high respect for the '*Rechtsstaat*', a peculiar German concept that links the rule of law to an efficient state.

Understanding the changing role of law at the European level is, therefore, key to understanding why the crisis is making political union less, not more, likely.

The Rule of Law

As the supranational rule of law is being eroded by a host of rescue measures that defy existing EU Treaty provisions (Böckenförde, 2010; Everson & Joerges, 2013; Kirchhof, 2014), the EU's democratic legitimacy suffers. The measures employed for the establishment of the European Stability Mechanism (ESM), for example, were characterised as consisting of 'contradiction, circumvention and conceptual gymnastics' (Tomkin, 2013). Only through such dubious means was it possible to maintain the legal fiction that the ESM – established with the sole purpose of bypassing the 'no-bailout clause' in the Maastricht Treaty – is compatible with the EU legal order. This has far-reaching consequences for the democratic legitimacy of the European project. As Tomkin summarised:

> It was argued that the ESM is not concerned with monetary policy – although its task is to save the euro; that the ESM falls outside the economic competence reserved to the Union – even though it is directly concerned with coordinating financial assistance to support the Union's single currency; that the establishment of a bail-out fund *requires* a Treaty amendment – yet the ESM may operate before the amendment takes effect. Arguably the accumulation of such contradictions and the circumvention of prohibitions contained in the Union Treaties represent a challenge to the Union's fundamental commitment to respect for the rule of law as enshrined in Article 2 TEU. (Tomkin, 2013, p. 81)

Such concerns find strong resonance particularly in Germany, throwing into disarray a long-held, elite consensus. For decades, the federalist vision for a supranational Europe offered a perfect fit for Germany in Europe (Wessels, 2003). The eurozone crisis created an insoluble dilemma for any German government. It is safe to hazard the following prediction in early 2014: The re-elected Christian Democratic chancellor Angela Merkel, supported by the Social Democrats in a grand coalition, will either disappoint her voters or the rest of Europe. If the government is serious about its intent to rescue the eurozone and, by extension, the European project, it will have to sacrifice its traditional (West) German commitment to the *Rechtsstaat*, because a number of measures deemed necessary for safeguarding the single European currency are clearly in violation of existing EU law. If, by contrast, the government is serious about protecting German democracy and the *Rechtsstaat*, as it is bound to do under the German constitution, it will be forced to abandon the eurozone, at least in its current form. What is particularly disturbing about these two conflicting scenarios is that they touch on the two fundamental commitments that have underpinned the reconstruction of West German democracy after the Second World War – European integration and the rule of law. Take one of them away and the German question re-emerges: What is Germany's relationship with Europe and what is its self-understanding?

 This explains why observers in Germany and Europe at large are concerned about the emergence of a fringe party, which almost made it into the *Bundestag* in the 2013 German federal elections, *Die Alternative für Deutschland* (AfD, The Alternative for Germany). The name encapsulates its political programme, which seeks to offer alternatives to what the present chancellor, Merkel, presented as necessary policies towards the eurozone (Scicluna, 2014). Particularly in German debates, the party tends to be dismissed as populist or even extreme right. In reality, the key aims of the party are very much focussed on the restoration of the EU's commitment to its own rules, including the no-bailout clause in the Maastricht Treaty. The party is seen as eurosceptic, yet its scepticism is not directed against the European Union as such, but rather against (what it sees as) the ill-conceived policies applied to the euro crisis. As one of AfD's founding members, the economist Joachim Starbatty, stressed, 'Europe's bequest is not the wrongly constructed single currency, but the *Rechtsstaat*, liberal democracy and friendly co-operation of sovereign states' (Starbatty, 2013, p. 307; Neuerer, 2013). Rather than populist, the AfD is a party of the rule of law.

Indeed, the AfD's stance echoes criticisms voiced by respected legal scholars, such as Professor Paul Kirchhof. Kirchhof, who was the judge-rapporteur in the Maastricht Treaty decision of the German constitutional court, argued that EU leaders' willingness to subordinate legal stability to economic and financial stability is misguided and dangerous. In fact, the very notion that there can be a trade-off between the two is a fallacy – legal stability is a necessary precondition of financial stability. It is the existence of reliable and enforceable legal norms that ensures that contractual obligations, including those surrounding the repayment of debt, will be honoured (Kirchhof, 2012b).[6]

Yet, outside Germany, there is a growing consensus that *Stricter Rules Threaten the Eurozone*, as the title of a policy paper put it (Tilford & Whyte, 2011). At the risk of making a generalisation, I would suggest that Irish and Slovak political cultures are, for better or worse, characterised by a more pragmatic approach towards compliance with rules. They are also less inclined to worry excessively about price stability. In a comprehensive study about *The Fall of the Celtic Tiger*, the authors, prominent Irish economists Donal Donovan and Antoin E. Murphy, appear remarkably relaxed about the ECB abandoning the 'no-bailout clause' (Donovan & Murphy, 2013, p. 97), and the way in which the International Monetary Fund has been willing to act against its own rules.[7] The authors envisage 'as part of the solution' the ECB pursuing monetary policies that would lead to higher inflation, notwithstanding its restrictive mandate as stipulated in the Maastricht Treaty (Donovan & Murphy, 2013, p. 286).

That being said, Donovan and Murphy are right to point out that the actual rules that are meant to govern the eurozone are problematic and reflect the ideological predispositions of their framers – particularly the German governing elites. The German proclivity to assign the state an important role in securing the right balance between freedom and order is reflected in the ideology of ordoliberalism, which became prevalent amongst economists and political leaders in the post-war Federal Republic. Just as the *Rechtsstaat* combines a firm commitment to the rule of law with the state (*Recht* = law, *Staat* = state), ordoliberalism conceives economic liberty as created and guaranteed by a strong regulatory state. Applied to the EU, as Christian Joerges compellingly argued, 'ordoliberal-monetaristic standards were Europeanized in the legal constitution of the monetary union, although it was not possible to Europeanize their societal conditions for functioning, which had developed over time' (Joerges, 2012, p. 12). This is why a number of policies implemented to address the crisis are bound to be seen as insufficiently ordoliberal in Germany, all the while being opposed by many Irish, Italian, Portuguese or Spanish people for being too rigid.

This is not just about conflicting political cultures though. At stake are also the conflicting material interests of the eurozone members, particularly between the debtor and creditor states. Sulík's German-style ordoliberalism, for example, reflects not just his upbringing in West Germany (Auer, 2013b), but also plausibly addresses Slovak economic interests, which appear to be best served in a close alliance with Germany. Even the Prime Minister Robert Fico, his strong Keynesian leanings notwithstanding, speaks in favour of strict rules for the eurozone, echoing the insights of ordoliberalism (Fico, 2013).

The conflicting views on various euro rescue strategies expose the fallacy – particularly popular in Germany – that the crisis can be solved through technocratic means. The increased politicisation of the ECB is a case in point. To be sure, the ECB was conceived as an apolitical body, with the Treaty of Maastricht clearly defining its restricted mandate. Yet, there is a growing consensus – particularly outside of Germany – that Mario Draghi's publicly declared commitment to do 'whatever it takes' to safeguard the single currency was as bold as it was necessary. Through this simple statement, Draghi was turned virtually overnight into the most powerful *political* actor in the eurozone. Indeed, following Schmitt's definition of sovereignty, Draghi is one of the few actors who may be considered truly sovereign in a crisis that has shown other political bodies to be constrained by their lack of credibility (i.e. the European Commission), historical legacies (i.e. the German government) or insufficient formal powers (i.e. the European parliament).

Against this background, repeated calls for increased transparency in the operations of the ECB governing council seem justified. This extends to suggestions to publicise the minutes of ECB governing council meetings (Steen, 2013). As a number of commentators in Germany argued, however, such an arrangement would result in ECB board members acting under the pressure of their national public opinions, rather than following their own technocratic reasoning of what is in the best interest of the eurozone as a whole (Schieritz, 2013; Zydra, 2013). Such arguments ignore the fact that the decisions of the ECB are not value neutral, and there are hence no clear technocratic criteria to ensure their 'correctness'. As Carl Schmitt understood well, in such situations there is no way of avoiding controversial value judgements. To present such judgements as objective may well amount to self-righteousness, leading to *The Tyranny of Values* and exacerbating conflicts:

> The subjective nature of ordering values is not overcome, and the objective values are not gained simply through a process, in which the subjects are concealed, in whose interests certain points of view and certain strategies for attack are offered by these same set of values. Nobody can value without devaluing, revaluing and exploiting. [Niemand kann werten ohne abzuwerten, aufzuwerten and zu verwerten.]. (Schmitt, 2011, p. 46)

With or without new measures to enhance the ECB's transparency, the bank and its board members are increasingly politicised.[8] Indeed, the very idea of an apolitical Central Bank is political, reflecting German preferences for ordoliberalism. Particularly in times of crisis, ECB decisions produce winners and losers; one course of action benefits one group of nations, or their various segments, more than others. Higher inflation, for example, produces more losers in Germany, the creditor nation, which is also a nation of savers, while the debtor nations benefit from the reduction of their debt burden at both national and individual levels (while the assets of individuals are less affected, because they are more likely to reside in properties, rather than bank savings).

This is one of the key aspects that the German Constitutional Court is currently considering as it has to pass judgement on the legality of ECB's bond-buying programme (Scicluna,

2014). Kirchhof may well be going too far by arguing that the ECB's unusually low interest rates are in violation of the German constitution and its provisions to protect the individual right to property (Kirchhof, 2012a, 2014). But there can be little doubt that his concern for depreciating savings is widely shared in Germany.[9] This raises the question of fairness, and whether and how it can be made compatible with demands for transnational solidarity.

Solidarity

Solidarity is an elusive, even intriguing, moral category. Located somewhere between obligation and voluntary act of generosity, it raises demands that cannot be easily defined. By restricting our obligations towards a community, however broadly this might be conceived, it appears to violate the moral imperative to act in a decent way towards humanity as such (Sandel, 2013). Yet no meaningful political community can exist without some sentiment of solidarity amongst its members. This is what poses a significant challenge for Europe as a supranational democracy in search of its own demos. Whether and how transnational solidarity can emerge among EU citizens, who face conflicting pressures depending on what country they live in, is uncertain. 'Solidarity', cautions Habermas, 'is not synonymous with "justice", be it in the moral or the legal sense of the term' (Habermas, 2013, p. 23). Yet, as mainstream politicians across Europe are experiencing, it is increasingly difficult to appeal to feelings of solidarity in situations that are manifestly unfair.

In fact, few politicians still dare to call on their citizens to demonstrate solidarity with fellow eurozone members. During the 2013 German election campaign, the euro crisis and strategies for its resolution were barely mentioned by the major parties. Rather than trying to win public support for her euro policies (whether through appeals to 'solidarity' or in some other way), Merkel preferred not to talk about them. Peer Steinbrück, whose *Sozialdemokratische Partei Deutschlands* (SPD, Social Democratic Party) had called for more solidarity and less austerity whilst in opposition (even countenancing the possibility of debt mutualisation), was also conspicuously silent on such topics during the campaign (Scicluna, 2014). What German politicians feared was a backlash from an electorate that had grown tired of their state accepting ever more responsibility for the (potential) financial liabilities of other member states.

While Germany is rightly considered to be the economic powerhouse of Europe, a recent comparative survey of wealth distribution across the eurozone produced by the ECB concluded that German households were indeed the poorest in the eurozone in terms of their overall median assets (ECB, 2013). To be sure, the study is open to criticism about its methodology, and some of its findings were indeed contested, particularly the emphasis that the method put on house-ownership, which is not nearly as significant in Germany culturally and legally (owing to high levels of tenant protection) as it is in other countries of the eurozone. What is more significant from my perspective is the fact that the release of the report was delayed owing to its potentially explosive nature in the midst of negotiations over a bailout package for Cyprus, whose citizens top the table of both median and mean wealth (Steltzner, 2013). This is yet another example of the ECB's growing politicisation.

The argument about the fairness of bailout packages is even more difficult to mount with respect to Slovakia, undoubtedly one of the poorest countries of the eurozone in terms of both its total GDP as well as its pro-capita income. This is why opposition towards euro rescue policies offered an attractive platform in the 2010 Slovak national elections. As the Finance Minister, Ivan Mikloš argued shortly after he took office, 'I do not consider it solidarity if it is solidarity between the poor and the rich, of the responsible with the irre-sponsible, or of tax payers with bank owners and managers' (Rettman, 2010). Yet, only two years later Mikloš felt obliged to comply with the EU pressure, as discussed above, and accepted Slovakia's contribution towards the second bailout for Greece.

The problem is not limited to creditor states. The countries at the receiving end of various bailouts, having been subjected to conditionality, had their room for democratic governance severely constrained. Whether this is a sufficient ground to call for a 'ban on solidarity', as a German commentator did, may well be questioned. There can be little doubt, however, that the calls for wealth redistribution across national boundaries raise difficult dilemmas with respect to fairness and whether the principles should apply to national communities or the individual citizens constituting these communities. Moreover, it is difficult to envisage a fair redistributive arrangement between different states that would not affect their power relationship:

> The ban on solidarity protects against the attacks of other states on the sovereignty of a nation. […] Whoever denounces the ban on solidarity as heartless must accept that the principle of self-government (sovereignty) strengthens the pride of a nation. (Hank, 2013, p. 24)

What these examples point towards are the limits of transnational solidarity. If sufficient feelings of commonality exist amongst citizens of a decently government democratic polity, arguments in favour of redistributive policies can be compelling. This corresponds with the ideal of liberal nationalism that can be traced back to John Stuart Mill, but remains relevant today (Miller, 1995). In order to apply a similar logic to the 'postnational constel-lations' that characterise contemporary Europe, existing social and political conditions would need to change rather dramatically. In particular, a sense of European identity would need to arise that would trump people's commitments to their nation – a proposition that has become less plausible through the crisis, which clearly polarises the nations of Europe (Auer, 2010, 2013a, pp. 123–124). Hence, the calls for a deeper political union lack plausibility, just as much as the desire to create a European demos lacks credibility.

The Folly of Demoi*cracy – Third Way or Dead End?*

What of alternatives? Can *demoi*cracy offer answers where the EU's ideal of supranational democracy has failed? This is arguably its most potent promise. Kalypso Nicolaïdis praises the concept as 'a *third way*, distinct from both national and supranational versions of single demos polities'. She defines *demoi*cracy as 'a Union of peoples, understood both as states and as citizens, who govern together but not as one' (Nicolaïdis, 2013, p. 351). At the heart of it is the republican ideal of freedom as non-domination that, applied to Europe, can be translated into the principle of 'transnational non-domination' (Nicolaïdis, 2013, p. 358). *Demoi*cracy too, just like democracy at the national level, is underscored by the principle of solidarity, albeit only 'under stringent conditions'. Indeed, Nicolaïdis and Viehoff (2012, p. 23) believe that 'solidarity can play a similar role in underpinning European integration in the future as peace played in the foundation years'.

The concept is as tempting as it is misguided. The adherents of *demoi*cratic theory for Europe are astute in identifying the shortcomings of the EU's system of governance and its further deterioration through the crisis. Bellamy (2013, p. 513), for example, argues that the new approach to economic governance in the EU:

> compounds the original democratic legitimacy problem. For in removing core budgetary decisions from domestic politicians, the discipline imposed by the Fiscal Pact and the EU's Six-Pack Regulations effectively insitutionalise a system of domination of the creditor over the debtor states – precisely the situation the EU exists to prevent.

Yet Bellamy appears unable to jump over the shadow of the solving-the-crisis-through-more-integration approach, since he still advocates 'An ever closer union among the peoples of Europe'. The key challenge, 'how to justify transfers between the member states without undermining the right of each people to be publicly and equally represented in national and international decision-making' (Bellamy, 2013, p. 514), remains unaddressed. In other words, their founding republican principle of non-domination notwithstanding, neither Bellamy nor Nicolaïdis is able to offer solutions that seem fair, let alone a viable governing mechanism, which could generate them. They fail to find them because they do not exist. Their theory is yet another example of a conceptual muddle born out of the assumption that the EU is a unique, unidentified and unidentifiable object, the beauty of which lies in its complexity. This might be exciting for researchers, but is pernicious for Europe's nations and citizens.

Concluding Remarks

The single currency created problems for all eurozone members. This is exemplified by the contrasting stories of three pro-EU nations, which have seen their European projects put on a collision course with their political traditions, expectations and material interests. Slovaks can no longer be confident in strengthening their post-communist democracy through its engagement with Europe. The pressure to demonstrate more 'transnational solidarity' with nations far richer than themselves contributed to Slovakia being ruled by a populist, who simply proved more compliant with the EU demands rather than his pro-western and significantly more liberally minded predecessors. In Germany, people are concerned that they can no longer trust their currency, the euro, let alone see it as the bedrock of economic and political stability. Perhaps more than citizens in any other nation, Germans are also profoundly worried about having both their own as well as the EU *Rechtsstaat* eroded through euro rescue measures, which are yet to prove their effectiveness. In Ireland, people who had experienced European integration as hugely beneficial both economically and politically have been forced to question their commitments. Their primary aim after the collapse of the Celtic Tiger is not just to restore the solvency and the economic viability of their nation, but reclaim as much self-government as possible.

Things were once different. Prior to the Treaty of Maastricht, when Europe proved capable of 'rescuing the nation state' (Milward, 1992), Irish, German and (for the sake of the argument somewhat ahistorically) Slovak interests and expectations, though varied, were compatible. No longer. The single European currency requires – if it is to continue to exist – levels of integration that will violate the carefully balanced principle of (shared?) sovereignty, damage EU rule of law and undermine the sense of solidarity. The push towards more integration – whether it be in the form of a political union advocated by Habermas or *demoi*cracy – is likely to create a backlash, resulting in its very opposite. To persevere and sustain a modicum of unity, Europe needs less integration, not more.

Notes

[1] Admittedly, this claim is not easily supported by hard evidence, especially when relying merely on EU official surveys. The *Eurobarometer* has documented a steady decline in public opinion on the European Union since 2007, with further rapid decline in 2011. Since then, however, 'indicators of membership to the EU and perceived benefits of membership (for which over 25 years of uninterrupted series of results are available) are no longer included in the survey' (Debomy, 2013, p. 1). Yet, alternative surveys leave little doubt that the public perception of the EU and its ability to deal with the crisis has significantly worsened further since 2011, including in Germany, Ireland and Slovakia (Debomy, 2013, pp. 10–11; BertelsmannStiftung, 2012).

[2] The unemployment level has more than tripled between 2006 (4.5per cent) and 2012 (14.7 per cent) (Andor, 2014), while sovereign debt is forecast to peak at 123 per cent of GDP in 2014 from 25 per cent of GDP in 2007 (Andor, 2014). Revealingly, EU leaders, including the Commission president José Manuel Barroso and the Commissioner for Economic and Monetary Affairs Olli Rehn, were instructed by the Irish government to stay away from the official celebrations of the exit from the EU–IMF bailout programme. As the *Irish Times* reported:

> the Government did not accede to the requests because it was felt that the presence of two such political figures associated with the troika – and its 2010 intervention that resulted in the loss of economic sovereignty – would not be appropriate. (14 December 2013)

[3] As Erika Harris argued, for example:

> If there ever was an argument about the limits of political conditionality for the purpose of accession, the return to power of two parties from the 1994–8 establishment, Mečiar's HZDS [The Movement for a democratic Slovakia] and the nationalists, must be it. This reward-based strategy by the EU to stabilize political changes and promote liberal-democratic norms was initially, in the pre-accession period, very effective in Slovakia, but lost its influence and domestic rationality very soon after accession. (Harris, 2010, pp. 191–192)

[4] Available on SaS's YouTube, <http://www.youtube.com/watch?v=y8KSBykRJl8>. It is worthwhile noting that the speech is published with both German and English subtitles, demonstrating Sulík's determination to reach beyond the Slovak electorate.

[5] In contrast, Werner Abelshauser argued that 'only nation state proved capable of responding to the economic state of emergency. ... All assumptions about the Westphalian system of governance being superseded through European, let alone worldwide integration process were proven wrong' (Abelshauser, 2010, p. 2).

[6] The affiliation between Kirchhof and the AfD goes beyond similarities in their viewpoints on the euro crisis. The AfD also advocates the radical simplification of the taxation system as proposed and developed by Kirchhof.

[7]

> The IMF is generally regarded as a fairly pragmatic institution. Once the IMF's major shareholders take a policy decision (in this case to finance the individual members of the euro area), supporting legal justifications are usually identified without too much difficulty. (Donovan & Murphy, 2013, p. 231)

This can be seen as insider knowledge of the IMF's *modus operandi*. Donovan was an IMF staff member between 1997 and 2005. See also his note from 31 March 2009 to Alan Ahearne, Special Adviser to the Irish Minister of Finance, in which he suggested mechanisms to 'ensure that the letter, if not the spirit, of the ECB prohibition on lending to member governments was not violated' (Donovan & Murphy, 2013, 304).

[8] The president of the German *Bundesbank*, Jens Weidmann, for example, widely publicised his opposition to the ECB's controversial bond-buying programme in a number of interviews and newspaper articles (Fischer & Szalay, 2012; Weidmann, 2012; Fichtner, 2014).

[9] A German writer, Eugen Ruge (2013), observes: 'everyone – just like myself – is afraid of inflation', which threatens 'to eat up this sum of money, which might otherwise safeguard my old age'.

References

Abelshauser, W. (2010) It's not the economy stupid! Die politische Ökonomie der europäischen Integration in der Krise, *ZSE Zeitschrift für Staats – und Europawissenschaften*, 8(1), pp. 1–23.

Andor, L. (2014) *Employment and Social Developments in Europe 2013* (Brussels: European Commission: Directorate-General for Employment, Social Affairs and Inclusion).

Auer, S. (2010) New Europe: Between cosmopolitan dreams and nationalist nightmares, *Journal of Common Market Studies*, 48(5), pp. 1163–1184.

Auer, S. (2013a) *Das Ende des europäischen Traumes und die Zukunft der Begrenzten Demokratie in Europa* [The end of the European dream and the future of Europe's constrained democracy], *Transit: Europäische Revue*, 44, pp. 122–141.

Auer, S. (2013b) Richard Sulík: A provincial or a European Slovak politician? *Humanities Research*, 19(1), pp. 81–100.

Beck, U. (2012) *Das deutsche Europa* (Berlin: Suhrkamp).

Beck, U. (2013) Merkel the European will wake up – once Germany's elections are over. *The Guardian*, 2 September.

Bellamy, R. (2013) An ever closer union among the peoples of Europe: Republican intergovernmentalism and democratic representation within the EU, *Journal of European Integration*, 35(5), pp. 499–516.

BertelsmannStiftung. (2012) *Deutsche zunehmend skeptisch über die Vorteile der Europäischen Union.* (BertelsmannStiftung). Available at http://www.bertelsmann-stiftung.de/cps/rde/xchg/SID-5FFD1F57–956E3FAA/bst/hs.xsl/nachrichten_113500.htm (accessed 24 January 2014).

Böckenförde, E-W. (2010) Kennt die europäische Not kein Gebot? *Neue Zürcher Zeitung*, 21 June.

Buraj, I. (2013, 27 March) Obyčajný rasizmus. *Sme*, 14 January.

Debomy, D. (2013, 27 March) EU no, Euro yes? European public opinions facing the crisis (2007–2012), *Policy Paper: Notre Europe – Jacques Delors Institute*, 90, pp. 1–24.

Donovan, D. & Murphy, A. E. (2013) *The Fall of the Celtic Tiger: Ireland and the Euro Debt Crisis* (Oxford: Oxford University Press).

ECB. (2013) The eurosystem household finance and consumption survey, *ECB Statistics Paper Series* (2).

Evans-Pritchard, A. (2013) EU Troika rule in Ireland worse than British empire, *The Telegraph*, 28 February.

Everson, M. & Joerges, Ch. (2013) Who is the guardian for constitutionalism in Europe after the financial crisis? *LSE Europe in Question Discussion Paper Series*.

Fichtner, U. (2014) Herr Nein: Der sture Währungswächter Weidmann, *Der Spiegel*, 20 January.

Fico, R. (2013) Tlačová konferencia po rokovaní Európskej rady v Bruseli. Available at http://www.vlada.gov.sk/tlacova-konferencia-po-rokovani-europskej-rady-v-bruseli/ (accessed 15 January 2014).

Fischer, P. A. & Szalay, C. A. (2012) Weidmann im Interview: Es bringt gar nichts die Dinge schönzureden, *Neue Zürcher Zeitung*, 25 September.

Giddens, A. (2013) *Turbulent and Mighty Continent: What Future for Europe* (Cambridge: Polity Press).

Guiso, L., Herrera, H. & Morelli, M. (2013) A Cultural Clash View of the EU Crisis, *CEPR Discussion Paper* (1314–04).

Habermas, J. (2013) Democracy, solidarity and the European crisis, *Social Europe Journal*, 7(2), pp. 18–25.

Hank, R. (2013) Solidaritätsverbot: Zur Theorie nationalstaatlicher Souveränität in Europa, *Merkur*, 67(1), pp. 14–24.

Harris, E. (2010) Slovakia since 1989. in: S. P. Ramet (Eds) *Central and Southeast European Politics since 1989*, pp. 182–203 (Cambridge: Cambridge University Press).

Joerges, C. (2012) Europe's economic constitution in crisis, *Zentra Working Papers in Transnational Studies*, (6).

Kirchhof, P. (2012a) *Deutschland im Schuldensog* (Munich: C. H. Beck).

Kirchhof, P. (2012b) Verfassungsnot!, *Frankfurter Allgemeine Zeitung*, 12 July.

Kirchhof, P. (2014) Geldeigentum und Geldpolitik. *Frankfurter Allgemeine Zeitung*, 13 January, 7.

Marsh, D. (2013) *Beim Geld hört der Spaß auf* (Berlin: Europa Verlag).

Miller, D. (1995) *On Nationality* (Oxford: Clarendon).

Milward, A. S. (1992) *The European Rescue of the Nation-State* (London: Routledge).

Neuerer, D. (2013) AfD gewinnt prominenten Euro-Gegner. *Handelsblatt*, 23 May.

Nicolaïdis, K. (2013) European demoicracy and its crisis, *The Journal of Common Market Studies*, 51(2), pp. 351–369.

Nicolaïdis, K. & Viehoff, J. (2012) The choice for sustainable solidarity in Post-Crisis Europe, in: G. Bajnai, T. Fischer, S. Hare, S. Hoffmann, K. Nicolaïdis, V. Rossi, J. Viehoff & A. Watt (Eds) *Solidarity: For Sale? The Social Dimension of the New European Economic Governance*, pp. 23–43 (Gütersloh: BertelsmannStiftung).

Pytlas, B. (2013) Radical-right narratives in Slovakia and Hungary: Historical legacies mythic overlaying and contemporary politics, *Patterns of Prejudice*, 47(2), pp. 162–183.

Rettman, A. (2010) Brussels rebukes Slovakia over Greek u-turn. euobserver.com, 12 August.

Ruge, E. (2013) Our viability is the thing in the crisis, in: C. E. Bruun (Ed) *The European Fall: 28 Essays on the European Crisis* (Copenhagen: Politikens Forlag).

Sandel, M. (2013) Solidarität, *Transit: Europäische revue*, 44, pp. 103–117.

Schieritz, M. (2013) Mehr transparenz in der EZB – Eine gefährliche Idee. *Zeit Online*. 31 July. Available at http:// blog.zeit.de/herdentrieb/2013/07/31/mehr-transparenz-in-der-ezb-eine-gefahrliche-idee_6308 (accessed 7 January 2014).

Schmitt, C. (1985) *Political Theology: Four Chapters on the Concept of Sovereignty*, Translated by G. Schwab (Chicago: The University of Chicago Press).

Schmitt, C. (2011) *Die Tyrannei der Werte* (Berlin: Duncker & Humblot).

Scicluna, N. (2014, 31 January–1 February) Domestic implications of reluctant hegemony: German euroscepticism and the euro crisis. Paper presented at the conference, Territorialisation of Interest Representation in Times of Economic Crisis, Willy Brandt Centre of German and European Studies, University of Wroclaw, Wroclaw, Poland.

Starbatty, J. (2013) *Tatort Euro: Bürger schützt das Recht die Demokratie und euer Vermögen* (Berlin: Europa Verlag).

Steen, M. (2013) ECB pressed to open up as officials back call to publish minutes. *Financial Times*, 29 July.

Steltzner, H. (2013) Arme Deutsche. *Frankfurter Allgemeine Zeitung*, 9 April.

Tilford, S. & Whyte, P. (2011) *Why Stricter Rules Threaten the Eurozone* (London: Centre for European Reform).

Tóibín, C. (2013) Once upon a time there was a dream about Europe, in: C. E. Bruun (Ed) *The European Fall: 28 Essays on the European Crisis* (Copenhagen: Politikens Forlag).

Tomkin, J. (2013) Contradiction circumvention and conceptual gymnastics: The impact of the adoption of the ESM treaty on the state of European Democracy, in: B. d. Witte, A. Héritier & A. H. Trechsel (Eds) *The Euro Crisis and the State of European Democracy*, pp. 64–81 (Florence: European University Institute).

Weidmann, J. (2012) Nur eine Stabilitätsunion kann den Euro retten, *Der Standard*, 26 June.

Wessels, W. (2003) The German debate on european finality: Visions and missions, in: S. Serfaty (Eds) *The European Finality Debate and its National Dimensions*, pp. 133–160 (Washington, DC: The Center for Strategic and International Studies).

Zydra, M. (2013) EZB und Demokratie: Ein Widerspruch. *Süddeutsche Zeitung*, 21 September.

From *Grexit* to *Grecovery*: The Paradox of the Troika's Engagement with Greece

ANNA VISVIZI

DEREE – The American College of Greece, Athens

ABSTRACT   *Locked in the commitments of previous governments and arrangements negotiated with the Troika back in 2010 and early 2012, the Greek government continues to channel the burden of fiscal adjustment towards the private sector, killing any nascent thoughts of investment and entrepreneurship in Greece. Simultaneously, bold structural reforms are kept hostage to the uncertain balance of the ruling coalition and negligible majority in the Greek parliament. Caught literally between a rock and a hard place, the authorities seek to attain a primary fiscal surplus, hopeful that this will help to bring an end to the essentially faulty economic adjustment programme for Greece in 2014. Surprisingly, the talk of fiscal surplus alone seems to have ignited positive expectations that the crisis might, in fact, be nearing an end. This suggests that in the same way as the crisis in Greece was provoked by irresponsible and inaccurate statements about Greece's fiscal position and Grexit was a viable option through 2011, discourses on Grecovery may prove constitutive of the end of the crisis. This paper explores this issue and by so doing contemplates the evolving nature of the core-periphery relations in the EU and its policy-making.*

1.   Introduction

Five years into supervision by the Troika of Greece's creditors (i.e. the European Commission, the European Central Bank and the International Monetary Fund, economic adjustment programmes (EAPs) for Greece), the economic situation in the country is worse than it was in 2010 when insolvency had become a viable possibility for Greece and the first of the two EAPs was launched. As a result of flaws in the design, implementation and supervision of the EAPs, since 2010 the Greek economy has contracted more than 20 per cent and the investment level has decreased by 86 per cent as compared to 2008 (IMF, 2013b). In early 2014 unemployment exceeded 28 per cent, whereby youth unemployment at 63 per cent made young educated people emigrate in masses. The uncertainty of making ends meet blended with growing exasperation of society with the continuous increases in taxation and with desperation about the seemingly no end to the ordeal that Greece was put through. Although the appropriateness of the Troika-led approach to the crisis in Greece has been repeatedly questioned (Blanchard & Leigh, 2013; EP, 2013;

IMF, 2013a) the Troika exerts a constant pressure on the Greek government to deliver on unfeasible objectives of the programme. In this way, locked in the commitments of previous governments and arrangements negotiated with the Troika back in 2010 and early 2012, the Greek government continues to channel the burden of fiscal adjustment towards the private sector.

Simultaneously, given that the plans of Greece's PM, Antonis Samaras to renegotiate the terms of the implementation of the programme failed in late 2012, the mounting fragility of the political scene turned structural reforms (including downsizing of the public sector and an overall liberalization of the economy) hostage to the uncertain balance of the ruling coalition. Today, literally caught between a rock and a hard place, through a range of sophisticated revenue-enhancing measures, the authorities seek to meet the EAP's fiscal objectives and to attain a primary fiscal surplus. The expectation being that – as a result – confidence and trust of the Troika towards Greece will consolidate and Greece will be able to put an end to the second EAP in 2014. Although the fiscal witch-hunt aimed at improving the returns on taxation kills any nascent thoughts of investment and entrepreneurship in Greece, the talk of fiscal surplus seems to have ignited positive expectations that the crisis in Greece might be over. Even if in some instances vehemently, an increasing number of leading EU-level political figures admits the possibility of Greece having attained a primary fiscal surplus and Greece's efforts are recognized. Notably, as credit ratings for Greece have improved slightly at the end of 2013 and elections to the European Parliament loom on the horizon, it is plausible that the same way as the crisis in Greece was provoked by irresponsible and inaccurate statements about Greece's fiscal position and *Grexit* was a viable option through 2011, discourses on *Grecovery*[1] may prove constitutive of the end of the crisis. This paper explores this issue. To this end, the argument is structured as follows. In the first section, the contentious issue of the 2009 revision of the general government deficit is elaborated and its implications for the subsequent developments in Greece are examined. In the discussion that follows a case is made that the Troika's role in managing the crisis in Greece constitutes a paradox that in some respects is indicative of some to the features of the evolving core-periphery divide in the EU. It is in this context that the possible constitutive impact of discourses vis-à-vis *Grecovery* is explored. Conclusions follow.

2. The 2009 Greek Deficit Issue and the Making of *Grexit*

The sudden deterioration of Greece's terms of lending in late 2009 and the deleterious malicious sequence of events that followed and resulted in viable concerns of *Grexit* have not attracted the degree of critical consideration in the literature that they should have. By means of enriching the debate, this section focuses explicitly on this issue. It is suggested that to a large extent, *Grexit* is the product of irresponsible and inaccurate discursive interventions by key Greek politicians who since late 2009–2010 employed an essentially anti-Greek discourse. Given the pre-existing negative stereotypes about Greece, this discourse fuelled the dramatic sequence of events that led Greece to the brink of insolvency in May 2010.

The negative image of Greece and ambivalent perceptions of its role on the EU forum on the eve of the eurozone crisis have been influenced by the experience of the first decade of Greece's membership in the EEC. Throughout the 1980s, the Greek authorities' attitude towards the EEC was at least defensive, focusing on a narrowly defined Greek interest and the promotion of Greek 'distinctiveness' (Mitsos, 2000, p. 61). The EEC was employed as a political resource in political competition at home, while a nearly exclusive focus on the intergovernmental and bilateral fora of decision-making rendered Greece incapable either of promoting its national interest in the EEC or of adjusting to the broader logic of cooperation within the grouping. The EEC itself and the process of European integration did not constitute a political priority for successive Greek governments. An introverted country, a passive receiver of European policies, caught between claims to exceptionalism and a self-imposed constraint (Verney, 1987; Ioakimides, 2000; Spanou, 2000), Greece contributed to the consolidation of its image as a peripheral state and Europe's 'odd man'. Following the disintegration of Yugoslavia and prior to eastern enlargement of the EU, significant efforts were made to recast Greece's role in the EU as a regional leader and a hub for investment in South-Eastern Europe. Sadly so, however, the developments that ensued after the shocking announcement of a bloated 2009 deficit turned Greece into a case-study in failed convergence, a fake promise of modernisation, and 'a warning about the perils of Europeanisation without deeper transformation' (Bechev, 2012, p. 6).

Early elections were called up in September 2009. In this way, the ruling government of Nea Democratia (ND), under the premiership of Konstantinos Karamanlis, sought to put an end to the enduring political stalemate on the Greek political scene and the resulting impossibility of implementing long overdue structural reforms and fiscal consolidation. During the electoral campaign, ND pointed to worsening state finance, and pledged auster-ity measures and deep structural reforms as the only way to address Greece's fiscal problem. The opposition movement (PASOK) ridiculed these pleas for austerity, promising instead more welfare-state and increased spending (Visvizi, 2012a, p. 21). Capitalizing on the image of his father, former PM of Greece, in 2009 George Papandreou led PASOK to victory with the populist slogan 'There is money [to be spent]!' hitting the sweat point of the electorate's expectations. Right after the elections, in a move designed to discredit the previous establishment and set a convenient benchmark for assessing the political effi-ciency of the new government, an official revision (from ca. 8 to 12.7 per cent) of the projected general government deficit was announced in early October 2009. At the same time, Papandreou pressed charges at the European Commission against the government of Karamanlis on account of it falsifying the fiscal data (Papathanasiou, 2010, pp. 9–15).

Former Greek minister of finance, Papathanasiou (2010) explains that the fiscal goal of the ND's government, as outlined in February 2010, was an ambitious, yet a feasible deficit of 6 per cent. In 2008 and 2009, due to the implications of the global financial crisis, over-shooting of fiscal data and their necessary revisions was a common practice across the EU. In Greece, these projections were aggravated mostly by a political stalemate that eventually led to early elections. During the electoral campaign, ND warned that if no appropriate measures were taken the deficit could reach the level of 8 per cent of GDP, i.e. ca. EUR 20 bn. Following the elections, PASOK claimed that ND concealed amounting to EUR 10 bn part of the deficit. As evidence suggests, once in power, the PASOK government deliberately spent on otherwise 'frozen' items of the budget an amount of EUR 10 bn in the last quarter of 2009. As a result the deficit increased and reached the level of 12.7 per cent in October 2009. The hysterical reaction of the markets that followed and the dele-terious sequence of events that made it necessary for Greece to request financial assistance from international creditors in May 2010 can be explained as follows.

The revised projections of the deficit produced a new picture of the situation in the Greek economy that surprised the markets. In combination with overt claims of the PASOK government that Greece was falsifying data, all prior assumptions that the market players had about Greece were undermined. The uncertainty that it caused destabilized the already shaky 'information equilibrium' on the market. A violent adjustment to the damaged at that point credibility of Greece was forced and manifested itself via rising spreads. Presumably, when in October 2009 the PASOK government decided to augment the official data on Greece's fiscal deficit to 12.7 per cent, it was driven by domestic policy purposes, i.e. it aimed to disgrace the previous government in the eyes of the Greek electorate. It seems that by embarking on this bold move, however, the government was ignorant about the consequences that such an irresponsible announcement, depicting lack of experience and incompetence, would have internationally. Upon the realization of the dismay that this news caused outside Greece, as a means of maintaining their credibility vis-à-vis Greece's international partners and, later, creditors, the socialist government of PASOK had no choice but to insist on subsequent recalculations of the deficit throughout 2010, i.e. even after the launch of the EAP. In this manner the size of the 2009 general government deficit escalated to an alleged 15.4 per cent in November 2010. As repeatedly stressed by former ELSTAT employees (Mandrou, 2011; SKAI, 2013), the enormous jump in the size of the general government deficit to 13.6 per cent in April 2010 and 15.4 per cent in November 2010), was the result of dubious practices and 'creative recalculations' of the data (Coronakis, 2013a). In short, contradicting the standard methodology employed by other EU Member States, the deficit officially announced by Eurostat in November 2010 included debts and deficits of the major deficit-generating state-owned enterprises as well as negative values of currency swap transactions that the government of Kostas Simitis was engaged with in 2001 on the eve of the adoption of the euro (Coronakis, 2013b).

3. Discourses and the Policy-Mix Implemented

Having sent the shockwave across the world, rather than addressing the emergency situation by some equally bold and resolute economic policy statements and actions to appease the markets' hysteria, somewhat surprisingly Papandreou embarked on a series of state-visits. These were complemented by interviews in top international opinion-making outlets; Papandreou did not miss Davos 2010 either. The multitude of Papandreou's discursive interventions in a variety of political and economic settings in Europe and elsewhere employed over the period October 2009–March 2010, formed an essentially anti-Greek discourse. Paired with nearly identical statements by Papandreou's minister of finance, George Papakonstantinou,[2] the arguments employed and the claims made in this discourse played a fundamental role in constructing a biased image of Greece and of the nature of weaknesses inherent in its economy. Importantly, these discourses proved constitutive of very specific policy responses to the emergency situation in Greece that was caused not by anything else but by artificially augmenting the size of the deficit over the period 2009–2010.

Specifically, the discourse that Papandreou developed oscillated around the following arguments: Greece is a corrupt country (Papandreou, 2009); corruption is the culprit responsible for Greece's fiscal imbalance and Greeks do not pay taxes (Papandreou, 2010a); Greece's major problem is credibility deficit (Papakonstantinou, 2009). In line with the Guardian, Papandreou is quoted to have said that 'it was the previous government, and not the euro, that was to blame for [Greece's] predicament' (Papandreou, 2010b). Given the delayed response of his government to the self-induced emergency situation at home, Papandreou succeeded in turning the escalating problems in Greece in a European challenge that required European solutions. Referring to the rising spreads, he argued that

> this is an attack on the eurozone by certain other interests, political or financial, and often countries are being used as the weak link, if you like, of the eurozone. We are being targeted, particularly with an ulterior motive or agenda, and of course there is speculation in the world markets. (Papandreou, 2010c)

This mirrors an earlier statement of Papakonstantinou (2009) who argued that 'We [Greece] happened to be at the forefront of this [i.e. ulterior market forces trying the resistance of the eurozone]'. As the terms of lending available to Greece continued to worsen and dismay regarding the developments in Greece prevailed, Papakonstantinou likened Greece to the Titanic. He said his task was like changing 'the course of the Titanic ... People think we are in a terrible mess. And we are' (Papakonstantinou, 2010). As Bloomberg reported, 'After the minister's comments, the yield on Greece's two-year bond rose to 5.230 per cent, compared with 5.1547 per cent on February 12' (Bodoni & Ross-Thomas, 2010).

The belated policy responses suggested by the PASOK government in February 2010 under an explicit pressure of the European Commission and subsequently approved by the Troika in May 2010 in the form of the EAP for Greece (Visvizi, 2012a, pp. 21–22), resembled a standard set of policy-measures designed to address a standard fiscal imbalance problem. Perversely so, however, the biased image of Greece that the anti-Greek discourse embodied was employed by the PASOK government instrumentally as a source of justification for a biased à la carte implementation of the programme. That is, the focus of the programme was shifted away from politically costly expenditure-reducing measures (and the necessity to downsize the public sector, PASOK's electoral base) to essentially measures that were politically neutral for PASOK revenue-enhancing. The emphasis on revenue-enhancing measures was further complemented by a discourse on a largely constructed problem of tax evasion in Greece (Visvizi, 2013, pp. 232–234). In this way, at the domestic level PASOK recast itself as a 'just' government introducing fiscal burdens also for the perceived rich.

In its relations with the Troika, by skilfully playing with arguments of alleged impunity of the alleged rich tax dodgers, PASOK convinced Troika that tax evasion was indeed the culprit responsible for Greece's economic problems and thus had a priority in the policy-mix implemented over other items on the agenda. In fact, the representatives of Greece's creditors seem to have been overwhelmed by the exaggerated and untrue images of Greece that matched the pre-existing stereotypical understandings of Greece as a holiday destination (Visvizi, 2012a, p. 33). It may be argued that the surprising announcement of a revision of the fiscal data followed by an essentially anti-Greek discourse led Greece to the verge of insolvency in 2010. Succeeding the launch of the EAP in May 2010, the same discourse, in which Greece was depicted as 'a corrupt country of tax dodgers', matched the pre-existing negative stereotypes of Greece as Europe's 'odd man' and a holiday destination. Capitalizing on this discourse, the PASOK government was then able to legitimately shift the focus of the Troika-supervised programme from politically costly expenditure-reducing measures to measures that were initially politically neutral for PASOK and revenue-enhancing.

Noteworthily, the validity of the claims and arguments employed by Papandreou in the discourse on Greece and thus the ability of his government to model the implementation of the EAP in line with his government's political preferences, were further boosted by an inexplicable credit of trust that Papandreou was granted by Greece's European partners. When constructing the negative image of Greece through discursive interventions – exemplarily depicted above – that undermined Greece's credibility, a practice unheard of for a PM, Papandreou certainly aimed at distancing himself from the reality that unfolded through his statements. In addition, by shifting the blame for the dramatic developments in Greece to the previous establishment as well as to market speculation and market forces, Papandreou wanted simultaneously to recast himself as a concerned, responsible, modern politician; as a cosmopolitan and citizen of the world; as the saviour of Greece and the European Union. Remarkably, while the negative image of Greece voiced openly by Papandreou was eagerly upheld and reproduced by media around the world, the Greek PM received positive feedback mixed with sympathy, empathy and support for his alleged efforts to save the country. Papandreou's talk of Greece as a corrupt country was welcomed as representative of 'straight talk' (Juncker, 2012). In October 2010 he was awarded the prestigious German Quadriga Award for 'The Power of Veracity' (sic!). In the same year, Papandreou was named as one of Foreign Policy magazine's Top 100 Global Thinkers for 'making the best of Greece's worst year'.

4. Exploring the Paradox of Troika's Role in Greece

As the Troika was unaware of the country-specific political circumstances and the motives behind Papandreou's government political actions were not questioned, the burden of fiscal adjustment designed to bypass the fiscal imbalance problem was channelled through the private sector. As a result, since the launch of the EAP, 260.000 companies closed down, unemployment surged from 8.9 per cent in 2009 to 28.3 per cent in late 2013, and – regardless of a generous debt-reduction scheme offered to Greece in 2012 – the debt of the general government is expected to rich the level of 175 per cent of GDP in 2014 (European Commission, 2013, p. 16) up from 115 per cent in 2009 and clearly overshooting the target of 146 per cent set in the programme in 2010 (MoF, 2010). The feasibility of the programme was questioned from its onset in that the target values set therein were considered overly ambitious and hence unrealistic. For a careful observer of the developments in Greece, though, the flaws inherent in the Greek EAP, and especially its missing of the structural weaknesses of the economy, had become apparent even before the programme started in May 2010. That is, although negotiations on the content of prospective assistance programme for Greece continued throughout April 2010, during the same period of time Papandreou's government rushed to have a significant tax reform approved by the Parliament. The tax law in question introduced multiple increases in taxation of income, revenue, luxury goods, real estate, set special levies, and presumptive taxation, criminalized the inability to deliver on fiscal obligations and established a variety of other measures of a detrimental impact on business activity in Greece. The law was published in the Official Government Gazette on 23 April 2010 (to apply as of 1 January 2010). The same day, i. e. on 23 April 2010, Greece extended an official request to the EU, ECB and the IMF for financial assistance to be granted.

Given the utterly negative impact of this tax law on for the Greek economy, at the time of its introduction the question was whether Greece's creditors, engaged with negotiations on the prospective assistance scheme for Greece, would approve of it. The point is that prior to its official arrival in Athens, the Troika could not bar the government from passing this law. However, as experts – interviewed by the author[3] – related to and familiar with the IMF argued, had PASOK attempted to pass this law once the official request for financial assistance was made, the Troika would not have consented to it. Another point is that, clearly, the way the programme was implemented, had nothing to do with liberal economic approach. Paradoxically, although the left-leaning critics of the programme and for that matter of the IMF specifically, linked the programme's failure to its alleged neoliberal logic, the EAPs implemented in Greece, rather than reducing the degree of state intervention, increased its abusive role in the Greek economy.

At the same time as the bloated inefficient public sector was left intact, exorbitant increases in taxation drained the tax base, extinguished economic activity in the country, created more than 1.5 million of unemployed in the private sector, and effectively barred prospects of growth in Greece.

Indeed, the initial expectation[4] was that the Troika, under the leadership of the IMF, would efficiently execute the implementation of the EAP in Greece. The implicit assumption of observers at that point was that the Troika constituted a coherent group of technocrats determined to pursue a very specific economic policy direction, and that the IMF's expertise would allow it to assume the role of an unquestioned leader of the Troika. It was only afterwards that internal cleavages and difference in approaches to economic policy had become apparent on the forum of the Troika. For the sake of maintaining its good image and not endangering Troika's credibility and capsizing its involvement with Greece, up to a certain point these internal divisions were successfully concealed. Retrospectively, as the scarce information on this issue depicts, at a certain point the IMF became aware of Papandreou's government strategy aimed at avoiding downsizing of the public sector and liberalization of the economy at the expense of the private sector. Accordingly, it was suggested by the IMF that a clause be added to the EAP so that the next Greek government can renegotiate EAP's terms and thus bring it back on track conducive to growth and fiscal adjustment. This suggestion – aimed at bypassing the problem of the Greek EAP falling hostage to Papandreou's government domestic politicking – was blocked by the IMF's European partners. In 2013, following the release of an ex-post critical assessment of the Greek EAP by the IMF (2013a), the split within the Troika became evident. On that occasion Oli Rehn, the EU Commissioner for Economic Affairs, commented: 'I don't think it's fair and just [for the IMF] to wash its hands and throw the dirty water on the European shoulders' (Fox, 2013).

Overall, irrespective of the IMF's attempts of getting the Greek EAP right, as a result of a biased policy-mix implemented in Greece since 2010 under the aegis of the Troika, today very little promises a happy end to the Greek ordeal. The programmes' implementation, consistent with channelling the whole burden of fiscal adjustment towards the private sector and resulting in crowding out private agents from the economy, bears no resemblance to the liberal principles of market economy. Rather, Troika's blind insistence on meeting Greece's quantitative obligations, complemented with a lax stance towards structural reforms throughout 2010–2013, turned the Greek EAP to a peculiar mix of policies that are closer to the logic of etatism than to anything else. In the name of economic liberalization and austerity measures, the Troika allowed the enormous public sector in Greece to consolidate and the state intervention in the economy to increase. The Troika proved unwilling to recognize the specificity of the Greek case and remained largely unaware of the Greek reality. It proved arrogant and tactless when dealing with the stakeholders in Greece and overall incompetent to deal with the complexity of the Greek predicament. Finally, internal divisions within the Troika and the inability to bypass them reduced the opportunity to get the programme on a proper track. Subsequently, rather than assisting Greece in overcoming specific weaknesses in its economy, the policies approved and supervised by the Troika led to the collapse of the Greek economy and society. While at the same time a shadow was cast on the credibility of Greece, the major challenge for the coalition government of Samaras and for Samaras himself following the June 2012 elections was to restore confidence and trust in Greece's relations with its European partners (Visvizi, 2012c, p. 8). How daunting a task it was, was revealed by the end of 2013 when the Greek authorities' claims of a projected primary fiscal surplus were received with irony and disbelief by several key EU-level actors who openly questioned them. Greece was pushed back to its politically and economically peripheral position in Europe.

5. Grexit, Grecovery and the Core-Periphery Divide

Certainly, claims of Greece's primary fiscal surplus, expected to be confirmed by the Eurostat on 23 April 2014, are bound to surprise given the fact that there is no economic activity in the country. The primary fiscal surplus is the product of exorbitant taxation imposed on natural and legal persons. Noteworthily, there is a direct correlation between the revenue attained by the government and the reduction in savings in the Greek banks. The bitter observation here is that although the primary fiscal surplus does not reflect the actual state of the Greek economy, irrespective of an initial disbelief, today it is welcomed and applauded by a great variety of actors on the EU political scene. Furthermore, while the fiscal witch-hunt accompanying the tax hikes kills any nascent thoughts of investment and entrepreneurship in Greece, the talk of fiscal surplus alone seems to have been enough to ignite positive expectations that the crisis in Greece might be over. Although there is no improvement in the economic standing of Greece, the leading figures on the EU political scene are ready to accept the partial depiction of the developments in Greece in order to consolidate their political future. Indeed, given the positive reactions of the capital markets (and rating agencies for that matter), it is plausible that Greece will be able to return to the capital markets in 2014, say 2015. This in turn suggests that the same way as the crisis in Greece was provoked by irresponsible and inaccurate statements about Greece's fiscal position and *Grexit* became a viable option in throughout 2011, discourses on *Grecovery* will enable the Greek government to take hold of the reform process in Greece.

In this view the sovereign debt crisis in Greece represents a very interesting case that sheds new light on the anatomy of Europe's progressing differentiationbetween the boundaries of the core and the periphery becoming increasingly blurry. It is also argued that although democracy and solidarity have become a frequently referred to item of political discourse at the EU-level, the oblivious of country-specific circumstances supranational policy responses to the crisis in Greece have played a fundamental role in inducing unwelcome political and economic dynamics in the country. As a result, today Greece is worse off than it used to be prior to 2010 when the EAP started, while its role in the EU once again needs to be referred to as peripheral.

The fact that Greece assumed the rotating presidency of the European Council in the first half of 2014 does not substantially change the status quo as the perceptions of Greece across the EU are shaped today by the arguments initially employed in the anti-Greek discourse launch by Papandreou in late 2009.

Although stereotypically the argument that Greece fiddled with fiscal data is common (Visvizi, 2013), nobody questioned the accuracy of the surprising 2009 announcement of Papandreou's government about the size of the budget deficit. Greece's European partners had not considered the possibility that – driven solely by domestic politicking purposes – Papandreou's government would produce and officially present data depicting a worse-than-real situation of Greece's public finance. From a different angle, by giving in to PASOK's arguments of an allegedly much higher deficit, the Eurostat cast a shadow on its credibility, because it allowed for a revision of data that it had previously approved in 2008 and 2009. Another point that needs to be raised is that Papandreou and his minister of finance, Papakonstantinou, were given an inexplicable credit of trust by Greece's European, and especially German, partners who questioned neither the validity of their arguments of the size of the deficit nor the shifting of the entire burden of fiscal adjustment to the private sector. The EU-wide consequences of Papandreou's claims and the ease with which they were accepted by the key EU actors are indicative of lack of leadership in the EU and confirm the thesis of Germany being a 'reluctant leader' (Schwarzer, 2010; *Economist*, 2013). A good case in point highlighting that granting the credit of trust to Papandreou was premature was revealed by Papandreou's attempt to call up a national referendum in Greece. Although it was never officially and explicitly spelled out, the question was to be roughly whether Greeks were for or against the second assistance package for Greece and a debt restructuring scheme negotiated with Greece's private creditors (Visvizi, 2012b). This attempted referendum outraged both Angela Merkel and Nicolas Sarkozy during the G20 Cannes Summit. At that point, i.e. in November 2011, it was too late to reverse the course of events that started in October 2009. Of course, it remains a great unknown to which extent exactly the internal divisions on the Troika's forum would have allowed to reverse the orientation, emphasis and policy-mix of the Greek EAP. The point remains, however, that had Papandreou's claims regarding 2009–2010 been received with more scepticism and suspicion by Greece's European partners, the dramatic deterioration of Greece's terms of lending and therefore the Eurozone crisis could have been avoided.

Notes

[1] To be specific, 'Grecovery' is a term employed for the first time by Antonis Samaras in his speech delivered in Helsinki in 2013 at the Economic Ideas Forum organised by the Centre of European Studies, where he stated 'Now, we are talking about Grecovery, not about Grexit'. In an interview for the Helsingin Sanoat on this occasion, Samaras argued that

> We worked hard to restore the credibility of our country, to reverse the fears of Greece's exit from the eurozone to consolidate its membership in it. From month to month, we strive to meet the fiscal adjustment objectives, we reduce the deficit, implement structural reforms and turn Greece into an investment-friendly country. (Samaras, 2013)

[2] Today, Papakonstantinou faces criminal charges on account of suspected infidelity in service, falsification of document as well as breach of duty. See: AMNA (2014) 'Time limit for former minister Papakonstantinou's offences has not expired', AMNA, 12 January 2014, at: http://www.amna.gr/english/articleview.php?id=4 /48

[3] I.e. the author's interviews with high-profile experts and decision-makers that consented for the interview on the condition of their anonymity preserved. The interviews took place in Athens, Washington and Brussels over the period 2010–2013.

[4] I.e. the author's interviews with high-profile experts and decision-makers that consented for the interview on the condition of their anonymity preserved. The interviews took place in Athens, Washington and Brussels over the period 2010–2013.

References

Bechev, D. (2012) The Periphery of the Periphery: The Western Balkans and the euro crisis, Policy Brief 60, European Council on Foreign Relations (ecfr), August 2012.

Blanchard, O. & Leigh, D. (2013) Growth Forecast Errors and Fiscal Multipliers, IMF Working Paper, WP/13/1, January 2013.

Bodoni, S. & Ross-Thomas, E. (2010) Europe Economy Chief Calls for More Steps by Greece (Update5), Bloomberg, 15 February 2010, Available at http://www.bloomberg.com/apps/news?pid=newsarchive&sid=aKPXdMFfM9Ok

Coronakis, B. (2013a) Eurostat's crafty ways of collaboration with governmental officials to swell Greece's public deficit and debt for the period 2005–2009, New Europe, No. 1062, 15–21 December 2013, Available at http://zoe-georganta.co.uk/wp-content/uploads/2013/12/191685964-New-Europe-Print-Edition-Issue-1062.pdf

Coronakis, B. (2013b) Eurostat's failures greatly increase the size of Greece's debt', New Europe No. 1057, 10–16 November 2013, Available at http://zoe-georganta.co.uk/wp-content/uploads/2013/11/New-Europe-Print-Edition-Issue-1057-1.pdf

Economist. (2013) Germany and Europe: The Reluctant Hegemon, 15 June 2013, Available at http://www.economist.com/news/leaders/21579456-if-europes-economies-are-recover-germany-must-start-lead-reluctant-hegemon

EP. (2013) Enquiry report on the role and operations of the Troika (ECB, Commission and IMF) with regard to the euro area programme countries, DRAFT REPORT, European Parliament (2013/2277(INI)), 17.12.2013, Available at http://www.europarl.europa.eu/sides/getDoc.do?pubRef=-//EP//NONSGML+COMPARL+PE-526.111+01+DOC+PDF+V0//EN&language=EN

European Commission. (2013) The Second Economic Adjustment Programme for Greece. Third Review – July 2013, European Economy: Occasional Papers No. 159/July 2013, European Commission, Brussels.

Fox, B. (2013) Rehn in war of words with IMF, euobserver, 7 June 2013, Available at http://euobserver.com/economic/120419

IMF. (2013a) Greece: Ex Post Evaluation of Exceptional Access under the 2010 Stand-By Arrangement, IMF Country Report No. 13/156, June 2013.

IMF. (2013b) IMF Executive Board Concludes 2013 Article IV Consultation, Public Information Notice (PIN) No. 13/64, June 5, 2013.

Ioakimides, P. (2000) The Europeanisation of Greece's foreign policy: Progress and problems, in: A. Mitsos & E. Mossialos (Eds) Contemporary Greece and Europe, pp. 359–372 (Aldershot: Ashgate).

Juncker, J. C. (2012) quoted in Kakissis, J. (2012) George Papandreou: Greece Had To Make Changes, NPR, 1 May 2012, Available at http://www.npr.org/2012/05/01/150804420/george-papandreou-greece-had-to-make-changes

Mandrou, I. (2011) Ο πρόεδρος του ΔΣΑ ζητά εφέτη – ανακριτή για τις καταγγελίες της Ζ. Γεωργαντά, 29 September 2011, Available at http://www.skai.gr/news/greece/article/181782/o-proedros-tou-dsa-zita-efeti-anakriti-gia-tis-kataggelies-tis-z-georgada-/#ixzz2tX5m6h83

Mitsos, A. (2000) Maximising contribution to the european integration process as a prerequisite for the maximisation of gains, in: A. Mitsos & E. Mossialos (Eds) Contemporary Greece and Europe, pp. 53–92 (Aldershot: Ashgate).

MoF. (2010) Hellenic Stability and Growth Programme Newsletter, Hellenic Ministry of Economy and Finance, 17 May 2010, pp. 2.

Papandreou, G. (2009) quoted in Barber, T., Hope, K. (2009) Papandreou says Greece is corrupt, Financial Times, 12 December 2009. Available at http://www.ft.com/intl/cms/s/0/6871e1e6-e6be-11de-98b1-00144feab49a.html#axzz2t90PiPNu

Papandreou, G. (2010a) in an interview with Der Spiegel (2010) SPIEGEL Interview with Greek Prime Minister Papandreou: It's a Question of Survival for Greece, Der Spiegel, 22 February 2010, Available at http://www.

spiegel.de/international/europe/spiegel-interview-with-greek-prime-minister-papandreou-it-s-a-question-of-survival-for-greece-a-679415.html

Papandreou, G. (2010b) quoted in Elliott, L. (2010) No EU bailout for Greece as PM promises to 'put house in order, *The Guardian*, 28 January 2010. Available at http://www.theguardian.com/business/2010/jan/28/greece-papandreou-eurozone

Papandreou, G. (2010c) quoted in Atkins, R. and Hope, K. (2010) Greece and the eurozone: Halcyon no more, *Financial Times*, 7 February 2010, Available at http://www.ft.com/cms/s/0/26739ae4–1410–11df-8847–00144feab49a.html#ixzz2qPolB8Dg

Papakonstantinou, G. (2009) quoted in Hughes, J. and Giles, C. (2009) Greek credibility deficit its key issue, *Financial Times*, 16 December 2009, Available at http://www.ft.com/intl/cms/s/0/97291246-ea3f-11de-aeb6–00144feab49a.html#axzz2tUKl619B

Papakonstantinou, G. (2010) quoted in Bodoni, S. and Ross-Thomas, E. (2010) Europe Economy Chief Calls for More Steps by Greece (Update5), Bloomberg, 15 February 2010. Available at http://www.bloomberg.com/apps/news?pid=newsarchive&sid=aKPXdMFfM9Ok

Papathanasiou, G. (2010) *Με τη γλώσσα των αριθμών: Η αλήθεια για την Οικονομία* [Talking numbers: the truth about the economy], Athens, November 2010.

Samaras, A. (2013) *Αντ. Σαμαράς: Μιλάμε πλέον για grecovery και όχι για grexit* [Now, we are talking about Grecovery, not about Grexit], Kathimerini, 6 June 2013. Available at http://www.kathimerini.gr/42049/article/epikairothta/politikh/ant-samaras-milame-pleon-gia-grecovery-kai-oxi-gia-grexit

Schwarzer, D. (2010) Germany and the Euro: a Reluctant Leader? in: R. Dehousse & E. Fabry (Eds) Where is Germany heading? Notre Europe, July 2010, pp. 13–20. Available at http://www.swp-berlin.org/fileadmin/contents/products/fachpublikationen/1007_where_is_germany_heading_swd_ks.pdf

SKAI. (2013) *Γεωργαντά: Λανθασμένες ευρωπαϊκές πρακτικές στα ελλείμματα – κριτική εισαγγελέων σε Παπανδρέου* [Georganta: Faulty European practices regarding deficits ...], SKAI News 24 January 2013. Available at http://www.skai.gr/news/greece/article/222364/georgada-lanthasmenes-europaikes-praktikes-sta-elleimmata-kritiki-eisaggeleon-se-papandreou/#ixzz2tX5BKEuH

Spanou, C. (2000) Greece: A truncated pyramid? in: H. Kassim, B. G. Peters & V. Wright (Eds) *The National Co-ordination of EU Policy*, pp. 161–181 (Oxford: Oxford University Press).

Verney, S. (1987) Greece and the European Community, in: K. Featherstone & D. K. Katsoudas (Eds) *Political Change in Greece: Before and After the Colonels*, pp. 253–270 (London: Croom Helm).

Visvizi, A. (2012a) The crisis in Greece and the EU-IMF rescue package: Determinants and pitfalls, *Acta Oeconomica*, 62(1), pp. 15–39.

Visvizi, A. (2012b) The crisis in Greece, democracy, and the EU, Carnegie Ethics Online, December 2012, Available at http://www.carnegiecouncil.org/publications/ethics_online/0076.html

Visvizi, A. (2012c) The June 17 Elections in Greece: Domestic and European Implications, *PISM Policy-Paper*, No. 31, June 2012. Polish Institute of International Affairs (PISM), Warsaw.

Visvizi, A. (2013) Addressing the crisis in Greece: The role of fiscal policy, in: B. Farkas (Eds) *The Aftermath of the Global Crisis in the European Union*, pp. 210–240 (Cambridge: Cambridge Scholars Publishing).

Portugal Is Not Greece: Policy Responses to the Sovereign Debt Crisis and the Consequences for the Portuguese Political Economy

JOSÉ M. MAGONE

Berlin School of Economics and Law, Berlin, Germany

ABSTRACT   *This paper delineates the changing environment from a benevolent to a conditionality-oriented. It uses the case study of Portugal and the implementation of the austerity programme to show how a semi-peripheral country of the European Union (EU) reacted to this changed environment. The first section shows how the EU has become more divided due to the growing cleavage between rich and poor member states. This is followed by the section on the making of the growing tensions between the European partners and the International Monetary Fund. Subsequently, the semi-peripheral economy of Portugal is analysed, before the policy responses of the Portuguese government are presented.*

Introduction: Towards a Europe of 'Haves' and 'Have-Nots'?

In the past 15 years, the European Union (EU) has moved from a community based on solidarity to one divided into 'haves' and 'have-nots'. The central and eastern enlargement has increased the divide between rich and poor countries. Moreover, the EU has become more heterogenous. Due to the lack of resources, the EU has been shifting from an attitude of benevolence to that of conditionality.

In order to understand the shift from a benevolent laissez-faire, laissez-passer to a conditionality-oriented EU and how it affected Portugal, we will first discuss this change of rationale within the EU. The subsequent section contextualises the problems of the Portuguese political economy and society. The subsequent three sections discuss how Portugal adjusted to the new regime of austerity imposed by the troika, which consequences emerged for the democratic institutional setting and the implementation of the austerity measures in the Memorandum of Understanding agreed with the troika. The paper will be finished with conclusions.

From Benevolent to Conditionality-Oriented EU

When the southern European countries joined the European Community in the 1980s, the supranational organisation was still dominated by member states. It was a west European club of democracies and still in the process of defining the future shape of the EU. It was a benevolent European Community able to support the fledging new democracies of southern Europe. The leadership of Spain under Felipe Gonzalez led to the emergence of the Club Med coalition (comprising Portugal, Spain and Greece), which was able to achieve a doubling of the European Commission (EC)/EU budget in 1988 and 1992 as a trade-off for support of the Single European Market (SEM) and the Economic and Monetary Union (see Magone, 2003, 2010; Closa & Heywood, 2004, pp. 188–201; Dinan, 2004, p. 226). For southern Europe, the EU is regarded as a 'vincolo esterno' (an external link) that after membership would solve or sort out all negative aspects of their economies and political systems. Membership has almost a millenarian dimension. The benevolent attitude of the other member states towards the new fledging democratic countries confirmed the perception of southern European countries (Carli, 1996, pp. 6–8; Dyson & Featherstone, 1996). The principle of a solidarity community became a predominant feature of European integration. Catching up of developing economies with the more advanced core European economies was a desirable goal. Power retreated from the considerations of the EU.

However, in the 1990s a new reality became to set in. The fall of the Berlin Wall opened an important structure of opportunity. Suddenly, apart from the Club Med, the Mezzogiorno and Ireland, the new democracies of central and eastern Europe were lined up to join the EU. The major problem was the lack of resources to finance the central and eastern enlargement. In spite of the integration of three net-payer countries, Sweden, Finland and Austria, with strong eurosceptic populations in 1995, it became more difficult for the EU to fund further enlargement. The central and eastern European enlargement was also characterised by a more tight conditionality-oriented process based on regular screening of progress. Moreover, the Agenda 2000 has frozen more or less any increase in the budget, in spite of more countries joining after 2004–07 (Magone, 2008, pp. 195–196). A general conflict between rich and poor countries emerged in the Berlin summit of 1999 to be continued in London 2005 and lately in the Brussels meeting of 2013. It means that since the turn of the century, a conflicting divide exists between the rich net-payer countries of the EU and the poorer member states, of which the southern Europeans are included. Southern, central and eastern Europe created a coalition of friends of cohesion against this growing alliance of net-payer countries.

As Martin Höpner and Armin Schäfer have analysed quite thoroughly, todays EU is considerably heterogenous to be an efficient SEM (Höpner & Schäfer, 2008, 2010). Indeed, as Dermott Cann shows, the national regulatory regimes are quite diverse across the EU (McCann, 2008). In the end, the crisis of the so-called PIIGS (Portugal, Italy, Ireland, Greece and Spain) is also a crisis of European social capitalism. There is a need for a reflection on the present development towards the SEM.

The sudden change of approach towards these countries, particularly Ireland, Portugal, Greece and Spain was a German idea. The German government did not trust the European institutions to oversee the reforms in the bailout countries and demanded a less benevolent international actor, the International Monetary Fund (IMF) to be part of the monitoring process. It seems that the main factor that may have changed substantially the nature of European integration was the inclusion of the IMF in the troika besides the EC and the European Central Bank. Allegedly, this was a demand of the German government in order to make sure that the bailout countries really comply with the conditions of the memorandum (Die Welt, 28 August 2012; Berliner Zeitung, 7 June 2013).

However, in 2012 one begins to see the emergence of differences of approach in relation to Greece, which considerably damaged the role of the troika. Moreover, both in 2011 and 2012, the IMF acknowledged that their computerised projections of the development of the Greek and Portuguese economies were far too optimistic. Such information does not come from the Europeans, but from the IMF under director Christine Lagarde. Reports of the IMF review the failure of the approach, and it is concluded that a softer approach among 'friends' would have been more conducive to reform (Tagesspiegel, 7 June 2013; IMF, 2013a, pp. 20–27, 2013b) There were general calls by European Stability Mechanism (ESM)-director Klaus Regling and European Commissioner Viviane Reding to take the IMF out of the troika mainly due to the criticism that they were exposed by the international organisation (Wirtschaftswoche, 14 June 2013; Reuters, 16 July 2013). Chancellor Angela Merkel's model of austerity is now under review, particularly when there was an expected third bailout for Greece in 2014, and probably Portugal (Handels-blatt, Berliner Zeitung, 7 June 2013). Meanwhile, Portugal is scheduled to come out of troika supervision by June 2014, however most likely has to submit to a precautionary transitional programme in her quest to return to the markets (Publico, 17 December 2013; Expresso, 8 March 2014; Diário de Notícias, 23 January 2014).

The Semi-Peripheral Economy of Portugal

The Portuguese economy can be characterised as a semi-peripheral one. According to Immanuel Wallerstein, a semi-peripheral economy has consumption patterns that are similar to those of developed economies, however the production structures are closer to those of developing countries in spite of some national business champions that are also internationally active. In long global commodity chains some countries have more periph-ery-like activities and others more core-like ones. In between are countries with a mix of both periphery- and core-like activities. These countries are called semi-peripheral (Waller-stein, 1985, p. 34; Santos, 2011, p. 21; Magone, 2014, pp. 38–39).

After the accession to the EU, Portugal was entitled to a large amount of structural funds that were used to build up the poor infrastructure of the country. Joining the EU was like a millenarian turning point in which the country was safe from further crisis. In 1979 and 1983, Portuguese governments had to deal with austerity programmes imposed by the IMF, which led to the pauperisation of the country. This experience should remain an important reminder that macroeconomic and monetary policies had to be sound to prevent a repetition of such intervention. Since 1986, the political economy of the country was quite dependent on the cohesion funds as strategic means to invest in the country, and they were also important to attract more foreign direct investment. The auto-mobile factory Autoeuropa set up by Volkswagen and Ford in 1991 has been so far the symbol of the post-accession Portuguese political economy. However, it showed also that on the turn of the new millennium it began to lose its strategic significance, particularly after Ford decided not to use the facility anymore. The Portuguese political economy is highly vulnerable to the withdrawal of foreign direct investment (Lima, 2009). The economy has a quite low research and development expenditure and it is highly dominated by the public sector, although in recent years the private sector was able to increase its share. Research and development expenditure increased to 1.5 per cent of GDP in 2011. The share of such effort is split equally between the public and private sectors. Private enterprises contribute about 0.7 per cent of the GDP (Pordata, 2014).

According to an excellent study by the Portuguese National Statistical Office, in 2010 there are a total of 1,262,168 enterprises in Portugal. Only 2.1 per cent are in the financial sector, while 97.9 per cent are in the non-financial sector. The financial sector enterprises have a larger number of employees per unit than the non-financial sector. Indeed, in both cases the average number of employees is quite low, with 4.73 full-time employees per enterprise in the financial sector and 3.36 in the non-financial sector, on average (INE, 2012, p. 12). The fragmentation of the entrepreneurial fabric clearly remains a significant problem for the development of economies of scale. According to the same study conducted in 2010, there were 1,144,150 small and medium-sized enterprises; however, a closer examination revealed that 96 per cent of these were micro-enterprises, and only 4 per cent could be considered small or medium-sized as defined by Eurostat. Just 1082 enterprises were considered large (more than 500 workers). In terms of the structure of employment, out of the total working population of 3,843,268 people employed in these enterprises, 44.3 per cent were employed in micro-enterprises, 34.4 per cent in small and medium-sized enterprises and 21.3 per cent in large enterprises (INE, 2012, p. 19).

Apart from the very fragmented structure, Portuguese enterprises show a very low level of productivity. Portuguese enterprises have one of the lowest productivity levels of the EU. According to a major study on the Portuguese economy, society and structural funds coordinated by Augusto Mateus with the title '25 years of European Portugal', Portuguese productivity has been declining since 1996, showing signs of exhaustion and stagnation in the new millennium. According to the study, one of the major factors leading to this situation is the lack of technological innovation in the enterprises. Apart from the exception of enterprises in the new branches of communication and new technologies, all other enterprises are affected by it. There are too many people employed in the economy that work much longer than the counterparts in Europe, however produce less. Portuguese workers in the industrial sector tend to earn one-third of what their counterparts in Germany earn (Vasconcellos e Sá, 2011, pp. 17–18; Mateus, 2013a pp. 57–58, 2013b, pp. 442–446). Ricardo Reis made aware that one factor that may also play a role in the low productivity of Portuguese workers is the poor quality of human resources management in the workplace. Human resources managers have poor social skills to organise more efficiently the available personnel. In this respect, Portugal and Greece have similar problems. The lack of motivation of workers seems to play a role in this respect (Reis, 2011, pp. 184–192; his findings are based on a survey by Bloom & van Reenen, 2010 which also include Greece; for Greece, see Featherstone & Papadimitriou, 2008).

As José da Silva Lopes asserts, Portugal has a dual labour market, in which a large proportion of the workers and employees in large enterprises and in the large public sector enjoy a high level of protection through relatively rigid legislation in the areas of hiring and firing, atypical work (such as temporary and fixed-term contracts) and regulation of collective dismissals; less privileged are workers in micro-, small, and medium-sized enterprises that generally do not respect any legislation and demonstrate a high level of flexibility in hiring and firing. In times of economic boom, this latter sector enables the absorption of a large number of workers, permitting a considerable reduction in unemployment; however, in times of crisis, many enterprises in that sector either shut down or summarily dismiss large numbers of workers and employees. This feature of the Portuguese labour market explains the rapid rise in unemployment in the country, similar to that has occurred in Spain and Greece (Lopes, 2003, pp. 276–277).

It will be quite difficult to come out of this crisis situation due to the fact that the education sector is suffering from a major crisis. In spite of investing considerably in the education sector in the past 40 years, the results have been poor. The Lisbon Strategy and the Programme of International Student Assessment have highlighted that the Portuguese schooling system is still mediocre, even if it has been making some progress in the past decades. Apart from school organisation issues, the Portuguese class society has been reproduced in the past four decades (Justino, 2011, pp. 81, 84–86). It means that social mobility has been happening, but too low to allow for substantial change of the structure of qualifications of the population. Two-thirds of the population have just basic education or less. Portugal can be compared to the educational structure in Turkey, Mexico and Brazil: only these three countries are catching up (see Table 1). Although progress has been made over the past decade, Portugal remains among the EU member states with the highest rates of early school leavers in secondary education (along with Malta and Spain). About 29 per cent of Portuguese secondary students dropped out of school in 2010, a figure that has stayed constant since 2009. However, in 2000, this figure was over 50 per cent. Figures for 2012 seem to suggest that such declined now to 23 per cent, however still quite high. Such statistical evidence shows that the Portuguese educational system truly needs a new paradigm and a complete overhaul if it is to change the structure of educational attainment in the coming decades. Thus far, change has been modest or negligible (European Commission, 2011, p. 4, 2012, p. 2).

An intelligent reform which is consensually agreed between the main political parties would be needed to overcome the stagnation and inertia of the crucial education sector. One further problem of the Portuguese economy is that it has comparative advantage in low research and technology products, which can be produced by several countries at lower prices. The top products of export are cork and artificial fibres. This is followed by shoes and textiles, cars mainly from international multinationals, some other machines and food products. Portugal would need to diversify and upgrade its economy to more high technological products in order to achieve more sustainability in the future. The Portuguese economy depends still largely on traditional products of semi-finished nature.

A piece of good news is that Portuguese exports have increased considerably in the past three years, while imports have gone down. This clearly helps to improve the trade balance, which has been traditionally negative. The reduction in imports has to do with the decline in consumption in Portugal due to the austerity situation in the country, while the increase in exports is related to the effort of many Portuguese enterprises to find new markets. Exports are up to 3 per cent in the first and second trimesters of 2013 in comparison to 2012 (Jornal de Negócios, 17 September 2013). One important area of investment for Portuguese companies is the lusophone countries, particularly Angola, Mozambik and Brazil. Unemployment is still quite high with 15.6 per cent in the third trimester of 2013, however there are some indications that this is slightly declining. Portugal was also able to profit from emigration not only to Angola, Mosambik and Brazil, but also to the UK, France, Luxembourg, Germany and Switzerland. All

Table 1. Educational attainment among the working population (ages 25–64) in OECD Countries (2010)

	Primary and lower secondary education	Upper secondary education	Post-secondary, non-tertiary education	Tertiary education
Australia	27	31	4	38
Austria	17	53	10	19
Belgium	30	34	2	35
Canada	11	26	12	50
Chile	28	45	–	26
Czech Republic	8	76	–	17
Denmark	24	44	–	34
Estonia	11	47	7	35
Finland	27	44	1	38
France	29	41		30
Germany	14	52	8	27
Greece	35	32	9	24
Hungary	18	59	2	20
Iceland	34	25	9	33
Ireland	26	24	12	38
Israel	18	37	–	46
Italy	45	39	1	14
Japan	–	55	–	44
Korea	22	41	–	39
Luxembourg	22	38	4	35
Mexico	64	19		17
Netherlands	27	38	3	33
New Zealand	27	21	11	40
Norway	19	40	3	37
Poland	11	62	4	23
Portugal	68	16	1	14
Slovakia	9	74	–	17
Slovenia	17	59	–	24
Spain	47	22	–	31
Sweden	13	46	7	33
Switzerland	15	45	6	35
Turkey	69	18	–	13
UK	25	37	–	38
USA	11	47	–	41
OECD average	26	44	–	30
EU 21 average	25	48	–	28
Brazil	59	18	–	11
China	82	13	–	4
Russia	11	34	–	54

Source: OECD (2012, p. 34).

this good news has encouraged the government to be more optimistic about the resili-ence of the Portuguese economy (Jornal de Negócios, 5 October 2013). Moreover, Por-tuguese immigrants tend to transfer quite a considerable amount of saved money to Portugal, so that the current account balance is in a better shape than the trade balance. In 2012, Portuguese emigrants sent €2.7 billion to Portugal. In the first six months of 2013, €1.7 billion were sent to Portugal, in comparison immigrants just sent €260 million out of Portugal (O Publico, 22 August 2013).

In summary, Portugal has a quite weak political economy that has been losing competi-tiveness in the past one and a half decades. The intervention of the troika was certainly regarded as the climax of this negative development related to a stagnating national economy and democracy.

'Portugal Is Not Greece': The Denial of the Political Elite of an Extremely Bad Situation

Portuguese political elites were for a long period of time in a mode of denial that the Portuguese economy was not competitive and national democracy was performing badly (for an excellent discussion of this denial see Aguiar, 2005; Santos, 2011). Economic stag-nation began to set in at the beginning of the millennium, however the problems may have started after 1993, when growth was induced mainly by the public sector. Between 2009 and 2011, the socialist government of José Socrates tried desperately to meet the growing demands related to the growth and stability pact of the EC. However, the sovereign debt crisis of Greece had strong contamination effects on Portugal. Moreover, the second José Socrates government was a minority government which was not able to rely on strong majority in the national parliament. On the contrary, two left-wing parties, the Communists and Greens (Partido Comunista Português-Partido Os Verdes (PCP-PEV)) and the Block of the Left (Bloco da Esquerda (BE)), were against any cuts and austerity policy, while the social democrats would give just a passive support at least through abstention. In 2009 and 2010, the budget was approved with the passive support of the main right-centre party the social democrats (Partido Social Democrata (PSD)). During 2011 it became more difficult for Portugal to get funding from the markets. After a failed vote of confidence at the end of March 2011, the interest rates for sovereign debt skyrocketed, making it imposs-ible for the government to get funding at reasonable rates.

Prime Minister José Socrates was determined not to ask for funding and follow the Greek example, which had to undertake two bailouts in 2010 and 2011–12. After con-siderable pressure from the banking sector, the social democrats, his own Socialist party (Partido Socialista (PS)), the EC and Eurozone counterparts, he requested a bailout. In spite of having resigned, the outgoing government was 'forced' by the political (includ-ing his own party) and economic establishment to do the negotiations with the troika (17 May 2012). In the end, a Memorandum of Understanding was adopted on 5 May 2011. Prime Minister José Socrates announced that the bailout agreement of €78 billion for three years was a better deal than those with Ireland and Greece (Reuters, 4 May 2011).

A major theme of successive governments was to distance the ailing situation of the country from that of Greece. 'Portugal is not Greece' was and remains a favourite slogan used by several governmental ministers and officials in Portugal. The theme remains alive up until the present day in the Portuguese government. Also, the Pedro

Passos Coelho coalition government used the 'Portugal is not Greece' slogan on several occasions. Greek Prime Minister George Papandreou government's announcement at the end of October 2011 that it would hold a referendum on the second Greek bailout and this led to the Prime Minister's statement that his government would not follow suit (Expresso, 2 November 2011; Visão, 2 November 2011). In early December 2012, the finance minister Vitor Gaspar repeated the slogan when Greece was offered an extension of deadline to comply with the objectives of the memorandum and the reduction in interest rates (Diario de Noticias, 3 December 2012). Also, foreign minister Paulo Portas in early February 2012 presented a positive picture of Portugal in relation to Greece using the same slogan (TVI online, 2 July 2012).

The other theme was that Portugal is a 'good pupil' (um bom aluno) in the EU and German chancellor Merkel's austerity policies in particular. There was always a competition between the leaders of the two main parties to be photographed with chancellor Merkel. The idea of being a 'good pupil' should contrast with the Greek example of a 'bad pupil'. In this sense, Greece was used domestically and internationally to show that the situation in Portugal was not as bad as that in Greece (Jornal de Negócios, 31 January 2012; Semanário, 13 November 2012).

The reality is a bit different. Although Portugal was quite successful in keeping the budget deficit at 4.2 per cent of GDP at the end of 2011 beyond all expectations, this was achieved by transferring quite a considerable amount of surplus funding from the public banking pension fund. However, Portugal ended 2012 with a budget deficit of 6.4 per cent, well beyond the original target of 4.5 per cent. The public debt had increased from 94 per cent of GDP in 2010 to dangerous 123.6 per cent. Only in March 2014, were there concrete figures on the budget deficit for 2013. According to official figures of the government, the deficit will remain at 4.5 per cent lower than the agreed target of 5.5 per cent. However, this was possible due to a considerable increase in taxation, which led to the collection of 35.5 per cent more revenue than was expected. Without the austerity measures attached to taxation, the deficit would be 6.6 per cent, which is similar to 2012 (Figures 1 and 2).

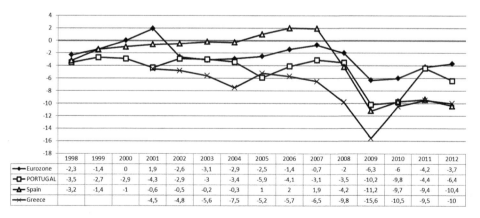

	1998	1999	2000	2001	2002	2003	2004	2005	2006	2007	2008	2009	2010	2011	2012
Eurozone	-2,3	-1,4	0	1,9	-2,6	-3,1	-2,9	-2,5	-1,4	-0,7	-2	-6,3	-6	-4,2	-3,7
PORTUGAL	-3,5	-2,7	-2,9	-4,3	-2,9	-3	-3,4	-5,9	-4,1	-3,1	-3,5	-10,2	-9,8	-4,4	-6,4
Spain	-3,2	-1,4	-1	-0,6	-0,5	-0,2	-0,3	1	2	1,9	-4,2	-11,2	-9,7	-9,4	-10,4
Greece				-4,5	-4,8	-5,6	-7,5	-5,2	-5,7	-6,5	-9,8	-15,6	-10,5	-9,5	-10

Figure 1. Budget deficit and surplus among Southern European member states (2000–2012)
Source: Eurostat (at http://epp.eurostat.ec.europa.eu/tgm/refreshTableAction.do?tab=table&plugin=0&pcode=tcina200&language=en), accessed 12 October 2012, 27 May 2013.

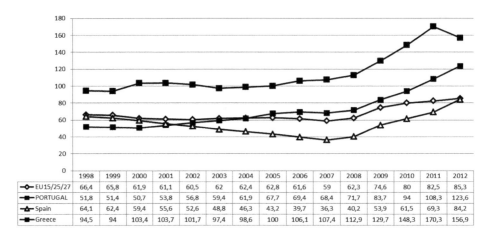

	1998	1999	2000	2001	2002	2003	2004	2005	2006	2007	2008	2009	2010	2011	2012
EU15/25/27	66,4	65,8	61,9	61,1	60,5	62	62,4	62,8	61,6	59	62,3	74,6	80	82,5	85,3
PORTUGAL	51,8	51,4	50,7	53,8	56,8	59,4	61,9	67,7	69,4	68,4	71,7	83,7	94	108,3	123,6
Spain	64,1	62,4	59,4	55,6	52,6	48,8	46,3	43,2	39,7	36,3	40,2	53,9	61,5	69,3	84,2
Greece	94,5	94	103,4	103,7	101,7	97,4	98,6	100	106,1	107,4	112,9	129,7	148,3	170,3	156,9

Figure 2. Public debt as a percentage of GDP in Southern European member states (1995–2011)
Source: Eurostat (at http://epp.eurostat.ec.europa.eu/tgm/table.do?tab=table&plugin=0&language=en&pcode=teina225), accessed on 12 October 2012, 27 May 2013.

Democratic Institutions and Government: The Veto Power of the Constitutional Court

One of the major problems for the Portuguese government was that the Constitutional Court rejected four proposals to reduce the deficit that affected the Portuguese civil service. Among the budgetary austerity measures, the Passos Coelho government intended to cut the Christmas bonus of civil servants. However, this was rejected by the Constitutional Court at the end of July 2012 because it was against the equality principle of pay between the public and private sectors. The bonus payment was regarded as a compensation for the lower wages of civil servants in relation to those of the private sector. This created major problems for the Passos Coelho government to find new areas to cut (Magone, 2013). In early April 2013, the Constitutional Court ruled again against some of the austerity measures in the budget. These four measures were the suspension of the payment of a holiday bonus to civil servants, in teaching contracts and pensioners because it violated the principle of equality between the public and private sectors in terms of pay. Furthermore, a fee on unemployment and health benefits was also rejected (TSF, 13 April 2013; Publico, 4 April 2013). The impact on the budget was considerable, because it was estimated that it would create a €1.4 billion shortfall (TSF, 13 April 2013; Publico, 5 April 2013). Such ruling was possible after several parties and the President of the Republic sent a request for a post-facto review on constitutionality of these austerity measures. The President had failed to do so in 2012 and was under considerable pressure not to make the same mistake for the 2013 budget. It meant that the Passos Coelho government had major difficulties to deal with the normal running of the democratic institutions. This was due to an absolute majority of the government parties PSD and CDS-PP and a president that supported its policies. The Constitutional Court remained as the only true veto player in Portugal. The second ruling of the Constitutional Court destabilised considerably the government leading to the resignation of the finance minister Vitor Gaspar, a crucial ally of Prime Minister Passos Coelho in the implementation of the memorandum. Gaspar resigned on 1 July 2013, however simultaneously he sent a very negative letter to

Prime Minister Pedro Passos Coelho stating a very difficult situation for Portugal (O Publico, 1 July 2013). He also leaked the letter to the press, which clearly led to the collapse of the government (Expresso, 1 July 2013). After the appointment of the new finance minister Maria Luis Albuquerque, the leader of the junior partner CDS-PP Paulo Portas left the coalition government leading to a major crisis. Within days, the markets reacted negatively to the situation in Portugal. However, Prime Minister Pedro Passos Coelho was able to renegotiate the coalition agreement by putting Paulo Portas, leader of the CDS-PP, the junior partner under considerable pressure. The result was the awarding of extra competences for Paulo Portas as a deputy prime minister. Moreover, he gained also more competences in economic and finance affairs overshadowing finance minister Maria Luis Albuquerque. In Portuguese governments, the finance minister post is a crucial top position, but the new arrangement undermined the position of Allbuquerque. The funding provided by the bailout is running out and there were then calls, particularly from the opposition Socialist party, to apply for the second bailout. However, the government of Pedro Passos Coelho wanted to avoid the second bailout in order to get the troika out of the country. At the end of August 2013, the Constitutional Court ruled against the law on the mobility of civil service that was crucial to reduce their numbers. This clearly also affected a major part of the programme related to friendly contract termination. The target was to reduce the existing 600,000 civil servants by 30,000. This created another shortfall of potentially €419 million. The markets reacted with an increase in the interest rates to the dangerous level of 6.8 per cent for sovereign bonds for 10 years duration. Under these circumstances, the Prime Minister did not exclude the possibility of the second bailout, although he wanted still to avoid it due to the implications for the country. The creditors might impose even worse conditions (Semanário Economico, 30 August 2013). However, it seems that the return to governmental stability has led to a decline in the interest rates to 6.55 per cent at the beginning of October. There is a general resolve by the Portuguese government to get access to the markets in 2014, one year later, as planned originally (Expresso, 4 October 2013). Pedro Passos Coelho is pushing forward the programme of restructuring the economy and is aware of the difficulties ahead (Expresso, 8 October 2013). There will be possibly a transition period supported by the ESM so that Portugal may return to the markets. However, President Anibal Cavaco Silva, who is an economist himself, urged the government to accept a precautionary programme when returning to the markets and not to follow the Irish example of outright direct access to the markets. Moreover, he informed the population that even after the troika monitoring ends in Portugal, the country will have to continue its austerity policies in order to repay most of the accumulated public debt, which emerged after the bailout. He projected that Portugal may have to continue this path of austerity for the next two decades (Expresso, 6 October 2013; Publico, 17 December 2013; Expresso, 8 March 2014). Klaus Regling, the director of the new permanent ESM, seemed to be quite optimistic about Portugal. He clearly does not see any indications that Portugal may need the second bailout, while Greece will certainly need the third one (Handelsblatt, 3 October 2013; Expresso, 8 October 2013).

However, in December 2013 the Constitutional Court ruled again against measures of the government related to the budget for 2014. The government proposed a law to cut the pensions above €1000 of present pensioners, which worked for the public service retrospectively. This was regarded by the Constitutional Court as breaching the principles of trust and protection guaranteed by the constitution. After this ruling, the government had to deal with a shortfall of €388 million (O Publico, 20 December 2013). In January 2014, the government made further proposals for future reform of the main national pension fund in order to compensate for the shortfall (O Publico, 2 January 2014).

Europeanisation by Stealth: Implementing the Memorandum of Understanding of the IMF

Here is not the place to discuss in detail the measures of the memorandum of understanding. Most of the short- and medium-term measures are economic and financial governance in order to improve the budget deficit and public debt (Table 1). One can group the measures in short–medium and long-term measures. The short-term measures led to a major privatisation programme of several public sector companies, such as the main electricity company (Electricidades de Portugal (EDP)). The Chinese Three Gorges Investment Company now owns 24.5 per cent of shares of the EDP. Also the company running Portuguese airports (Aeroportos de Portugal (ANA)) was sold to the French consortium Vinci for €3 billion. However, the Portuguese government will be entitled to receive a small share of the profits for a decade. Other companies have not been so successful. Particularly, the ailing, highly indebted national airline TAP did not find an adequate buyer (Magone, 2014, p. 16).

In the long term, the more problematic reforms will be in the judiciary, the highly indebted health sector and the local government. In the latter, a majority of parishes and also about half of public enterprises owned by the local government, a source of patronage and political corruption due to the lack of proper legislation and control, were shut down (Magone, 2014, pp. 192–194) (Table 2).

Portugal will come out of this crisis in a much slimmer state. The number of civil servants has been declining since 2005, even before the austerity measures were introduced. In the past decade, a reduction of about 200,000 civil servants was achieved. On 30 June 2013, there were still 574,946 people working for public administration at different levels, a considerable reduction from the original 750,000. However, 74.5 per cent were still in the central public administration and just 20 per cent at the local level, the remaining 5.5 per cent were in the autonomous islands of Azores and Madeira. A lot has been done to reduce the size of the bureaucracy by merging structures or reviewing the adequacy of human and financial resources (DGAEP, 2013, p. 2).

In summary, losing sovereignty over economic affairs was a major traumatic experience in Portugal. The political elite never expected that it would be in this situation within a benevolent EU. However, the survival struggle of the euro changed the context towards one of conditionality-oriented EU. The Portuguese government of Pedro Passos Coelho took this quite seriously, however the dynamics of external factors, such as the permanent crisis in Greece, has led to a continuing comparison of the performance of the two countries. Portugal is not Greece, but financially and economically has become more similar to it.

Conclusions: 'Portugal Is Not Greece', but Quite Similar

This article sought to show how a small semi-peripheral country dealt with a changing global and European environment during the finance and Eurocrisis. It also delineated how it became an important agent of Europeanisation by stealth. The policies of the Portuguese focused only on fulfilling the conditions set out by the troika. At the same time, it

Table 2. Portugal's adjustment programme negotiated with the IMF (2011–14)

Area	Objective
Short-term measures	
Fiscal policies	
Budget deficit reduction	From 9.5 per cent of GDP to below 3 per cent in 2013 (now: 2014)
	Streamlining of budgetary framework and use of strategic management to overview expenditure
Internal debt commitments	Control, transparency, and speedy payment of debt obligations to the private sector by the state
Financial sector	
Banking sector	Upgrade and reform of regulation and supervision; bank crisis as an important factor in budget deficit
Medium-term reforms and measures	
Market de-regulation	
Liberalisation of markets for goods and services	• Energy markets • Telecommunications and postal services • Transport and other service sectors • Housing market
Business culture	• Improvement in competition mechanisms • Improvement in public procurement • Improvement in business environment
Labour-market reform	• Improved flexibility in the labour market • Reform of unemployment benefits • Measures against long-term unemployment • Reduction in severance costs (from 20 to 12 days per year of work as compensation) • Wage reform • Active labour-market policies
National health service	
Pharmaceuticals	• Monitoring and reduction of debt to the pharmaceutical industry • Cheaper online purchase of pharmaceuticals
Public economic sector	
Public–private partnerships	Review of public–private partnerships and freezing of new contracts
Public-enterprise sector	• Improvements in governance of the public-enterprise sector • Reduction in subsidies • Managerial best practices (according to international standards) • Debt ceilings • Privatisation (a) Portuguese airlines (TAP) (b) main electricity company (EDP) (c) airport management (ANA) (d) oil company (GALP) (e) energy company (REN) (f) postal service (Correios de Portugal) (g) freight branch of national railways (h) insurance company (Caixa Seguros) (i) nationalised bank (BPN)

(Continued)

Table 2. Continued.

Area	Objective
Long-term reforms	
State reform	
Taxation administration	Streamlining and unification of revenue administration through the merging of various existing units
Central public administration reform	• Leaner public administration (a) reduction in top executive positions (b) non-replacement of retiring civil servants (c) streamlining accounting at the regional and local levels (d) continuation of reduction in services and administrative units (e) enhanced flexibility and mobility of human resources
Local government reform	• Reduction in parishes (new local government map) • Introduction of new public-management philosophy • New electoral law • Reduction in number of elected offices • Reform of the local public-enterprise sector (reduction in enterprises)
Judiciary	
Reform of the judiciary sector	• New judiciary map • Introduction of new managerial philosophy in the micro-court system
Education and training	
Education	Reduction in number of school leavers in the secondary education
Training	Improvement in vocational training

Source: Own compilation based on European Commission et al. (2011).

had to deal with growing resistance of the population and other democratic institutions, particularly the Constitutional Court. The main aim of the government under pressure was to achieve success in implementing the measures set in the Memorandum of Understanding so that Portugal could as soon as possible get rid of the stringent monitoring of the troika. Portugal tried to present itself as a positive example, a 'good pupil' which implements the necessary structural reforms in order to achieve a more competitive economy. It used Greece as the opposite negative example that Portugal was not. However, during this process of change by stealth it became clear that Portugal is still closer to the Greek model to that of more developed economies.

References

Aguiar, J. (2005) *Fim Das Ilusões Ilusões do Fim 1985–2005* (Lisbon: Aletheia Editores).

Bloom, N. & van Reenen, N. (2010) Human resource management and productivity, in: O. Ashenfelter & D. Card (Eds) *Handbook of Labor Economics*, Vol. 4B, pp. 1697–1768 (Amsterdam: Elsevier).

Carli, G. (1996) *Cinquant'Anni di Vita Italiana* (Roma: Laterza).

Closa, C. & Heywood, P. (2004) *Spain and the European Union* (Basingstoke: Palgrave).

Dinan, D. (2004) *Europe Recast. A History of European Integration* (Basingstoke: Palgrave).

Direcção Geral de Adminstração e Emprego Público (DGAEP). (2013) Boletim do Emprego Público No. 9. Available at http://www.dgaep.pt/upload//DEEP/BOEP09/DGAEP-DEEP_BOEP_09_outubro_2013. pdf (accessed 17 November 2013).

Dyson, K. & Featherstone, K. (1996) Italy and EMU as a Vincolo Esterno: Empowering the technocrats transforming the state, *South European Society & Politics*, 1(2), pp. 272–299.

European Commission (2011) *Tackling Early School Leaving: A Key Contribution to the Europe 2020 Strategy.* Brussels 31.1.2011 COM (2011) 18 (Brussels: European Commission).

European Commission (2012) Progress in reducing early school leaving and increasing graduates in Europe, but more efforts needed. Press Release IP 12/577, Brussels, 7 June 2012.

European Commission, European Central Bank & International Monetary Fund (2011) Memorandum of Understanding on Specific Economic Conditionality. Available at http://economico.sapo.pt/public/uploads/ memorando_04–05–2011.pdf (accessed 11 September 2012).

Featherstone, K. & Papadimitriou, D. (2008) *The Limits of Europeanization. Reform Capacity and Policy Conflict in Greece* (Basinstroke: Palgrave).

Höpner, M. & Schäfer, A. (2008) Grundzüge der politisch-ökonomischen Perspektive auf die europäische Integration, in: M. Höpner & A. Schäfer (Eds) *Politische Ökonomie der europäischen Integration*, pp. 11–54 (Frankfurt a. M.: Campus).

Höpner, M. & Schäfer, A. (2010) Grenzen der Integration-wie die Intensivierung der Wirtschaftsintegration zur Gefahr für die politische Integration wird, *Integration* (1), pp. 3–20.

Instituto Nacional de Estatistica (INE) (2012) Evolução do Sector Empresarial em Portugal (2004–2012) (Lisboa. INE). Available at http://www.imf.org/external/pubs/ft/weo/2012/02/pdf/text.pdf (accessed 2 December 2012).

International Monetary Fund (IMF) (2013a) Greece: Ex post evaluation of exceptional access under the 2010 Stand-by Arrangement, IMF Country Report, 13/156, June. Available at http://www.imf.org/external/pubs/ft/ scr/2013/cr13156.pdf (accessed 6 October 2013).

International Monetary Fund (IMF) (2013b) Greece: Third review under the extended arrangement under the extended fund facility – staff report, staff statement; Press release and statement by the executive, IMF Country Report, 13/153, June. Available at http://www.imf.org/external/pubs/ft/scr/2013/cr13153.pdf (accessed 6 October 2013).

Justino, D. (2011) *Difícil é Educá-los* (Lisboa: Fundação Francisco dos Santos).

Lima, M.P.C. (2009) Autoeuropa workers reject works council pre-agreement, document ID PT0906059I, 25 September. Available at http://www.eurofound.europa.eu/eiro/2009/06/articles/pt0906059i.htm (accessed 11 September 2012).

Lopes, J. da S. (2003) The role of the state in the labour market: Its impact on employment and wages in Portugal as compared to Spain, in: S. Royo & P.C. Manuel (Eds) *Spain and Portugal in the EU: The First Fifteen Years*, pp. 269–286 (London: Cass).

Magone, J.M. (2003) *The Politics of Southern Europe. Integration into the European Union* (Westport, CT/ London: Praeger).

Magone, J.M. (2008) Leaderless enlargement? The difficult reform of the new Pan-European political system, in: J. Hayward (Ed.) *Leaderless Europe*, pp. 188–207 (Oxford: Oxford University Press).

Magone, J.M. (2010) The role of the EEC in the Portuguese, Spanish and Greek transitions, in: D. Muro & G. Alonso (Eds) *Politics and Memory of Democratic Transition in the Case of Spain*, pp. 215–235 (London: Routledge).

Magone, J.M. (2013) Living with the crisis in Southern Europe, in: A. Agh & L. Voss (Eds) *European Futures: The Perspectives of the New Member-States in the New Europe*, pp. 69–138 (Budapest: Budapest College of Communication and Business).

Magone, J.M. (2014) *The Politics in Contemporary Portugal. Evolving Democracy* (Boulder, CO: Lynne Rienner).

Mateus, A. (Ed.) (2013a) *25 Anos de Portugal Europeu. A economia a sociedade e os fundos estruturais* (Lisboa: Fundação Francisco Manuel dos Santos).

Mateus, A.M. (2013b) *Economia Portuguesa. Evolução no contexto internacional (1910–2013)* (Lisboa: Principia).

McCann, D. (2008) *The Political Economy of the European Union* (Basingstroke: Palgrave).

Organisation for Economic Cooperation and Development (OECD) (2012) *Education at a Glance* (Paris: OECD). Available at http://www.uis.unesco.org/Education/Documents/oecd-eag-2012-en.pdf (accessed 3 June 2013).

Pordata (2014) Despesas em actividades de investigação e desenvolvimento (I&D) em % do PIB: por sector de execução – Portugal. Official data from the Ministry of Education and Science, General-Directorate of

Statistics in Education and Science. Available at http://www.pordata.pt/Portugal/Despesas+em+actividades+de +investigacao+e+desenvolvimento+(I+D)+em+percentagem+do+PIB+por+sector+de+execucao-1133 (accessed 2 April 2014).

Reis, R. (2011) Solução Para Portugal. Fazer Mais Com os Portugueses, in: J. Vasconcellos e Sá (Ed.) *Portugal e o Futuro*, pp. 177–195 (Lisboa: Vida Económica SA).

Santos, B. De S. (2011) *Portugal. Ensaio Contra A Autoflagelação* (Lisboa: Edições Almedina).

Vasconcellos e Sá, J. (2011) Introdução, in: J. Vasconcellos e Sá (Ed.) *Portugal e o Futuro*, pp. 15–20 (Lisboa: Vida Económica SA).

Wallerstein, I. (1985) The relevance of the concept of semiperiphery to Southern Europe, in: G. Arrighi (Ed.) *Semiperipheral Development. The Politics of Southern Europe in the Twentieth Century*, pp. 31–39 (Beverly Hills/London: Sage).

The Tale of Two Peripheries in a Divided Europe

BELA GALGOCZI

ETUI, Belgium

ABSTRACT *This article addresses one of the major fault lines that emerged with the controversial crisis management practices in a divided Europe. Much attention has been paid to divergences between the Eurozone core (Germany and other surplus countries) and the crisis-ridden southern periphery of the monetary union. The crisis and its aftershocks that hit Central Eastern European countries in 2009 had also been addressed extensively. Less attention had, however, been paid to the different characteristics of the 'two peripheries' of Europe, the one in the South and the other in the East. This article focuses on the differences in their economic structure and most importantly the different role these peripheries play in the division of labour within the European economy. The conclusions we can draw are not only important for the understanding of the challenges these peripheries are facing, but they also deliver lessons to the whole process of European crisis management practices.*

Introduction

While the term 'two-speed Europe' was first coined simply to distinguish between the member states displaying a *faster* pace of integration and those managing to move forward only at a rather *slower* pace, the emphasis in this respect has recently shifted to a commitment to *more* integration. The new distinction became particularly apparent with the conclusion of the Euro+ Pact in March 2011 and the Fiscal Pact agreed at the EU Summit in December of the same year (European Council, 2012). It is as a consequence of the Euro Area crisis that the call for a closer degree of European integration has been reiterated, with the current focus being on economic governance and even fiscal union. Such deeper integration would, in the first instance, involve members of the Economic and Monetary Union (EMU) (plus any non-EMU member states that join voluntarily) and would thus result in a two-speed Europe not in quantitative terms alone but in terms of a more qualitative form of political and institutional integration. In this article, we examine various aspects of European economic integration in the specific fields of trade, finance and production regimes. Our focus, in so doing, will be on the prospects for growth and development of the European 'periphery' which encompasses the previously 'converging' countries of eastern and southern Europe that have been particularly harshly affected by the crisis of 2008 and its still ongoing consequences. Here, it is a question not merely of different economic *growth rates* among member states but of differing economic *models* that were differently affected by the crisis of 2008. The adjustments that came in the wake of this crisis (including austerity policies and competitiveness-enhancing measures based predominantly on wage cuts) also had differing implications for individual economic models, so that what we see currently is a 'patchwork Europe' with fault lines zigzagging around among a variable combination of country groups. The practices imposed in the context of the adjustments are affecting the so-called deficit countries asymmetrically, as these are the countries suffering a loss of national sovereignty as a result of interference from European institutions such that an accompanying feature of this development is a democratic deficit.

From Convergence to Divergence – Where Is the EU Heading for?

There is a fundamental clash between Europe's social ambitions and the way adjustment is under way. The conditionality of any bailout or support from the European Stability Mechanism is geared clearly in one direction: austerity, cost cutting and undermining of social standards, this all means 'rebalancing' downwards. Greece has lost 25 per cent of its GDP during this process up till now.

The idea of the European Social Model has always taken the back seat in the process of European integration. A bunch of political science literature (Streeck, 2000; Scharpf, 2002; Martin and Ross, 2004) argued that while the single market project has always been the hard core of the integration backed by hard law and its flagship project the EMU, albeit on base of an incomprehensive architecture as we bitterly learned during the crisis, the social dimension has always been based on declarations, wish lists and well, Open Method of Coordination. More than that was just based on ad hoc ideas, as e.g. some sort of a tax harmonisation, or even corridors of budget redistribution ratios, although the latter should not be seen as a totally unrealistic idea. While the EMU has clearly been a new stage of integration and much of the underlying regulatory framework was based on fiscal rules (by far not satisfactory as we again learned during the recent crisis), it is hard to imagine seriously that one can have a common fiscal platform among member states that have public expenditure ratios of GDP in the range between 34 and 57 per cent of GDP. And indeed, some elements of social spending get under scrutiny during the rebalancing act: pension systems and social spending is under huge pressure, but again the direction is downwards.

Besides debt consolidation and fiscal austerity, the other main dimension of crisis management focuses on the adjustment in the divergence of competitive positions among EMU members. The therapy here is also biased into one direction: downwards. On the one hand, adjustment policies are asymmetrical with the whole burden of correction put on deficit countries, while surplus countries are not involved seriously. On the other hand, the correction in the competitiveness gap (gap in unit labour cost developments) is forced out through the price channel (dominantly through a cut in labour costs, i.e. wages), while non-price aspects of competitiveness (economic and export structure, productivity and quality) are ignored. This again results in a downward bias.

All this leads to asymmetric and downward adjustment, where mostly peripheral, lower income countries are affected. The result of this crisis management strategy is a persistently growing gap between surplus and deficit countries that manifests itself in a diverging Europe.

Where Has the Big European Dream about Convergence Been Lost?

Besides the historical founding principle of the EU as a peace-keeping project, it was the prospect of convergence that gave a true substance to the European idea for millions of people. This also seemed to work for several decades. Now that Europe's flagship project, the single currency, is in trouble to respond to the external shock posed by the financial crisis and adjustment therapy forces its member states into a diverging downward spiral, this essential and fundamental mission seems to be evaporating.

The promise of income convergence – between poorer and richer member states and among the poorer and richer regions within them – has been an underpinning feature of European integration from the outset. In this respect, a glance back over 50 years of EU history up to the crisis provides confirmation of an unprecedented feat. As stated in a recent World Bank (2012) report: 'The European convergence in consumption levels in the last four decades is unmatched. Except for East Asia, the rest of the world has seen little or no convergence'. Indeed, already by the early 1990s, the incomes of more than 100 million people in the poor south – Greece, Southern Italy, Portugal and Spain – had grown and moved closer to those of the more prosperous areas of Europe. Similarly, between the late 1990s and the mid-2000s, the income levels of 100 million people in Central Eastern Europe were dynamically converging towards levels in the richer part of the continent. Figure 1 offers a historical glance at the economic divide in Europe, showing that Central Eastern European (CEE) countries still have substantially lower per capita GDP levels (at purchasing power standard (PPS)) than the EU27 average. The data also indicate milestones in the last 15 years, showing the varying convergence dynamic of individual countries in the different periods.

Most of the convergence took place between 2000 and 2007, after which it lost momentum or even went into reverse. It is apparent also from the graph that Greece and Portugal

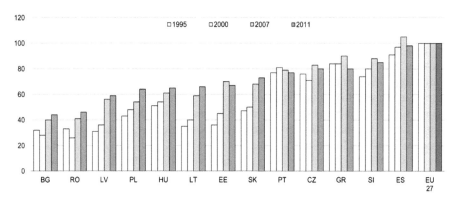

Figure 1. Income gaps and convergence: GDP/capita as percentage of EU27 total for selected years and countries (based on market prices at PPS)
Notes: Data for BG and RO: latest year 2010. *Source:* Eurostat (2012).

stand out as having displayed no convergence whatsoever over the whole 15-year period. The year 2008, with the onset of crisis, marked a halt in these processes of convergence achieved via a catching up of the less prosperous countries and regions, placing a question mark over the continuing sustainability of some of the progress achieved in the earlier phases of European integration.

Although 2008 was a common point of fracture for both East and South, the experience of these two regions was significantly different. While convergence ground to a definite standstill in Southern Europe, in the CEE countries, the much stronger impetus towards convergence came to a more abrupt halt which, in some cases, nonetheless proved no more than temporary. Indeed, in most CEE countries – and particularly those with the lowest per capita GDP levels – a rapid process of catching up had been observable in the years before the crisis. In Southern Europe, however, the picture had been more mixed, even during the boom period, with Spain having achieved significant convergence, while Greece and Portugal had tended to stagnate. Latvia and Lithuania, the two countries which suffered the most dramatic falls in output in 2009 (17.7 and 14.8 per cent, respectively), nonetheless showed still impressive overall convergence for the 1995–2011 period as a whole, with per capita GDP levels relative to the EU27 rising from 31 to 59 per cent for Latvia and from 35 to 66 per cent for Lithuania.

The picture for Southern Europe is much bleaker: between 1995 and 2011, the region showed no convergence – in the case of Greece and Portugal – or, in Spain, only limited convergence to EU27 levels. Thus, while Spain still achieved some convergence over these 16 years, from 91 to 98 per cent, Portugal saw none over the entire period (77 per cent in 1995 and still in 2011), while Greece actually suffered a loss of convergence (from 80 per cent in 1995 to 77 per cent in 2011). All three countries suffered significant setbacks in the wake of the crisis, most particularly Greece with a 14 per cent point drop in its relative income level between 2008 and 2011.

The Role of the Structure of the Economy

What matters for competitiveness is economic structure, not just labour costs. The different pattern in the catching-up process in the East and the South is the result of a number of underlying structural differences among European countries that have affected their respective economic integration. We take a look at four important drivers of economic integration that played a key role in convergence: exports; the balance-of-payments situation and its structure; foreign direct investment (FDI) and the role of credit flows.

Currently, most pronounced division in Europe appears between 'surplus' and 'deficit' countries, as determined by their balance-of-payments position within the Euro Area, with the core 'surplus countries' clustered around Germany and the 'deficit' ones around the Mediterranean. A similar distinction applies beyond the Euro Area, with a number of CEE countries belonging to the 'surplus' core (e.g. the Czech Republic and Poland) and the more peripheral CEE crisis-ridden countries (e.g. the Baltic States) falling into the 'deficit' group. This division between surplus and deficit countries thus cuts across the historical divisions between the East and the West of the continent.

The Czech Republic, Hungary and Slovakia had broadly balanced trade even before the crisis, whereas Latvia, Bulgaria, Greece, Romania and Portugal were, during this period, used to have persistent and double-digit trade deficits.

The balance of payments includes all of a given country's financial flows with the outside world, including trade in goods and services, various forms of capital, asset and income flows and credits. We address here one of its most important components that played a crucial role for deficit countries both before and during the crisis, namely, balance of trade in goods and services. The balance in the trade of goods (both in 2007 and 2011) reveals substantial differences between individual member states. A negative trade balance means that a country imports more than it exports and that the difference has to be financed. Persistent deficits not financed from other transactions within the balance of payments create debt, as happened in the cases of Latvia, Bulgaria and Greece, as shown in Figure 2.

The data also allow assessment of the degree to which countries were able to adjust to the crisis of 2008. The Czech Republic, Hungary and Slovakia had broadly balanced trade even before the crisis, whereas Latvia, Bulgaria, Greece, Romania and Portugal were, during this period, having to contend with persistent and double-digit trade deficits. During the crisis, most CEE countries were able to adjust by cutting their deficits substantially or by achieving a positive trade balance. In most cases, this happened through the decrease in imports that was a consequence of slowing growth or even recession. A balancing act achieved by the 'deep-freezing' of certain types of activity (such as, consumption, investments and imports) can produce signs of fast adjustment, but cannot be regarded as a long-term solution. Moreover, it is still an open question to what extent adjustments in CEE deficit countries (e.g. the Baltic States) have a longer term structural impact. Greece and Portugal, in any case, even after having absorbed a large dose of measures for a 'deep-freeze', continued to show high trade deficits still in 2011, thereby revealing a much more limited ability to adjust in either of the abovementioned ways.

When looking at key features of 'deficit' and 'surplus' countries on the periphery more in detail, we see further important structural differences in their economies. While 'surplus' countries in the East had a large-scale FDI into their productive sectors, this was less the case for southern European crisis states. According to the World Investment Report by UNCTAD (2013), while in 2012 Slovakia, the Czech Republic, Hungary and Estonia had an FDI stock in their economy between 60 and 80 per cent of their GDP, for Greece, this was just 9 per cent.

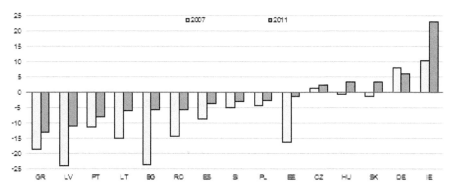

Figure 2. Balance-of-payments component: trade in goods (per cent of GDP)
Source: Eurostat (2012).

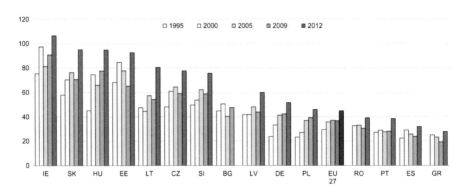

Figure 3. Exports of goods and services (per cent of GDP)
Source: Eurostat (2013).

Central Eastern European countries also tend to have a high export share in their GDP that again is not the case for the deficit countries in the South. For illustration, Figure 3 shows export shares for this group of countries.

While in 2012 Slovakia, Hungary and Estonia had an export share of around 90 per cent of their GDP, in the case of Greece, this was 27 per cent.

There are also substantial qualitative differences in the export profiles of individual countries. One important feature is the share of 'complex sectors' within the total exports of individual member states. The classification of export structures according to Standard International Trade Classification categories corresponds roughly to the level of technological sophistication of the products being exported. Accordingly, the 'complex sectors' include machinery and transport equipment, pharmaceuticals and scientific instruments. The classification is merely indicative, insofar as it does not take into account the role of the country in the division of labour within the sector or its R&D or innovation content. In terms of sectoral composition, Hungary and the Czech Republic thus had a higher rate of export complexity than Germany with a share of complex sectors of around 60 per cent of their total exports (with their high export share this corresponds to close to 50 per cent of their GDP). Greece had the lowest share of complex sectors in its exports (13.8 per cent in 2011), while Bulgaria, the Baltic States and Portugal also had comparably low shares (between 20 and 30 per cent in 2011). During the four years of the crisis, a further downgrading of what were already, in terms of complexity, relatively low export profiles took place in Greece, Lithuania, Portugal and Spain. By contrast, Romania, Estonia, Bulgaria and Latvia were able to upgrade their export profiles during this period. Export complexity thus supplies a further indication of the role of countries in the division of labour in Europe, and small peripheral countries with scarce domestic capital – like most of the CEEs – can achieve high export complexity through FDI.

Besides the size and composition of trade and FDI, the geographical orientation of exports also matters. As Germany currently represents the economic core of Europe, the share taken by it in the exports of individual countries is a decisive factor.

Based on Eurostat data (2013), Hungary, Poland and the Czech Republic have one-quarter to one-third of their exports directed to Germany, with a slightly decreasing trend over the years. Greece and the Baltic States, meanwhile, have values of below ten per cent. Three further CEE member states (Slovakia, Slovenia and Romania) had a German exports share of around 20 per cent, while the rest of the countries examined (including Portugal and Spain) have values closer to ten per cent.

Summarising the above, as regards foreign trade characteristics, the following trends emerge from the data: Central Eastern European exporters tend to have balanced trade or even trade surpluses; they have a high share of their GDP generated by exports and, in the case of the Czech Republic, Slovakia and Hungary, a substantial part of their exports consists of complex products, while a high proportion of their exports is oriented to Germany. These countries also have high FDI penetration in their tradable sectors, with much of their manufacturing FDI originating from Germany (automobile, components and electronic sectors). On the other hand, the Baltic States and the Southern European states examined here show lower export shares, varying levels of trade deficit, low levels of export complexity and limited trade relations with Germany. All of this supports the view that, among the different fault lines in crisis-ridden Europe, one decisive division is between the surplus and the deficit countries, with core CEE countries (in this context, the Czech Republic, Slovakia and Hungary) being part of the Germany-centred core region in terms of trade and investment patterns within the European division of labour.

Within this framework, Western (mostly German) multinationals have benefited from cheap sourcing from Central Eastern European locations and have used this to strengthen their market positions and competitiveness on a global level. The longer term sustainability of this model poses serious questions, however. It can be maintained only if CEE subcontracting activities become higher value added in terms of both R&D and local value-added content. Though signs of such a trend were apparent in the mid-2000s (Broadman, 2005), the process was interrupted by the crisis and nowadays the mainstream adjustment strategy as reflected in the European Semester (European Commission, 2011) is focused on low-wage competition. This is anything but promising for the future.

Wages Are Just One Factor of Competitiveness

Moreover, data also indicate that even if wage and unit labour cost developments showed a high grade of divergence in the decade up to the crisis when the competitive positions of periphery countries (both in the East and the South) deteriorated substantially in comparison to Germany, there is no fundamental cost competitiveness problem if we look at the levels of productivity and wage costs in their tradable (manufacturing) sector. Figure 4 shows that based on the manufacturing sector, periphery countries would not have a cost competitiveness problem with Germany. The problem some have is more of structural nature: the share of manufacturing and exports in general is very low in their economy.

The case of the two peripheries in Europe demonstrates that the competitiveness problem of some of the Mediterranean countries is much more due to deeply rooted structural problems than just price and cost levels. Since the therapy is focused almost exclusively on cost and wage cuts, not addressing their structural problems, it is not only that their previous achievements in convergence are wiped out, but their future perspectives are also put at stake.

Although tackling these structural problems through cost adjustment (wage and spending cuts) can deliver temporary results in cost competitiveness at the price of a dramatic increase in poverty and unemployment, in the end, these inevitable 'side effects' also

Country	Apparent labour productivity*	Average personnel costs	Wage-adjusted productivity (%)
		(EUR 1000 per employed)	
EU27	46	34.5	132.1
Czech Republic	22	14.0	154.6
Hungary	23	11.7	199.6
Greece	42	28.0	150.6
Germany	57	47.2	120.7
Portugal	23	15.8	146.7
Slovakia	17	12.3	134.7
Spain	48	35.1	137.2

Figure 4. Wage-adjusted productivity in manufacturing in selected countries, 2009
Note: *Apparent labour productivity is defined as value added at factor costs divided by the number of persons employed. *Source:* Eurostat (2012).

jeopardise the success of the entire adjustment. Cost adjustment is simply not an adequate way of addressing the longer term structural problems (such as the share of manufacturing in the whole economy, export shares, qualitative composition of exports, place in the international division of labour, etc.).

The problem, to put it bluntly, was not that consumers in the surplus countries had been buying less olive oil and port wine due to rising unit labour costs in Greece or Portugal. In other words, the cure chosen to date is one that tackles the symptoms but not the causes of the problem.

Even if part of the achieved convergence before the crisis can be deemed as not sustainable, this also points to a policy failure. European institutions in a series of reports and communications were proud to give account of growing employment and income convergence in many of the periphery countries up to 2007. This progress was also seen as partial achievement of the Lisbon targets. If much of this was not based on a real performance, it is also a strong criticism to EU policies. European leaders cannot just shrug their shoulders and say, sorry, what we believed and welcomed as achievement turned out to be (partially) fake. It was just an illusion, we can wipe this out. It is a matter of fact that much of the unsustainable expansion was due to a huge capital allocation problem resulting also from irresponsible finances and lending practices (dominantly through banks in surplus countries). Now ordinary working people should pay the price and those who blew the bubble are safeguarded without any future perspective.

Conclusions

The crisis has highlighted the diversity of economic models and of their sustainability during hard times and external shocks in the European 'peripheries'. Convergence of income levels between poorer regions in the South and the East towards the level of rich countries in the centre has been one of the big European objectives and seemed to function for several decades. This also strongly contributed to the legitimacy and the public support of the European Union (EU). Convergence although mostly driven by economic processes had also been a fundamental factor to maintain a European Social Model amid diversity at member state level.

While divergence in the economic catching-up processes, particularly after 2008, showed an East–South division, the multiple fault lines characterising the diversity of political and economic structures can be shown to cut across historical and geographic country groups. The credit crunch of 2008 highlighted the division between the countries with current account surpluses, the European 'core' around Germany including also the Central Eastern European exporters, and the 'deficit' countries, including Mediterranean countries and a number of countries in Central Eastern Europe. Given the lack of effective adjustment mechanisms in the Euro Area, the surplus–deficit divide quickly turned into the difficult creditor–debtor relationship. The 'debtor' countries then experienced a prolonged agony of negotiated and imposed adjustments in the context of crisis-driven Euro Area institution building. Given the unequal power relations between debtors and creditors, the concerns of the latter inevitably came to dominate the nature of the adjustment efforts made.

What we clearly see now is that if convergence is driven by economic processes only, the result will not be enduring and balanced, more political and institutional integration is needed, the Single Market alone will not do the job. The paradox and most worrying phenomenon is that political integration in the form of the economic governance that evolves through the current crisis management practice of the EU is precisely doing the opposite: it drives diversity further up to the point that may tear the Eurozone and the EU apart.

References

Broadman, H. (2005) *From Disintegration to Reintegration: Eastern Europe and the Former Soviet Union in International Trade* (Washington, DC: World Bank).

European Commission (2011) Annual Growth Survey 2011. Available at http://ec.europa.eu/economy_finance/articles/eu_economic_situation/pdf/2011/com2011_11_annex1_en.pdf (accessed 14 February 2014).

European Council (2012) The Treaty on Stability. Available at http://european-council.europa.eu/eurozone-governance/treaty-on-stability (accessed 14 February 2014).

Eurostat (2012) Manufacturing Statistics. Available at http://epp.eurostat.ec.europa.eu/statistics_explained/index.php/Manufacturing_statistics_-_NACE_Rev._2 (accessed 13 December 2013).

Eurostat (2013) Data. Available at http://epp.eurostat.ec.europa.eu/statistics_explained/index.php/International_trade_in_goods#Intra-EU_trade (accessed 13 December 2013).

Martin, A. & Ross, G. (2004) Introduction: EMU and the European social model, in: A. Martin & G. Ross (Eds) *Euros and Europeans. Monetary Integration and the European Social Model*, pp. 1–19 (Cambridge: Cambridge University Press).

Scharpf, F. (2002) The European social model: Coping with the challenges of diversity, *Journal of Common Market Studies*, 40(4), pp. 645–670.

Streeck, W. (2000) Competitive solidarity: Rethinking the European social model, in: K. Hinrichs, C. Offe, H. Kitschelt & H. Wiesenthal (Eds) *Kontingenz und Krise*, pp. 245–261 (Frankfurt am Main, New York: Campus).

UNCTAD (2013) *World Investment Report, Global Value Chains for Investment and Trade Development* (New York and Geneva). Available at http://unctad.org/en/publicationslibrary/wir2013_en.pdf (accessed 13 December 2013).

World Bank (2012) *EU11 Regular Economic Report: Coping with External Headwinds* (Zagreb: World Bank Office).

Poland under Economic Crisis Conditions

MACIEJ DUSZCZYK

Institute of Social Policy, University of Warsaw, Poland

ABSTRACT   *Poland is perceived as the European Union (EU) country that copes very well with the consequences of the crisis that started in late 2008. This is corroborated by statistical data related to, among others, economic growth and unemployment rate. This article provides analyses of Poland's responses to the two phases of the crisis so far. It attempts to identify the determinant factors that helped Poland avoid adverse consequences of the crisis and to answer the question whether the priorities adopted in the two phases thereof differ. In particular, the article ventures an analysis of the impact of Poland's membership in the EU on its economic situation. The undertaken analyses have been supplemented with the description and evaluation of the major instruments applied by the Polish government in the period 2009–13 and presentation of the economic and social situation in this regard. The article also verifies the thesis of Poland's good economic standing. On the basis thereof, conclusions for future development scenarios have been drawn up.*

Introduction

Despite numerous optimistic statements by politicians and experts heralding the end of the economic crisis[1] faced by the world since 2008, many states have decided both to continue measures taken thus far and to propose new instruments aimed at economic revival, which would help offset the incurred losses and improve the security and quality of the lives of their citizens in the future. Poland has been the only European Union (EU) member state not to record economic recession and it can boast economic growth throughout the entire crisis duration so far. Simultaneously, it has faced several dilemmas when making the decisions related to the directions of economic and social policies. On the one hand, it was drawn to seemingly attractive proposals to pursue economic reforms aimed at reducing public spending, and consequently at decreasing public finance sector deficit, as recommended by the European Commission (2009) and the International Monetary Fund (2009). On the other hand, Poland analysed the effects of the packages stimulating economic revival introduced, among others, by the USA or Germany. In the following years, of equal importance was the analysis of the outcomes of the crisis for the functioning of the welfare state. Those issues were presented in the works, inter alia, of Vis et al. (2011), Farnsworth and Irving (2012) and Anioł (2011). Eventually it seems that Poland

has come up with its own model of response to the economic crisis, using various instruments of economic, financial and social policies, and above all by taking advantage of its
membership in the EU.

This text aims to analyse Poland's responses to the economic crisis and demonstrate
their effects as well as to identify the elements that determined the undisputed success
of Poland in coping with the consequences of the crisis. An attempt will be also made
to answer the question whether there are far-reaching differences between Polish government's responses to the first and the second waves of the crisis. And if yes, what they followed from. The analysis is supplemented with demonstration of potential long-term
consequences of the decisions made during the crisis for the social and economic situation
in the future.

Two Waves of the Economic Crisis

The fall of Lehman Brothers bank in September 2008 spurred the first global economic
crisis of the twenty-fist century, which was compared to the worldwide events that took
place in the 1930s (de Córdoba & Kehoe, 2009; Roubini & Mihm, 2010). Five years
after its onset, we can identify two phases of the crisis. The first one took place in the
period 2008–09, when negative consequences of the perturbations in the US financial
sector were manifested (The Economist, 2013). It ended in relative stability of the financial
and banking sector being secured. The second wave of the crisis started in early 2011, when
it became evident that the assistance provided to Greece so far to protect it against bankruptcy had been inadequate and it became necessary to provide another aid instalment to
that country (European Council, 2011). In contrast to the first phase of the crisis, the
second one is characterised by problems with solvency of states' public finance systems
instead of issues with the stability of the private financial sector. The hypothesis of two
phases of the crisis is corroborated also by conclusions from the analysis of economic
growth in the period 2008–13. They demonstrate that we experienced the greatest problems
in 2009 and 2011. In this connection, it seems justified to analyse and present the consequences of the crisis as well as the responses of the states affected separately for the first
and second phases.

Poland's Response in the First Period of the Crisis and the Socio-Economic Effects of the Undertaken Measures

The fact that the crisis failed to be envisaged by a decisive majority of economists
resulted in declining trust in the offered recipes and, more generally, in the ability of
economic sciences to propose exit strategies. The disputes as regards the causes of,
and methods of coping with, the crisis are well illustrated by the discussion inspired in
2009 by the article of Krugman (2009).[2] In his opinion it was a mistake to assume
that to prevent crises it suffices just to reduce government interventions in the
economy and to make sure that the Central Bank takes care of constant increase of
money supply. Therefore to recover from the crisis it is central to increase the government
spending (market intervention), which is tantamount, with some obvious modifications, to
the concept of Keynes (1936). Such an approach had been put forward by Krugman also
in his fundamental critique of neo-liberalism published two years before (Krugman,
2007). Meanwhile proponents of neo-classical economy tried to prove at that time, in

response to the stimulus package of President Obama, that government spending would not translate into adequate private spending increase, and consequently would fail to contribute to economic revival, while simultaneously resulting in increased state indebtedness and growing imbalance of the public finance system (Barro, 2009). The discussion of economists was transposed directly into debates of politicians, who have supported one or the other party of the dispute. A discussion on the best strategy for Poland to combat the crisis rolled also across the Polish political scene. On the one hand, politicians of left-wing and right-wing parties alike called for drafting of a generous stimulus package, mainly targeted at enterprises operating in the industry. On the other hand, though, the government of that time (composed of centre-leftist Civic Platform party and a peasants' party – the Polish Peasants' Party), which was appointed in late 2007, assessed that a potential stimulus package would be costly, while its effects – limited. This does not mean that the government espoused the neo-liberal approach. It decided against any fundamental spending reduction, although at that time several major reforms were carried into effect, such as raising retirement age to 67 for both women and men.

As the central approach in the measures constituting Poland's response to the economic crisis, the government chose intermingling of economic processes and internationalisation of the effects of financial and economic policy decisions made in particular states. This concerns in particular the states and international organisations that play a central role in the global economy. Here, we can quote Mazurek (2007, p. 8), who states that economic recession spreads out easily in geographic dimension in the globalised world, and it does not matter whether the countries concerned border with each other or not. This explains why the crisis that started in the US banking sector was carried to Europe so swiftly. Simultaneously, it should be pointed out that the proliferation of the effects of economic processes concerns not only crisis phenomena but also economic recovery. Just as the crisis moves from state to state, improvement of the economic standing and economic optimism in some states brings about positive effects in others. Therefore, Polish policy-makers decided that actions taken in other markets and in the frames of the EU – rather that a national stimulus package – will have a decisive impact on the Polish economy. The analysis of the government's positions and statements by politicians of the ruling parties indicates that two arguments were of central importance when decisions were made against introduction of a stimulus package.

First, a large portion of the Polish economy is closely connected with the German economy. Over 25 per cent of Polish exports go to Germany (Table 1). It was assumed that the German stimulus package (the Pact for employment and stability), passed by the Angela Merkel government in 2009 (Bundesregierung, 2009), would bring positive outcomes for Poland too. It was hoped that the investments made in Germany would result in increased volume of orders for Polish enterprises cooperating with German companies, and this will help keep the jobs. It is true that early on into the crisis, that is in 2009, Poland recorded a decline of exports to Germany, but already in 2010 the export increased again, reaching a level comparable to 2008 (Table 1). This means that the government was correct to assume that the German stimulus package would translate into growth of Polish exports, and would consequently affect Poland's economic situation.

It is also worthwhile pointing out that economic connections between Germany and Poland translate into political cooperation. Schweiger (2014, pp. 5–7) points out that enhanced economic and political cooperation between those two states is highly significant

Table 1. Export from Poland to Germany in the period 2005–12

Year	Export (USD million)	Share of Germany in export from Poland (per cent)
2005	25,204.6	28.2
2006	29,806.9	27.2
2007	35,945.3	25.9
2008	42,384.2	25.0
2009	35,800.0	26.2
2010	41,696.7	26.1
2011	49,654.6	26.1
2012	46,349.8	25.1

Source: Elaborated by the author on the basis of the data from the Central Statistical Office (2007, 2009, 2011, 2013).

not only for bilateral relations, but also for the future of the EU, because it testifies to the growing importance of Poland in the international arena.

The second factor that determined resignation from pursuance of a stimulus package was the assumption that such a role could be played by transfers from the EU budget in the frames of investments co-financed from structural funds and the Cohesion Fund. It was expected that the largest volume of such funding will come to Poland in the period 2009–12. Therefore, top priority was assigned to the use of structural funds, particularly as regards investments in road infrastructure and human capital (Ministry of Regional Development, 2006).

The analysis of the trends presented in Table 2 and Figure 1 demonstrates that the government forecasts of 2008 and 2009 proved to be correct. In the period 2009–12, Poland received over EUR 36 billion more than it paid as contributions to the EU budget. In that period spending from the Cohesion Fund and structural funds was the main item on the list of financial flows between Poland and the EU.

Depreciation of Polish currency was an important factor with positive impact on Polish export and the scale of transfers from the EU budget. In 2009, the average exchange rate of Polish zloty to the euro and US dollar was 23.1 per cent and 29.3 per cent, respectively, weaker than the annual average exchange rate of Polish currency in 2008 (Ministry of Economy, 2010). The weakening of Polish currency at the turn of 2008 and 2009 improved

Table 2. Net transfers from the EU budget to Poland in the period 2004–12 (EUR)

Year	Net amount (balance)	Cohesion fund	Structural funds
2004	1,158,651,353	0	840,975,083
2005	1,615,700,832	0	775,489,907
2006	2,712,352,921	255,730,261	1,624,939,595
2007	4,581,863,142	939,736,508	3,448,257,787
2008	3,986,437,621	1,332,079,814	3,446,708,115
2009	6,011,906,999	2,269,217,223	3,726,732,940
2010	7,737,593,561	2,163,929,765	5,377,936,911
2011	10,492,317,046	2,610,487,227	7,114,227,955
2012	11,869,627,863	3,174,473,034	7,270,509,259

Source: Elaborated by the author on the basis of data from the Ministry of Finance.

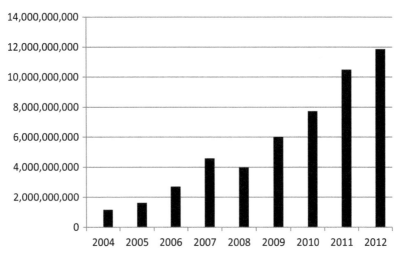

Figure 1. Balance of settlements with the EU in the period 2004–12
Source: Elaborated by the author on the basis of data from the Ministry of Finance.

the competitiveness of the goods manufactured in Poland and of the services rendered by Polish economic entities. Therefore, it should be assumed that Poland's non-membership in the eurozone had a positive impact on how Polish companies coped with the outcomes of the crisis. What is very interesting is that as late as in September 2008 Prime Minister Donald Tusk declared that the government he headed would aim to accede to the eurozone in 2011 (Tusk, 2008). He has never withdrawn this declaration, but simultaneously even in early 2009 it turned out that adoption of the single currency in Poland in 2011 would be impossible. Presently no specific date of membership in the eurozone is given. The government does declare that accession to the eurozone is among its priorities, but simultaneously it admits that a date of the adoption of a single currency cannot be precisely determined until the crisis ends (Polish Press Agency, 2013).

Thus the German stimulus package, transfers from the EU budget reinforced by Poland's non-participation in the eurozone, was a significant impulse for maintenance of economic growth and of jobs in the first years of the crisis. Simultaneously, with a view to preventing negative effects of the crisis, in early 2009 the government decided to undertake legislative actions that would allow for support to the enterprises that might fall into difficulties as a result of the economic slowdown. The government decided to adopt a package of instruments aimed at avoiding the fall of businesses experiencing temporary problems. In reality in 2009, for the first time in Poland's history, a decision was made to introduce preventive measures. Spytek-Bandurska and Szylko-Skoczny (2012) think that starting from the beginning of transformation in Poland that is since 1989, preventive measures were underestimated in economic policy and preference was given to measures stimulating creation of new jobs instead of applying instruments protecting the existing jobs. At the same time, several papers indicate that in the times of crisis it is better to support employers in maintenance of employment than to finance social benefits and occupational activation instruments (European Commission, 2010, Schmid, 2013).

It must be also stressed that the anti-crisis measures introduced in 2009 were developed via a social dialogue. At that time the government adopted a rule that it would introduce only the solutions developed in the frames of the works of the special commission (the Tripartite Commission for Social and Economic Affairs) composed of the representatives of trade unions, employer organisations and government. The following should be listed as the major instruments among those eventually contained in the so-called 'anti-crisis' act (The Act on ... 2009):

- Extension of the working time settlement period to a maximum of 12 months, which enabled entrepreneurs to plan a diversified number of working hours in particular months. The periods of longer work had to be offset by periods of shorter work in the adopted settlement period that is in the maximum period of 12 months.
- Introduction of the option to conclude any number of employment contracts for a definite time within a period of 24 months, but only if the breaks between particular contracts are shorter than 3 months.
- Provision of financial support to entrepreneurs who were recognised as 'being in a difficult situation', consisting of payment of benefits to their employees in partial settlement of remuneration in the outage period.

The aforementioned instruments may be considered as ones improving the flexibility of the work organisation and beneficial first and foremost for entrepreneurs, because on the one hand they gave them immense freedom in the organisation of working time, while reducing the costs of pursuance of business activity on the other (e.g. no need to pay additional remuneration for overtime). According to the act, the instruments contained therein were in force until 31 December 2011, because when the bill was drafted it was assumed that the economic crisis would be of a temporary nature and flexible solutions under labour law would not have to be applied in the longer term.

The data sourced from the Polish Ministry of Labour and Social Policy and from the State Labour Inspection suggest that the period of application of the instruments contained in the 'anti-crisis' act was very limited. Only slightly over 1000 entrepreneurs took advantage of them (State Labour Inspection, 2011). Most of them were interested in extension of the settlement period. To a much smaller extent, entrepreneurs were interested in taking advantage of the benefits to cover remuneration costs.

The analysis of the instruments intended to be Poland's response to the economic crisis allows for formulation of a conclusion that employers were supposed to be their main beneficiaries. Legislation measures went in the direction of making labour law more flexible, giving to employers a greater freedom in the management of their staff. This, however, failed to bring about the expected effects. Simultaneously, the government decided against introduction of protective packages or increased transfers to the unemployed. It needs to be stressed yet again, however, that the direction of reinforcement of employers was accepted at that time by a prevailing majority of trade unions. This can be explained by fear of the expected effects of the crisis and adoption of the priority of the existing jobs. As the future was to demonstrate, this approach was dramatically changed in the period 2013–14, when already the second package of measures was ready; it was aimed to provide an impulse for the Polish economy during the second wave of the crisis.

In recapitulation, a decisive, positive impact on Poland's economic and social situation in the first period of the crisis was exerted by general economic processes related to participation in the single market and use of EU structural policy. Poland took advantage, among others, of the stimulus package introduced in Germany and transfers from the

EU budget in the frames of cohesion policy. At the same time, legislative measures, particularly the so-called 'anti-crisis' act, had definitely much less influence on prevention of negative outcomes of the economic crisis.

Polish Economy and Government's Actions during the Second Wave of the Crisis

The relative good standing of the Polish economy in the first period of the crisis, particularly compared to other states of the region, afforded hope that also during the second wave spurred by the events in Greece, Poland would not record economic recession, and the situation on the labour market would not deteriorate, particularly because the largest transfers from the EU budget were expected in the period 2011–13. As a result the government postponed its response to the second wave of the crisis until early 2012. Simultaneously, the internal situation proved to be much more complex at that time. The negotiations on legal regulations proposed by the government were broken off by the trade union side. Representatives of employees came to a conclusion that the government failed to take their postulates into account and continues adopting a direction accordant with the postulates of employers (Związki poza … , 2013). In their opinion, the time had come to introduce instruments that both reduced labour law flexibility and increased employment stability. What is interesting is that the intention of the government adopted in late 2013 and announced for 2014 seems to respond to a much greater extent to postulates of trade unions than those of 2009. Simultaneously, the package of government proposals presented in 2013 was supposed, just as in 2009, to complement economic measures. The analysis of government strategy (Chancellery of the Prime Minister of Poland, 2013; Ministry of Labour and Social Policy, 2014) suggests that in the forthcoming years it will focus on the following actions aimed at exerting a positive impact on the Polish economy and coping with the consequences of the crisis:

- Fast launch of the European funds under financial perspective 2014–20.
- Increase in pro-developmental spending in the expenditure of the government and local government sector institutions, which should translate into competitiveness growth.
- Assurance of public finance stability through a change of pension reform.
- Re-launch of mechanisms improving the flexibility of employment conditions accompanied by presentation of proposals targeted at employees.

Adoption of such a catalogue of priorities shows that the government upheld its position accordant to which the standing of the Polish economy depends to the largest extent on external factors. Therefore, Poland should use first and foremost its competitive advantages and membership in the EU. A new element comprises introduction of significant changes in labour market policies, which were intended to lead to restoration of the solutions that had been contained in the anti-crisis act of 2009 but expired on 31 December 2011 on the one hand, while also leading to regular salary increases and reduction of the attractiveness of hiring employees on contracts not based upon Labour Code. Simultaneously, as I have already pointed out, legislative measures are supposed merely to supplement measures of general economic nature.

In reference to the first priority connected with transfers from the EU budget, it should be noted that as a result of the negotiations on the financial perspective 2014–20, Poland obtained the net amount (after deduction of the contribution to the EU budget) of over

EUR 70 billion (European Council, 2013). In practice, it use will be possible starting from 2015. At the same time, the investments financed under the previous financial perspective are completed now in 2014. This means that Poland has a chance to move smoothly from one financial perspective to another, which should secure uninterrupted inflow of financing from the EU budget for deployment of investments. According to government proposals, financing from the EU budget is to be spent on four major priorities (Ministry of Regional Development, 2013).

- Increasing innovativeness of the economy, among others, by ensuring conditions for growth of demand for the results of scientific research.
- Increasing the use of digital technologies as support to dissemination of innovation and creativity on the one hand, and as an element conducive for activities in the area of social inclusion on the other.
- Development of human capital, comprising the basis for creativity and innovation of the society.
- Increasing the external and internal transport accessibility – as a completion of the process of modernisation and extension of transport connections between voivodeship cities and those helping incorporate national networks into 'TEN-T'.

The analysis of the aforementioned priorities shows that with the use of funding from the EU, Poland intends to change its economic policies into a more innovative one. This is indirectly related to experiences of coping with the outcomes of the crisis. This is accordant with the approach presented in the strategic documents of the government, pointing out to the necessity to improve the competitiveness of the Polish economy so that it could take even better advantage of the single market within the EU and compete against other states of the world. So the transfers are to be used to stimulate Polish economy in the time of crisis, at the same time lending to it an impulse to modernise.

Similar targets are to be accomplished under the second priority of Poland's response to the second wave of the crisis, that is, increased share of development spending in the expenditure of the sector of government and local government institutions. According to government strategy, the share of development spending is to rise from 36.2 per cent in 2010 to 41 per cent in 2015 (Chancellery of the Prime Minister of Poland, 2013, p. 65). Public investments in science and research, culture and health were recognised as the main areas of development spending. Simultaneously, it was assumed that social transfer will decrease as a result of increased wages and occupational activity, which will in turn lead to greater self-sustainability of households. It was also stressed that 'EU funds are important but they are not and will never be a sufficient guarantee of development' (Chancellery of the Prime Minister of Poland, 2013, p. 67), which necessitates pursuance of a policy of balance in public finance. Such an approach contends that the period of the second wave of the crisis was to be used for consolidation of public spending so as not to lose financial solvency and to avoid, given the very negative assumptions, the Greek or Cypriot scenario. Therefore, it was assumed that the increase in development spending will be financed from transfers of funding between particular priorities and not from debt growth.

Maintenance of public debt at a low level was to be achieved also by the introduction of far-reaching changes in pension reform, which was introduced in Poland in 1999. The tri-pillar pension introduced back then was based upon individual pension accounts. The first pillar is managed by a public institution, namely the Social Insurance Institution, and is of repartition nature. The second pillar comprises open pension funds, which received 7.3 per cent of remuneration in the period 1999–2011. Private and voluntary pension insurance comprises the third pillar. Present changes in the Polish pension system concern mainly the second pillar. From 1 May 2011, the share of the contributions transferred to open pension funds was decreased from 7.3 per cent to 2.3 per cent. The remaining 5 per cent goes to a separate, individual account in the Social Insurance Institution. Another reform was carried out in 2013. It consists of far-reaching changes, which may in practice put an end to the three-pillar structure of the system. According to the reform Poles can make a decision by the end of July 2014 whether they want to remain in open pension funds or prefer to transfer their savings to the Social Insurance Institution. Moreover, the money collected in open pension funds will no longer be allowed to be invested in state treasury bonds, which was possible before the changes entered into force. The main argument in support of the introduction of the pension reform is the costs of the functioning of the existing pension system for the state budget. In practice, it was the government who had to bear the costs of disbursement of present pensions that were acquired under *pay as you go* principle, which required issuing of bonds to cover the deficit in the budget of the Social Insurance Institution. The bonds were in turn eagerly purchased by open pension funds. This model brought extremely negative consequences to the level of public debt. At the same time introduction of the reform translates in practice into departure from the model based on combination of the repartition (first pillar) and capital (second pillar), which offers greater security for disbursement and level of pensions in the future, but, as has been already stressed, is very costly in the introduction phase (Ministry of Labour and Social Policy and Ministry of Finance, 2013). Analyses and opinion have emerged in the public debate that without the pension reform the public debt is likely to exceed 60 per cent in the forthcoming years, which would be very negative for the Polish economy. Simultaneously, the increase in public debt is directly related not to the crisis but to non-action on the spending side of the state budget (Denderski & Paczos, 2013). Some experts argue that had the government used the times of the crisis to limit the privileges of certain social groups, e.g. farmers or unformed services (because this expenditure generates state indebtedness), introduction of changes in the pension system would not be necessary (Bitner & Otto, 2013). In recapitulation, by introducing the pension reform the government avoided the risk in which the second wave of the crisis causes insolvency of public institutions and it has thus avoided spending cuts, which such countries as, e.g., Greece, Ireland or Spain had to do. Simultaneously, it seems that considering the fact that the crisis protracts, reduction of spending, e.g. under social policy, will be still necessary.

In the case of the fourth priority concerning re-launch of the solutions known from the 'anti-crisis' act of 2009, a question arises about arguments supporting such a decision. As has been already pointed out, solutions consisting of the extension of the settlement period or the rules of employees' remuneration during so-called economic outage have not enjoyed interest of employers so far. In contrast to tripartite negotiations of 2009, this time government proposals encountered resistance from the trade unions that end in negotiations break-off. Eventually those solutions entered into force, but it is expected that their relevance for coping with the second wave of the crisis will be again very limited (Act … , 2013).

Proposals related to employment terms and combating unemployment are much more interesting and have much greater potential. In January 2014, the Minister of Labour and Social Policy announced adoption of several instruments aimed at increasing employment stability, generating regular wage rises and improving the chances for the unemployed to find jobs (Polish Press Agency, 2014). The following elements are to contribute to those targets:

- Changes in commission contracts (contracts concluded on the basis of the Civil Code, not Labour Code) through introduction of the obligation to pay social insurance contributions, which will make such contracts less attractive.
- Further consistent raising of the minimum salary.
- Introduction of the facility to obtain financial support by the persons who decide to undertake employment outside their place of residence.
- Provision of employment vouchers to youth (people under 30), which will help them to obtain the first job by lowering the costs borne by the employer.
- Reform of labour offices, which should improve the quality of services and shorten the time for which people remain unemployed.

The first two of the aforementioned proposals give rise to the greatest controversies. In the case of changes in commission contracts, one can fear that the costs of social insurance contributions will be transferred to employees, which will adversely affect the amounts of remunerations. Simultaneously, further continuing the current situation might have very negative consequences in the future because persons hired pursuant to commission contracts will have very low pension benefits, thus dramatically increasing their risk of poverty. Moreover, creditworthiness of such persons is very limited. The loan offer for persons employed pursuant to commission contracts governed by the Civil Code is more expensive than the offer targeted at people with employment contracts, as banks collect additional amount to insure the loans, thus increasing their costs. The government proposal addresses the problems related to abuse by employers of commission contracts in hiring employees in the situations when employment contracts would be more appropriate.

Similar controversies are aroused by the position concerning continued rises in the minimum salary (Table 3). Within the recent three years (2011–13) it has increased by over 15 per cent (notwithstanding inflation). In the same period, average salary in the national economy rose by 7.9 per cent. This means that the minimum to average salary ratio has improved. In the period 2011–13, this ration improved for the benefit of minimum salary by 2.8 percentage points. At the same time, trade unions continue to put forward the postulate that minimum salary should correspond to 50 per cent of

Table 3. Changes in minimum salaries in Poland in the period 2011–13 in polish zloty (PLN)

Year	Amount of minimum salary (PLN) as of 1 January	Amount of average salary (PLN) as of the end of Q1	Minimum salary as a percentage of average salary
2011	1386.00	3466.33	39.98
2012	1500.00	3646.09	41.14
2013	1600.00	3740.05	42.78

Source: Elaborated by the author on the basis of data from the Central Statistical Office (2007, 2009, 2011, 2013).

average salary in the national economy (Inicjatywa ... , 2013). In this case it can be feared that further rise in minimum salary may result in growth of employment in a grey economy or reduce competitiveness of some sectors that build their advantages on low salaries. Simultaneously, the minimum salary rise programme is accordant with the priority to modernise the Polish economy, which is to be based more on innovation than low salaries in the future.

The proposals presented in January 2014 demonstrate that the government is willing to meet the postulates of trade unions. The proposed instruments should increase the stability of employment for those groups of employees who are currently very rarely hired pursuant to contracts for indefinite time. In my opinion, negotiation break-off by trade unions is just one of the factors that resulted in elaboration and publication of new government proposals. The main argument was constituted by realisation of the fact that one of the consequences of the crisis is lack of employment stability among large social groups (e.g. youth) and the risk of 'working poor' phenomenon (Duszczyk, 2009). Therefore, balance in the labour market should be restored. This purpose is also to be served by regular rises of the minimum salary, that is, by stimulation of salary growth.

Poland's Response to Two Waves of the Crisis – An Attempt at Recapitulation

The analysis of Poland's response to two waves of the crisis shows both fundamental similarities and differences. In both cases, the impact of Poland's participation in the single market on the economic and social situation in Poland was recognised as a central concern. Therefore, the government focused on maintenance of the competitiveness of enterprises operating in Poland and promotion of their export activities through actions improving labour law flexibility. Similar are also the actions concerning the use of financing from the EU budget as a stimulus for Polish economy, although in the case of financial perspective 2014–20, priority was definitely given to innovation growth. The main difference is to be found in the priorities for legislative measures. In 2009, priority was definitely assigned to growth of labour market flexibility and promotion of measures targeted at meeting the needs of entrepreneurs; on the other hand, in 2013, besides flexibility instruments, there emerged new regulations as postulated by trade unions, particularly those targeted at employment stability growth and remuneration-level increase. This shows the evolution of the discussion and acceptance of the arguments that for the response to the crisis to be adequate it is important to ensure equilibrium in the labour market as regards employment terms. It must be also stressed that during both phases of the crisis the government decided against reforms reducing spending from the public finance system, deeming them unnecessary in the Polish situation.

Poland's Socio-Economic Situation during the Crisis

In the debate about the economic crisis, Poland is very often highlighted as an example of a state that copes best with its consequences among all EU member states (The Economist, 2012; La Republica, 2014). The analysis of statistical data corroborates this opinion. Simultaneously, we cannot consider that Poland has not been affected by negative consequences of the crisis. On the one hand the data concerning economic growth show that in the period 2009–13 Poland recorded stable economic growth (Figure 2). This helped close the gap between Poland and best developed EU member states.

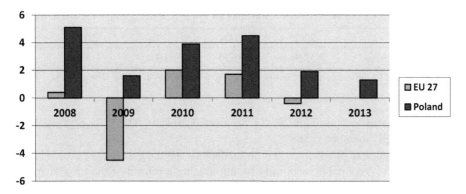

Figure 2. Real GDP growth rate in 2009–13 in Poland and UE (27)
Source: Eurostat.

Also the analysis of the consequences of the crisis for labour market shows that the unemployment rate in Poland remained at the level of EU average, while exceeding it slightly in the case of youth unemployment (Table 4). It must be borne in mind that as late as in 2005 the unemployment rate in Poland amounted to almost 20 per cent and was the highest in the Community at that time.

On the other hand, though, those two indicators, which are most frequently presented in the discussions about the effects of the crisis for Poland, fail to fully reflect the present economic and social situation. As an example, the analysis of the scale of emigration and return migration shows that despite the indisputable success of Poland in combating the crisis, the number of Poles residing in other EU member states has not declined, and in the period 2011–12 it started to rise again (Table 5). This shows that Polish migrants still perceive the situation in receiving states as more stable than the one in Poland. This also means that despite absence of drastic unemployment growth in Poland and a really good situation in the Polish labour market compared, e.g., to such countries as Ireland or Spain, which received large groups of emigrants from Poland in the past, this has not provided sufficient impulse for them to return.

Similar conclusions as to ambiguity of the socio-economic situation of Poland can be drawn from the analysis of the data showing the risk of poverty. In the period 2009–12, the percentage of households at risk of poverty, after social transfers, did not decline

Table 4. Total and youth unemployment rate (under the age of 25) in Poland (PL) and the UE (27) in the period 2008–13

Year	Total unemployment rate PL	Total unemployment rate EU	Youth unemployment rate PL	Youth unemployment rate EU
2008	7.1	7.1	17.2	15.8
2009	8.1	9.0	20.6	20.1
2010	9.7	9.7	23.7	21.1
2011	9.7	9.7	25.8	21.4
2012	10.1	10.5	26.5	22.9
2013 (November)	10.2	10.9	27.9	23.6

Source: Eurostat.

Table 5. Changes in the number of emigrants temporarily residing in the EU (thousands)

Year	2008	2009	2010	2011	2012
Number of emigrants	1820	1690	1607	1670	1720

Source: Elaborated by the author on the basis of the data from the Central Statistical Office (2013).

and still amounted to approximately 17 per cent (Eurostat). This is one of the highest figures for all EU member states.

Also the standing of public finance is unsatisfactory and the government avoided the risk of losing control over public debt only by introducing a reform of the tri-pillar pension system and taking over a majority of funds collected in open pension funds.

In recapitulation, Poland has so far coped quite well with the consequences of the economic crisis, but at the same time there is still a serious risk that the situation will change and the potential third wave of the crisis will cause serious disturbances in the Polish economy. It must be borne in mind that in the forthcoming years the demographic situation of Poland is going to change. As consecutive age groups retire, increased expenditure will be generated; so Polish government may face the necessity to introduce reforms in the public finance system. The uncertainty concerning a positive scenario for the development of the Polish economy is also evidenced by the fact that Poland maintains access to a special, flexible credit line of the International Monetary Fund, which may be launched in the case of difficulties with servicing the public debt.

Conclusion

Poland's membership in the EU and use of competitive advantages of Polish enterprises has proven decisive in coping with the consequences of the economic crisis in both its phases. Maintenance of high export levels and inflow of financing from the EU budget have proven to be sufficient impulses to keep economic growth during the crisis. At the same time, the undertaken legislative actions have turned out to be hardly useful. Presently, it is very difficult to foresee a future development scenario for Poland. It will depend on whether the forecasts heralding imminent end of the crisis prove to be correct. If those forecasts materialise, in the forthcoming years Poland is likely to continue advancing on a further development path and come closer to the EU average and improve the living quality of its citizens. Simultaneously, if following phases of the crisis come about, it may turn out that the measure taken so far have been inadequate and absence of structural reforms will make it extremely difficult to find funding for development measures. Nevertheless, presently the former scenario seems much more likely.

Notes

[1] Throughout the text I use the term 'economic crisis' in its colloquial sense, while being well aware of the fact that from 2007 to 2013 we can rather speak of economic recession, because some of the member states recorded GDP decline in real terms for at least two consecutive months. From such a view, Poland has recorded economic slowdown characterised by economic growth pace slump and not recession per se.

[2] Similar views to Krugman's are shared also, among others, by Joseph Stiglitz and Edmund s. Phelps.

References

Act of 1st July 2009 *on relieving the outcomes of economic crisis for employees and entrepreneurs* (Journals of Laws of 2009 No. 125, item 1035).

Act on 11th October 2013 *on particular solutions connected with job protection* (Journal of Laws 2013 item 1291).

Anioł, W. (2011) *Kryzys finansowy w Europie. Reperkusje dla polityki społecznej*, Polityka Społeczna No. 4 (Warsaw: Institute of Labour and Social Affairs).

Barro, J. R. (2009) Government spending is no free lunch. Now the democrats are peddling voodoo economics, *The Wall Street Journal*, 22 January.

Bitner, M. & Otto, W. (2013) *OFE – pytania i odpowiedzi* (Warsaw: Civic Committee for Pension Security).

Bundesregierung. (2009) *Pakt für Beschäftigung und Stabilität in Deutschland zur Sicherung der Arbeitsplätze, Stärkung der Wachstumskräfte und Modernisierung des Landes* (Berlin: Bundesregierung).

Chancellery of the Prime Minister of Poland. (2013) *Trzecia fala nowoczesności. Długookresowa Strategia Rozwoju Kraju*, (Warsaw: Chancellery of the Prime Minister of Poland).

Central Statistical Office. (2013) *Informacja o rozmiarach i kierunkach emigracji z Polski w latach 2004–2012* (Warsaw: Central Statistical Office).

Central Statistical Office. (2007, 2009, 2011, 2013) *Yearbook* (Warsaw: Central Statistical Office).

de Córdoba, G. F. & Kehoe, T. J. (2009) *The Current Financial Crisis: What Should We Learn from the Great Depressions of the Twentieth Century?* Federal Reserve Bank of Minneapolis Research Department Staff Report 421.

Denderski, P. & Paczos, W. (2013) Czy zmiany w OFE to przygotowanie do bankructwa kraju? *Gazeta Wyborcza*, 31 August (Warsaw: Agora).

Duszczyk, M. (2009) Pogłębianie nierówności. Grupy społeczne zagrożone a kryzys gospodarczy, in: M. Księżopolski, B. Rysz-Kowlaczyk & C. Żolędowski (Eds) *Polityka społeczna w kryzysie*, pp. 145–156 (Warsaw: The Institute of Social Policy of the Warsaw University).

The Economist. (2012) Learning from abroad. Don't forget Poland, 18 December.

The Economist. (2013) Crash course, 7 September.

European Commission. (2009) *Communication of 4th March 2009 for European Council Summit on 19-20 March* (Brussels: European Commission).

European Commission. (2010) *Employment in Europe 2010* (Luxemburg: Publications Office of the European Union).

European Council. (2011) *European Council Conclusions from the Meeting on 23rd-24th June 2011, EUCO 23/1/ 11 REV 1* (Brussels: European Council).

European Council. (2013) *European Council Conclusions from the Meeting on 7th-8th February 2013, EUCO 3/ 13* (Brussels: European Council).

Farnsworth, K. & Irving, Z. (Eds.) (2012) *Social Policy in Challenging Times: Economic Crisis and Welfare Systems* (Bristol: Bristol Policy Press).

Inicjatywa ustawodawcza 'Podnieśmy Polakom płacę minimalną'. (2013) Available at http://www. placaminimalna.pl/index.php/o-inicjatywie-ustawodawczej (accessed 22 January 2014).

International Monetary Fund. (2009) *Review of Recent Crisis Programs* (Washington, DC: International Monetary Fund).

Keynes, M. J. (1936) *The General Theory of Employment, Interest and Money* (New York: Palgrave Macmillan reprint 2007).

Krugman, P. (2007) *The Conscience of a Liberal* (New York, London: W.W. Norton and Company).

Krugman, P. (2009) How did economists get it so wrong? *The New York Times Magazine*, 2 September.

La Repubblica. (2014) Polonia l'Europa senza euro, 19 January.

Mazurek, S. (2007) *Mechanizm międzynarodowej transmisji kryzysów gospodarczych* (Wrocław: Economic University in Wrocław).

Ministry of Economy. (2010) *Rozwój wymiany towarowej Polski z zagranicą w latach 2005-2009* (Warsaw: Ministry of Economy).

Ministry of Labour and Social Policy. (2014) *Pakt dla pracy* (Warsaw: Ministry of Labour and Social Policy).

Ministry of Labour and Social Policy and the Ministry of Finance. (2013) *Przegląd funkcjonowania systemu emerytalnego* (Warsaw: Ministry of Labour and Social Policy and the Ministry of Finance).

Ministry of Regional Development. (2006) *Narodowe Strategiczne Ramy Odniesienia 2007-2013* (Warsaw: Ministry of Regional Development).

Ministry of Regional Development. (2013) *Programowanie perspektywy finansowej 2014-2020 – uwarunkowania strategiczne* (Warsaw: Ministry of Regional Development).

Polish Press Agency. (2013) *Prezydent Bronisław Komorowski i Premier Donald Tusk za wejściem Polski do strefy Euro – komunikat po posiedzeniu Rady Gabinetowej w dniu 26 lutego 2013 roku* (Warsaw: Polish Press Agency).

Polish Press Agency. (2014) *Kosiniak-Kamysz: w 2014 r. zaproponujemy pakt dla pracy.* Available at http://www.pap.pl/palio/html.run?_Instance=cms_www.pap.pl&_PageID=1&s=infopakiet&dz=gospodarka&idNewsComp=138832&filename=&idnews=142143&data=&status=biezace&_CheckSum=1675479203 (accessed 22 January 2014).

Roubini, N. & Mihm, S. (2010) *Crisis Economics: A Crash Course in the Future of Finance* (New York: Penguin Press).

Schmid, G. (2013) *Inclusive Growth: What Future for the European Social Model?* OSE Opinion Paper No. 15 (Brussels: European Social Observatory).

Schweiger, Ch. (2014) Poland, variable geometry and the enlarged European Union, *Europe-Asia Studies*, 66(3), pp. 394–420.

Spytek-Bandurska, G. & Szylko-Skoczy, M. (2012) *Ocena wykonania ustawy antykryzysowej,* Polityka Społeczna No. 1 (Warsaw: Institute of Labour and Social Affairs).

State Labour Inspection. (2011) *Informacja na temat stosowania przepisów ustawy z dnia 1 lipca 2009 r. o łagodzeniu skutków kryzysu ekonomicznego dla pracowników i przedsiębiorców* (Warsaw: State Labour Inspection).

Tusk, D. (2008) *Wystąpienie na Forum Ekonomicznym w Krynicy w dniu 3 września 2013 r* (Warsaw: Government Information Centre).

Vis, B., van Kersbergen, K. & Hylands, T. (2011) To what extent did the financial crisis intensify the pressure to reform the welfare state, *Social Policy & Administration*, 45(1), pp. 338–353.

Związki poza Komisją Trójstronną. (2013) Available at http://www.solidarnosc.gda.pl/aktualnosci/z-ostatniej-chwili-zwizki-poza-komisj-trjstronn/ (accessed 22 January 2014).

Hungary and the Eurozone – the Need for a More Systemic Approach

OLIVÉR KOVÁCS

ICEG European Centre, Budapest, Hungary

ABSTRACT   *This contribution purports to illustrate why a more systemic approach is needed when it comes to considering the Eurozone accession in case of Hungary. The paper first dwells on the issue of macroeconomic instability in case of Hungary from a regional perspective by devoting attention to its 'lagging behind' phenomena which call our attention to the necessity of a more holistic approach in supporting the Hungarian Eurozone accession. Then it emphasises that the challenges we are facing today imply that the role of governance and the quality of state are heavily appreciating; and we argue that Eurozone accession needs good governance which incorporates the issue of public-sector innovation in a more dedicated way in tackling old and new challenges in supporting sustained growth and development as prerequisites of Eurozone accession as well.*

1. Introduction

The current problem of the Eurozone lies to a large extent in its history in the sense that the sheer fulfilment of the entry criteria in algebraic terms does not guarantee the successful integration afterwards. With the advent of the Great Recession due to the juggernaut effect of the recent financial and economic crisis as well as the lacklustre crisis management entailed with wicked policies, uncertainty over the future started to rise.

Importantly, uncertainty is not an independently existing phenomenon (*objectum*) that should be identified and estimated; it is therefore the dynamically evolving pattern of perceptions (*subjectum*) over economic policies. Since the importance of a momentum can be even higher if it generates significant differences in the experience and perceptions of another momentum, uncertainties become a complex web of mutually reinforcing phenomena perceived dynamically over time. This was explicitly the case after the eruption of the Greek crisis when financial markets' confidence with regard to Spain and Portugal was also crumbled because their tolerance level against the degree of macroeconomic instability (linked to international competitiveness and sustainability of public finances) lowered substantially.

As a corollary, the fervent need for macroeconomic stability was not reversed into the oblivion; all the more, the role of national states has been heavily appreciating in supporting not only the meaningful Eurozone accession but also macroeconomic stability that can dampen uncertainties.

Hungary must also act in a similar vein, where the socio-economic development has been showing a certain sign of deterioration and what is more, the real convergence seems to be stuck. We approach the issue of the Hungarian Eurozone accession in a new-fangled way. Our paper purports to illustrate why a more systemic approach is needed when it comes to considering the Eurozone accession in case of Hungary.

The paper *first* addresses the issue of macroeconomic instability in case of Hungary from a regional perspective by devoting attention to its 'lagging behind' phenomena which call our attention to the necessity of a more holistic approach in supporting the Hungarian Eurozone accession. *Second*, it then emphasises that the challenges we are facing today imply that the role of governance and the quality of state are appreciating. *Third*, we argue that Eurozone accession needs good governance which incorporates the issue of public sector innovation (PSI) in a more dedicated way in tackling old and new challenges in supporting sustained growth and development as prerequisites of Eurozone accession.

2. Macroeconomic (in)Stability from the Regional Perspective

When it comes to the issue of what kind of perspective does Hungary have with special attention to the potential Eurozone accession, the issue of catching up arises. Since approaching the EU average in terms of GDP per capita is often seen as a relatively proper indicator of maturity for Eurozone entry, we take a mere glimpse into that by looking at the so-called Visegrád countries (Czech Republic, Hungary, Poland and Slovakia). While the Hungarian catching up process has followed a relatively fast trajectory up until the middle of the 2000s, Slovakia and Poland shifted to an even higher pace and eventually outdid the Hungarian performance by 2010.

Figures 1 and 2 convey clearly the message that the catching up process of Hungary reached its inflexion point in 2006 and then it got stuck. Since 2006, the Hungarian path has been completely diverging from the trends of the Visegrád countries.

Let us underscore that the seemingly dynamic growth trajectory in the period 2000–06 was mainly driven by increasing indebtedness (Figure 3). As a corollary, the Hungarian fiscal governance was by and large pro-cyclical and lax; thus concerns over the sustainability of public finance came to the forefront.

Another equally important fact is that foreign indebtedness became a decisive feature of the Hungarian socio-economic development and growth. Net foreign debt-to-GDP ratio was growing swiftly as discernible in Figure 4.

As far as the governance intention is concerned to mitigate the indebtedness process, the structural primary balance offers a helping hand. This indicator reflects the stabilisation objective of the government and it showed that substantial surpluses were realised after 2011 due to fiscal adjustments (expenditure cuts and tax hikes) (Figure 5).

We would like to add that although fiscal sustainability-related economic literature suggests that fiscal consolidations are needed after a certain level of deficit and accumulated public debt, we can claim with due diligence that pro-cyclical fiscal policy with the aim of stabilising inexorably on mechanistically derived deficit targets via one-off measures[1] cannot and should not be considered as *panacea*, because it can easily lead to a stabilisation that is more like destabilisation.[2] This type of destabilisation can be captured by looking at the growth performance shown in Figure 6. Real GDP growth declined

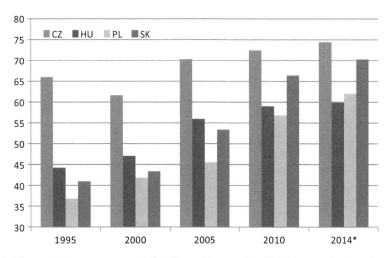

Figure 1. The catching up process of the Visegrád countries (GDP per capita, based on public-private partnership (PPP), EU15 = 100)
Source: Eurostat, National Accounts.

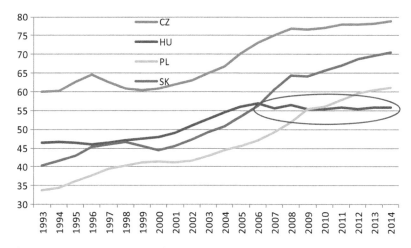

Figure 2. Getting stuck phenomena of Hungary (GDP per capita, based on PPP, reference year 2005, EU15 = 100)
Source: Eurostat, National Accounts.

significantly after 2011 by 2012, that is to say, debt-to-GDP ratio could not go through a significant and sustainable amelioration (the slight improvement by 2012 was just ephemeral).

Mainly expenditure-based fiscal consolidation – in the period 2009–12, see Figure 7 – interspersed with unconventional economic policies led to growing uncertainties that paved the way of shrinking net investments (Figure 8), depressed internal demand (that per se strengthened uncertainties), and these altogether manifested in the dispiriting close-to-zero potential economic growth.

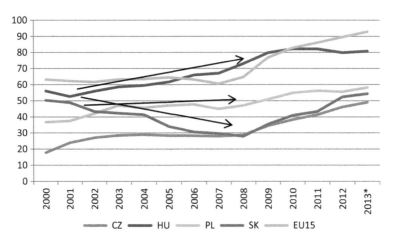

Figure 3. The trajectory of gross public debt (per cent of GDP)
Source: Eurostat, National Accounts.

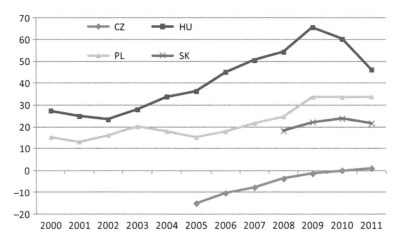

Figure 4. The development of net foreign debt (per cent of GDP)
Source: Eurostat, National Accounts.

Albeit many Hungarian economic practitioners having the predilection to interpret the realised surplus in current account balance as a benevolent phenomenon, it is mainly due to the depressed internal demand and investment activity (Figure 9).

As far as inflation is concerned, its low level seems to meet the target of the Maastricht Treaty; however, it is worth mentioning that exchange rate stability does not seem to be a priority of the government as it can be seen from its highly volatile nature. And as Bloom (2013) emphasised, volatility can be seen as a certain sign of uncertainty (the 270 EUR/HUF exchange rate of September 2009 skyrocketed to over 320 along 2011) (Table 1).[3]

Apart from the fact that Hungary seems to meet the inflation and deficit targets of the Maastricht Treaty in algebraic sum, it can be stressed that this kind of achievement merely gives Hungary a misleading feeling of comfort. Meeting deficit target *via* one-off

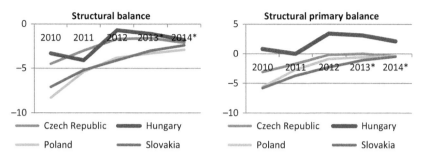

Figure 5. Budgetary development in Hungary (structural and structural primary balance per cent of GDP)

Source: European Commission (2013), AMECO database.

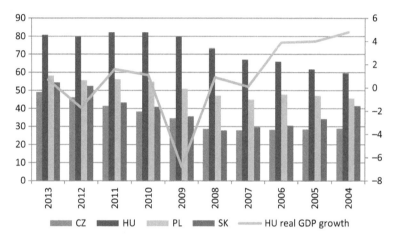

Figure 6. Gross debt and real GDP growth in Hungary (per cent of GDP)

Notes: Left axis refers to gross debt data, while right axis refers to the real GDP growth rate in case of Hungary. Data for 2013 are estimations.

Source: Eurostat, AMECO database.

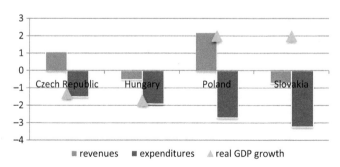

Figure 7. Changes in cyclically adjusted revenues and expenditures and real GDP growth (in percentage points) between 2009 and 2012

Source: Eurostat.

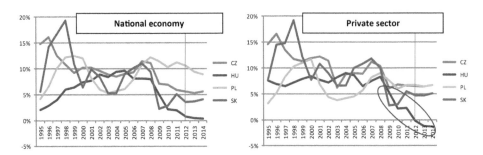

Figure 8. Net investment (per cent of GDP without amortisation)
Source: National Accounts, Oblath (2013).

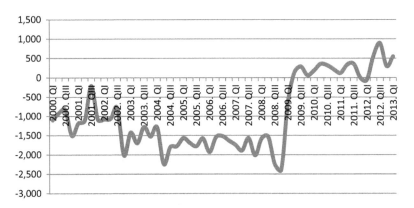

Figure 9. Current account balance (millions of EUR)
Source: The Central Bank of Hungary.

Table 1. Status of criteria for Euro adoption

	HICP inflation rate (12-month average of annual rates)	Budget deficit (per cent of GDP)	Gross public debt-to-GDP ratio	Long-term interest rate (12-month average of 10-year bond yields)	ERM II member
		Public finance			
Reference rate	max. 2.5 per cent	max. 3 per cent	max. 60 per cent, or approaching the reference rate sufficiently	max. 4.81 per cent	min. 2 years
Hungary	September 2013: 1.3 per cent	2012: 1.9 per cent	2013. Q1: 82.4 per cent	April 2013: 7.23 per cent	No

Notes: HICP, harmonised indices of consumer prices; ERM II, exchange rate mechanism II.
Source: Author's own compilation.

measures can be regarded as Pyrrhic victory, which does not drive Hungary sufficiently towards euro adoption. In addition, so far, the Hungarian government has not declared and announced a target date to be pursued for Eurozone accession.

The presented analysis directs us towards at least five recognitions: (i) The Hungarian catching up has been based mainly on unsustainable fiscal governance coupled with external imbalances. (ii) Pro-cyclical fiscal adjustment is not conducive to economic growth. Fiscal consolidations invoked to fend off excessive deficits proved to be futile undertakings if we look at the catching up (lagging behind) process, which was transformed into a 'getting stuck' phenomena (zero-close potential economic growth). (iii) Although external imbalance was reversed, it was predominantly determined by lowering real investments. (iv) There is no stipulated target date for euro adoption pursued by the government which undermines the commitment towards the European Monetary Union (EMU). And last but not least, (v) a *more systemic approach* would be essential in targeting euro adoption meaningfully, which enshrines the concept of *cultivating good and more effective national governance*.

3. A More Systemic Approach is Needed – the Appreciating Role of National Governance

Our reasoning is rooted in the well-documented consideration that despite the fact that we have to address wicked problems, the fundamental role of national state and governance cannot be questioned. There are wicked problems, complex problems spanning across the borders of national states by calling for international solutions, some sort of global governance. The wicked problems are as follows: (i) demographic challenge; (ii) climate change; (iii) the changing characteristics of emerging markets; (iv) secular decline in productivity and (v) the *sui generis* sovereign debt crisis.

3.1. *Wicked Challenges*

Demographic challenge is important from many aspects; one of the main reasonable side effects of the ageing population is the need for greater mobility, i.e. stream of active labour force paying taxes due to the worsening financial base of traditional European social systems that will be undermined by the decline in European employment levels.

Climate problem can be captured by many ways, but its *pièce de résistance* is that according to the common view of ecologists, mankind's only chance of survival is to provide the sustainability of Earth's biosphere. In this respect, some argue that cross-country, optimally global governance seems to be needed to dampen emissions, to enhance more climate-resilient economies.

Additionally, forgetting the fact that the *characteristics of emerging markets are changing* would be a Hayekian fatal conceit if for no other reason than because it will presumably have significant impetus on the economic performance of the EU, as well. There is a more and more observable shift in the economic paradigm of the Chinese economy; that is to say the economic paradigm based exclusively on the manufacturing sector and export-led growth do not seem to fit the requirements of the country any longer. The recent 5–Year Plan alludes to the required shift towards a more consumption- and service sector-based paradigm; it was discernible *expressis verbis* in the plan.[4]

As regards *productivity*, it has become common knowledge that Europe's labour productivity has been worsening as compared to that of the USA since the mid-1990s. Still, Innovation Union Scoreboard 2013 reported that Europe has closed almost half of the innovation gap with the USA, but the gap is yet gaping (IUS, 2013). Interestingly, it is often neglected that total factor productivity, which captures innovation dynamics, has been deteriorating since the mid-1970s in the USA. This weakening is more and more often attributed by scholars, having a holistic approach, to the secular withering of innovations (Cowen, 2011; Atkinson & Ezell, 2012; Gordon, 2012; Kasparov et al., 2013), contributing, therefore, not so spectacularly and intensively to the improvement of well-being and welfare. In this respect, the 'bridging-the-gap' phenomenon can be reinterpreted by considering that the European performance is catching up and associated with the fact that the global innovation performance has been undergoing a deterioration phase (i.e. Europe closes the gap more vehemently when the US economy is suffering from worsening innovation and thus productivity, hence growth performance) (see: Kovács, 2013b). Consequently, to a large extent, the EU Member States have to enhance the European labour productivity. One of the most expedient ways seems to be the stimulation of an innovation-based growth model.

The flame of the era of Great Moderation, coined by Stock and Watson (2003) in the period 1992–2007, has seemingly gone out with the eruption of the 2008 financial and economic turbulence and its ensuing *sui generis sovereign debt crisis*. The Great Recession (Coibion & Gorodnichenko, 2010) was here to stay with serious macroeconomic fluctuations. The debt crisis calls for long-standing fiscal consolidations that are painful enough to be cushioned by the more effective and innovative public sector which can feed into the trust base of citizens. Reinvigorating trust is of paramount importance for peripheral countries (southern Europe) that have not fared well due to their structural weaknesses. The core versus periphery dichotomy in terms of competitiveness was not dampened significantly by the European integration. Apart from the fact that the EMU is not a monetary and fiscal union, creating credible coercive power to conduct prudent fiscal policies and such structural reforms that are geared towards improving peripheral countries' international competitiveness was beset with difficulties.[5] It establishes a claim for deeper international coordination and surveillance (Shafik, 2013); however, the history of EMU conveys that member states are inclined to preserve their sovereignty and they require a solution which bolsters the fiscal discipline without endangering the transfer of sovereignty. As a consequence, due fiscal governance remains a priority at national level (Di Fabio, 2011, p. 464; Csaba, 2012).

3.2. *On the Impossibility of Efficient and Effective Global Governance*

Importantly, it would be naïve to think that the above-deciphered insights are directing us towards the recognition that a more dedicated and effective global governance is feasible.[6] For sure, a systemic approach seems to be a sine qua non of an effective crisis management, to tackle grand challenges and to have a promising way for euro adoption as well.

However, desiring effective and efficient global governance can be deliciously tempting, but this would be the wrong inference pervading a good deal of abstract thinking and forgetting the real-world nuances and complexities. Some sort of global governance (i) should be based on wide political consensus which is not the case even in the European Union, either (Szemlér, 2009), (ii) should be as democratic as it would be requested by citizens and (iii) should possess all the necessary relevant information to overlook and fully understand nonlinear economic processes.[7] We add to the latter one that it seems to be impossible mainly because of our limited rationality (Simon, 1957, 1986) to understand the whole in its entirety by overcoming the world's complexity and its nuances, especially when the

highly globalised world created an intensively integrated world interspersed with interconnectedness and mutual interdependence by making the system ever more complex to be
reckoned with. Consequently, higher-level international cooperation relies on whether
the expectations on functions and capabilities are realistic enough as Frieden et al.
(2012) ascertained.

Concerning the issue of capability, as the Nobel-laureate Kahneman (2013) pointed out,
the predictive power of our knowledge reaches its diminishing marginal returns relatively
fast. There is no gainsaying the fact that this time-tested psychological finding holds
especially in case of predicting nonlinear processes evolved in the complex global
system interspersed with growing interconnectedness and interdependency and the
current dominance of uncertainties (e.g. estimating *ex ante* the value of fiscal multiplier
precisely is particularly cumbersome as it was admittedly the case, see Blanchard and
Leigh (2013)). As a corollary, even if the national state can be seen as the antiquated heri-
tage of the French revolution, it still remains responsible for conducting pro-growth fiscal
consolidations efficiently geared towards short-term stabilisation as well as medium- and
longer-term sustained recovery alike.

In an era of growing uncertainties, when crisis management triggered even higher unemployment including youth unemployment – which has been associated with declining trust
and confidence level of citizens in states and their institutions (Figure 10) – *reinvigorating
trust* is of key importance. As Stevenson and Wolfers (2011) pointed out, every time unemployment rose in history, the trust level declined, that is to say, the democratic deficit just
deteriorated. This time is not different in this regard. As Nobel-laureates Akerlof and
Shiller (2009) emphasised, socio-economic development relies heavily on the trust
infrastructure.

The question of how to stabilise and give impetus at the same time remains a central
issue of contemporary European studies. For sure, the role of the state is appreciating.
The question of 'how to make the state to be a trust builder channel in a more dedicated
way' can be linked to the issue of *PSI*. It also implies that the view of simply dismantling

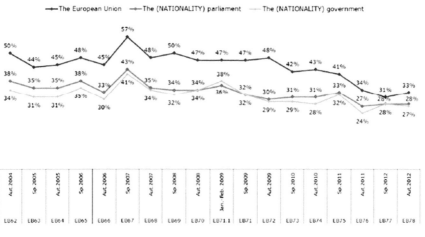

Figure 10. Declining trust base of European citizens
Source: Standard Eurobarometer 78, p. 14.

the Hobbesian Leviathan states through fiscal adjustments that are targeting numerical objectives should also be replaced by a more nuanced one that enshrines the idea of *making public sector itself to be more effective and innovative to increase societal welfare.*

4. Innovation is a *de rigueur* Aspect in the Public Sector

Innovation is considered as a prerequisite of socio-economic development and sustained economic growth. In times of crisis, supporting all type of private-sector innovation is of crucial importance (e.g. offering dedicated external financial resources).[8] In this regard, fiscal policy should conduct fiscal consolidations that spark firms' innovation activity through support measures (e.g. innovation credit, direct financial support, innovation voucher, etc.). Let us underscore that innovation is not linked exclusively to the private sector; it should be nourished even in the public sector.

Innobarometer 2010 considers PSI as '[...] any novel, or significantly improved (without indicating precisely what a "significant improvement" might be) service, communication or organisational method' (European Commission, 2010, p. 13). As in the case of private-sector innovation, PSI has also various forms (innovations in services; process innovation; organisational innovation and communication innovation).

PSI may help to maintain the quality of service provision, to reduce excessive expenditures while not imposing additional burdens on labour and the economy as a whole. PSI may lead to more efficient public services with improved quality and accessibility through which it cultivates trust building in time when painful measures (e.g. fiscal adjustments and structural reforms) are inevitable.

As a consequence, Hungary would need a public sector which pursues innovation in a more vigorous way. Of course, innovation in public sector cannot and should not be imagined onto the manner of how innovation happens in the private sector because of its specific features decipherable by building on the insights of new political as well as institutional economics.[9] Without being exhaustive, our paper highlights four things:

- One of the most fundamental differences between public and private innovations is linked to the issue of *evolution of innovation*, i.e. the rise and, most importantly, the fall of innovations. There is no 'invisible hand' in the public sector that would eliminate the failed innovations as an embedded mechanism. Moreover, the contestable market principle (Baumol, 1982) does not apply, and the Hayekian *trial and error* (Hayek, 1988) does not exist with the same vehemence.
- *Measuring the outcome of PSI is rather difficult.* Innovation within the public sector cannot be expressed in terms of algebraic sum in each case. Despite this shortcoming, following the guidance of Lord Kelvin and that of the Chicago School: 'if you can't measure it, measure it anyway' would be instructive if we want to specify whether what we do is useful or not. However, in case of measurement the main message of Werner Karl Heisenberg and his uncertainty relations seem to be worth remembering, namely that measurement affects the phenomenon that we measure. In the context of PSI, measuring the European PSI in a particular moment – as the European Public Sector Innovation Scoreboard does[10] – will offer the opportunity for respondents (public servants) to correct their earlier statements during the next measurement because the public sector is accountable and so does not like to be seen to fail.

- Due to accountability and visibility, there is an embedded risk aversion or failure avoidance inbuilt into the public sector that hampers risky innovations. The cost of their failure is great. Therefore, public organisations tend to stick to the status quo, old routines (known options) of low performance, rather than risky solutions of potentially high efficiency.
- The great level of heterogeneity within the public sector is also of key importance. The great level of heterogeneity may hamper the policy learning because of the more and more complex system that should be overlooked and understood.

In spite of these specific features of PSI, there is a continuously expanding empirical backing saying that certain techniques and methods are more likely to increase the innovativeness of the public sector (e.g. workplace innovation, team-based organisational structure; applying boundary-crossing management and careers, awards; putting customers' perspectives and needs into focus; deploying innovative public finance, public-private-innovation, innovative procurement and involving all the beneficiary community (European Commission, 2012)). What is more, as we indicated earlier, Europe faces a series of challenges (demographic, climate, debt crisis, etc.) that are establishing a claim for PSI in Europe. These innovations are expected to provide significant cost-reducing opportunities without any decline in service quality as well as accessibility.[11] PSI can lead to improvement in quality and accessibility and may lower public-sector expenditures. Thus, PSI can constitute a trust builder and maintainer channel.[12]

The notion of governance has, therefore, to be reconsidered by accepting that we should be prepared for constant social learning by resorting to trial-and-error methods. The main message decipherable is that PSI should be continuous and directed towards resilient governance and public sector to bear the burden determined by the permanent learning through trials and errors.

5. Conclusion

In this paper, we illustrated that a more systemic approach is needed when it comes to considering the Eurozone accession in case of Hungary. Behind the curtain of the 'getting stuck' phenomena is the Hungarian macroeconomic instability which has resulted in non-fulfilment with regard to the requirements of euro adoption.

After contemplating the Hungarian catching-up process, we devoted special attention to the issue of whether global governance is feasible in tackling wicked challenges. We argued that since omnipotent global governance can be considered as a wishful concept, national governance remains fundamental in achieving macroeconomic stability and Eurozone accession as well. At this point, the issue of making public sector itself more efficient and effective in providing higher-quality services with increased accessibility through innovations was raised. Along the course of our paper, at least four implications can be deciphered.

First, the old wisdom stating that there must be an Eucken-like interdependency, in our case, between fiscal and monetary policies still holds. Both should behave in a symbiotic way by being tailored towards macroeconomic stability.

Second, fiscal consolidation is needed in a more holistic and strategic way. It is not the matter of principles or ideologies; it is the question of extent, composition and thus that of direction. Pursuing mechanistically the deficit and debt targets being regarded as optimal objectives would be a Hayekian fatal conceit in supporting fiscal sustainability and sustained growth. There is a solid claim for some kind of *aurea mediocritas* fiscal consolidation with a more systemic approach by addressing powers that are of paramount importance in the new techno-economic paradigm (Perez, 2009) like R&D, innovation, education through fiscal impulse to resuscitate private sectors' similar activities to propel sustained growth. A mixture of pro- and anti-cyclical measures is, therefore, seen as an instructive way forward (i.e. expenditure cuts in unproductive fields like social transfers and public-sector salaries, additional spending on R&D and innovation on which today's growth depends the most). Hungary carried out a mixture of fiscal consolidation pervaded by the view of increasing R&D and innovation spending; however, the inconsistent and one-off, thus unsustainable measures triggered uncertainties that impede a healthy innovation milieu in the private sector.

Third, in times of debt when painful adjustments are needed, unfolding the potential of PSI is essence. To a certain extent, our paper is an innovation policy's clarion call for fostering innovation not only in the private but also in the public sector at all levels of governance in order to increase the quality of public services, to increase people's well-being and to reduce costs through more sustainable public services. With PSI, governance can signal its commitment towards increasing the well-being of people and their trust base. In case of Hungary, a matured PSI mindset is still lacking. Although the Hungarian government accepted the new innovation policy strategy document[13] during the summer of 2013 – whose merit is the recognition that the Hungarian public sphere is weak in innovation – it leaves at loose ends the instruments and techniques that are more likely to direct the public sector towards pro-active innovation.

Fourth, Eurozone accession needs to be pursued by all-time Hungarian government *via* credible plans and actions. The EU's external anchoring mechanisms do not by any means offer enough pressure towards the Euro; hence cultivating internal commitment is essential (e.g. stipulating and announcing a target date).

Economic history teaches us that development and decay are spontaneous and nonlinear processes. Still, governments always have the opportunity to emit right signals at the right time in the right measures. It can be manifested in credible fiscal consolidations being armed with pro-growth measures as well and a variety of economic policies geared towards longer-term development. In an era of uncertainties, public debts, growing asymmetrical interdependency and complexities, national public sectors should *toujours à l'affût* more innovation not only in supporting its citizens' trust and confidence level, but also to have an ameliorated ground for euro adoption.

Acknowledgements

This research was realized in the frames of TÁMOP 4.2.4. A/2-11-1-2012-0001 'National Excellence Program – Elaborating and operating an inland student and researcher personal support system'. The project was subsidized by the European Union and co-financed by the European Social Fund.

Notes

[1] Imposing big taxes on the banking system as well as crisis taxes on certain sectors like the pharmaceutical industry, nationalisation of private pension funds, etc. As Csaba (2011) sensitively illustrated:

Interventionism is detectable in every corner, from micromanaging the consequences of the environmental catastrophe in Transdanubia to the highly differentiated application of crisis taxes, by the sector and by the market players. Capping the remuneration of public officials across the board, no matter how popular, rewrites long term contracts, and so does the nationalization of private pension funds. Re-tailoring taxes accruing to local municipalities was yet another case in point.

[2] A lesson learned from the current European crisis management is that eschewing public debt can be as harmful as letting debt-to-GDP ratio to grow since austerity could not pervasively resurrect investors' confidence in certain countries due to the fact that expenditure cuts triggered GDP declines leading to increase in public debts (Kovács, 2013a).

[3] See: European Central Bank, historical data. Available at http://www.ecb.europa.eu/stats/exchange/eurofxref/ html/eurofxref-graph-huf.en.html (accessed 12 December 2013).

[4] Due to the shift, the economic growth will go through a dampening process, which is now the case. This is completely in line with the results of Barry Eichengreen and his co-authors emphasising that economies tend to slow down as they reach the 17,000 dollar per capita income level (Eichengreen et al., 2012). It can be anticipated by 2015, in case of China. Another potential repercussion will be the change in the European import structure, and the price-moderating effect of the cheap Chinese products will also be lower.

[5] Apart from the fact that softening the Stability and Growth Pact was equal to worsening credibility, particularly by the early 2000s when two non-complying countries (Germany, France) were not sanctioned, we argue that EMU framework acted as a mechanism which was on the one hand benefiting for core countries like Germany and France, and it was a counter-incentive for such countries like Portugal in implementing necessary fiscal adjustments and structural reforms. Since the indebtedness in southern Europe, helped by Germany and France, fostered their imports, a contrario, it also triggered the German exports; and thus this system appeared to be a desirable one. Therefore, the well-documented design failure (De Grauwe, 2013) was not only the result of human action, but to a certain degree also that of human deliberation. Nonetheless, the surplus cash stemming from strengthening exports was being to a large extent re-allocated to the southern countries in the form of loans. The reason for the EMU not serving completely as an external enforcement framework is that the German and French governments would have blocked the flow of increasingly risky loans to the peripheral countries, but their interest groups would not have left it without a word because this would have led to additional economic slowdown determined by a decline in demand and workforce layoffs. For this reason, the creditor countries were not interested in the break-up of this *status quo* and therefore closed one of their eyes to the fiscal indisciplinarity.

[6] As Temin and Vines (2013) repeatedly reaffirmed, in the absence of a hegemonic power, global governance seems to be a desired but not realistic option. Even the World Economic Forum has just recently played down a scenario for global governance without clearly specifying its feasibility. See Nye (2013)

[7] As the Austrian economists ravelled out long ago, this cannot be the case. von Mises (1929|1996) argued that interventionism even at national level generates unintended negative consequences, i.e. generates uncertainties. Hayek (1945) associated this issue to the shortcomings in utilising information when it comes to coordination (i.e. to have all the necessary knowledge to overlook the process of interventions).

[8] In an era of growing uncertainties, certain firms are more likely to postpone their R&D and innovation activities; however, as economic history suggests, some firms consider the crisis as an opportunity and innovate and spend on R&D in a more emphatic way if external finance is provided (Stone & Stein, 2012). It was documented in the Great Depression by Mowery and Rosenberg (1998) as well as Field (2003, 2011). It seems that scarcity together with more constrained conditions serves as an enforcement mechanism of new or significantly improved goods and services and processes, ultimately that of innovation and imitation. Plastic and television were also invented during the uncertainties of the 1930s (Nanda & Nicholas, 2013). Crisis is always an opportunity to be seized. Business cycle analyses also confirmed that inventions are often brought to life during downturns (Kondratieff, 1935).

[9] See for instance: Downs (1957), Niskanen (1971) and Tullock (1980).

[10] EPSIS Report is available at http://ec.europa.eu/enterprise/policies/innovation/files/epsis-2013_en.pdf (accessed 10 December 2013).

[11] According to the model of 'radical efficiency' coined by Gillinson et al. (2010), significant service-quality improvement can be reached with substantial (approximately 20–60%) cost savings. This requires the recognition that new insights, the re-conceptualisation of customers and their roles in public service delivery, and last but not least new resources are needed.

[12] A potential approach towards reinvigorating trust through PSI is the well-known participatory budgeting which gained momentum not only in Brazil (Porto Alegre) but also in more and more European cities (e.g. Eindhoven, Seville, etc.) which is able to increase the trust base of citizens by engaging them in expressing their opinions on urban development-related priorities.

[13] The document is called Investment in the Future – National Research and Development and Innovation Strategy 2013–2020. Available at http://www.nih.gov.hu/download.php?docID=25559 (accessed 10 December 2013).

References

Akerlof, G. A. & Shiller, R. J. (2009) *Animal Spirits: How Human Psychology Drives the Economy, and Why It Matters for Global Capitalism* (Princeton, NJ: Princeton University Press).

Atkinson, R. D. & Ezell, S. J. (2012) *Innovation Economics: The Race for Global Advantage* (New Haven: Yale University Press).

Baumol, W. J. (1982) Contestable markets: An uprising in the theory of industry structure, *The American Economic Review*, 72(1), pp. 1–15.

Blanchard, O. & Leigh, L. (2013) Growth Forecast Errors and Fiscal Multipliers. *IMF Working Paper* No. 1.

Bloom, N. (2013) Fluctuations in Uncertainty. *NBER Working Paper* No. 19714.

Coibion, O. & Gorodnichenko, Y. (2010) Does the Great Recession Really Mean the End of the Great Moderation? *VoxEU.org*. Available at http://www.voxeu.org/index.php?q=node/4496 (accessed 4 December 2013).

Cowen, T. (2011) *The Great Stagnation: How America Ate All the Low-Hanging Fruit of Modern History, Got Sick, and Will (Eventually) Feel Better* (New York: Dutton Adult).

Csaba, L. (2011) The challenge of growth, *Hungarian Review*, 2(3). Available at http://www.hungarianreview. com/article/the_challenge_of_growth (accessed 13 December 2013).

Csaba, L. (2012) Revisiting the crisis of the EMU: Challenges and options, *Zeitschrift für Staats- und Europawissenschaften*, 10(1), pp. 53–77.

De Grauwe, P. (2013) Design failures in the Eurozone: Can they be fixed? *LEQS Paper* No. 57.

Di Fabio, U. (2011) Europa in der Krise, *und Europawissenschaften*, 9(4), pp. 459–464.

Downs, A. (1957) An economic theory of political action in a democracy, *Journal of Political Economy*, 65(2), pp. 135–150.

Eichengreen, B., Park, D. & Shin, K. (2012) When fast-growing economies slow down: International evidence and implications for China, *Asian Economic Papers*, MIT Press, 11(1), pp. 42–87.

European Commission. (2010) Innobarometer 2010 – Analytical Report. Innovation in Public Administration. Available at http://ec.europa.eu/public_opinion/flash/fl_305_en.pdf (accessed 20 November 2013).

European Commission. (2012) *Policies Supporting Innovation in Public Service Provision*. An INNO-Grips policy brief by ICEG European Center, Budapest.

European Commission. (2013) *Annual Macro-Economic Database*, AMECO. Available at http://ec.europa.eu/economy_finance/ameco/user/serie/SelectSerie.cfm (accessed 18 April 2014).

Field, A. (2003) The most technologically progressive decade of the twentieth century, *American Economic Review*, 93(4), pp. 1399–1413.

Field, A. (2011) *A Great Leap Forward: 1930s Depression and US Economic Growth* (New Haven, CT: Yale University Press).

Frieden, J., Pettis, M., Rodrik, D. & Zedillo, E. (2012) *After the Fall: The Future of Global Cooperation. Geneva Reports on the World Economy 14* (Geneva: International Center for Monetary and Banking Studies).

Gillinson, S., Horne, M. & Baeck, P. (2010) Radical Efficiency – Different, Better, Lower Cost Public Services. *Research Paper*. Innovation Unit, NESTA, The LAB.

Gordon, R. J. (2012) Is US Economic Growth Over? Faltering Innovation Confronts the Six Headwinds. *CEPR Policy Insight* 63.

Hayek, F. A. (1945) The use of knowledge in society, *American Economic Review*, 35(4), pp. 519–530.

Hayek, F. A. (1988) The Fatal Conceit: The Errors of Socialism, in: W. W. Bartley (Ed) *The Collected Works of F. A. Hayek*, Vol. 9 (London: University of Chicago Press (US), Routledge Press (UK)).

IUS. (2013) Innovation Union Scoreboard 2013, European Commission, DG Enterprise and Industry. Available at http://ec.europa.eu/enterprise/policies/innovation/files/ius-2013_en.pdf (accessed 14 December 2013).

Kahneman, D. (2013) *Thinking, Fast and Slow*. Reprint edition (New York: Farrar, Straus and Giroux).

Kasparov, G., Levchin, M. & Thiel, P. (2013) *The Blueprint: Reviving Innovation, Rediscovering Risk, and Rescuing the Free Market* (New York: W. W. Norton & Company).

Kondratieff, N. D. (1935) The long waves in economic life, *Review of Economic Statistics*, 17(6), pp. 105–115.

Kovács, O. (2013a) Message in a Battle – Austerity in Europe and Lessons for Central and Eastern European Member States. ICEG European Center, *News of the Month*, No. 61, pp. 8–18. Available at http://icegec.hu/download/news/nom_november_2013.pdf (accessed 10 December 2013).

Kovács, O. (2013b) Black Swans or Creeping Normalcy? – An Attempt to a Holistic Crisis Analysis, *Eastern Journal of European Studies*, 4(1), pp. 127–143.

von Mises, L. (1929|1996) *A Critique of Interventionism. Irvington-on-Hudson* (New York: Foundation for Economic Education).

Mowery, D. & Rosenberg, N. (1998) *Paths of Innovation: Technological Change in Twentieth Century America* (Cambridge, MA: Cambridge University Press).

Nanda, R. & Nicholas, T. (2013) Did Bank Distress Stifle Innovation During the Great Depression? Harvard Business School. *Working Paper* 12–106.

Niskanen, W. A. (1971) *Bureaucracy and Representative Government* (New York: Aldine-Atherton).

Nye, J. S. (2013) Governance in the Information Age, Project-Syndicate. Available at http://www.project-syndicate.org/commentary/joseph-s–nye-examines-three-potential-scenarios-for-governance-in-2050 (accessed 12 December 2013).

Oblath, G. (2013) Makrogazdasági instabilitás és regionális lemaradás – Magyarország esete Conference presentation: Economic Policy Roundtable, 12 April 2013.

Perez, C. (2009) Technological Revolutions and Techno-economic Paradigms. *TOC/TUT Working Paper* No. 20.

Shafik, N. (2013) Smart Governance: Solutions for Today's Global Economy. Speech delivered on 5 December 2013 at the University of Oxford. Available at http://www.imf.org/external/np/speeches/2013/120513.htm (accessed 13 December 2013).

Simon, H. (1957) *A Behavioral Model of Rational Choice, in Models of Man, Social and Rational: Mathematical Essays on Rational Human Behavior in a Social Setting* (New York: John Wiley & Sons).

Simon, H. (1986) Rationality in psychology and economics, *The Journal of Business Part 2: The Behavioral Foundations of Economic Theory*, 59(4), pp. 209–224.

Stevenson, B. & Wolfers, J. (2011) Trust in public institutions over the business cycle, *American Economic Review, American Economic Association*, 101(3), pp. 281–287.

Stock, J. H. & Watson, M. W. (2003) Has the Business Cycle Changed and Why? *NBER Macroeconomics Annual 2002*, 17. Available at http://www.nber.org/chapters/c11075.pdf (accessed 10 November 2013).

Stone, E. & Stein, L. (2012) The Effect on Uncertainty on Investment, Hiring and R&D: Causal Evidence from Equity Options. The University of Chicago, *Working Paper*.

Szemlér, T. (2009) Future prospects of the European Union, *Revista de Economía Mundial*, no. 22, pp. 127–138.

Temin, P. & Vines, D. (2013) *The Leaderless Economy: Why the World Economic System Fell Apart and How to Fix It* (Princeton: Princeton University Press).

Tullock, G. (1980) Efficient rent-seeking, in: J. M. Buchanan, R. D. Tollison & G. Tullock (Eds) *Toward a Theory of the Rent-Seeking Society*, pp. 97–112 (College Station, TX: Texas A&M University Press).

Index

For Product Safety Concerns and Information please contact our EU
representative GPSR@taylorandfrancis.com Taylor & Francis Verlag GmbH,
Kaufingerstraße 24, 80331 München, Germany

Batch number: 08158490

Printed by Printforce, the Netherlands